# River
# Passage

# River Passage

by p.m.terrell

Published by Drake Valley Press
USA

ISBN 978-1-935970-28-6 (Paperback, 2nd Edition)
ISBN 978-0-9728186-0-5 (Paperback, 1st Edition)
ISBN 978-0-9728186-7-4 (eBook)

Author's web site: www.pmterrell.com

# ACKNOWLEDGEMENTS

Special thanks to the following people and organizations who provided research, assistance, or editorial support:

Barbara Kimberlin Broach

Barbara Condrey

Ken Fieth, Metro Nashville Archives, Metro Archivist

Kenneth R. Johnson, Ph.D., Professor Emeritus of History, Florence, Alabama

Charles E. Moore, Florence, Alabama City Archeologist

John W. Neelley, Jr.

John W. Neelley, Sr.

Thomas Robertson

Donald Terrell, Sr.

D.E. Ward, Jr., M.D.

JoAnn Weakley of Historic Collinsville, Tennessee

Milly Wright

# Foreword

This is a work of historical fiction. It is based on true events as recorded in Colonel John Donelson's Journal and other journals and records kept by the settlers who accompanied Colonel Donelson on his harrowing voyage of 1779-1780. Though it was necessary to use imagination to fill in details and provide dialogue, I attempted at all times to remain historically accurate.

# Prologue

## Sycamore Shoals,
## The Watauga Settlement, 1775

They appeared at dawn, rising like apparitions through the mist. The morning dew clung to their bronzed bodies as their sinewy arms sliced paddles through the water in a rhythmic motion borne of hours of toil. They moved silently on the glistening current, their black eyes alert, ever searching for others along the shore and in the gathering canoes. When at last they rounded the final bend, they were greeted with the ghostly vision of braves pulling ashore, their lean, taut bodies gliding out of the vessels, their flat, bare feet touching the cold ground without leaving as much as a footprint on the pristine shore. The canoes were lined up wordlessly, their wooden bodies pressed side by side as dozens and then hundreds gathered.

The men greeted one another with a quiet nod, their eyes meeting for the briefest of moments before they began trotting through the thickening woods. Their figures seemed to morph from the very tree trunks that concealed them into a forest that came alive with their bodies, the branches swaying ever so slightly as they completed a journey across lands where their forefathers' spirits still roamed.

Their feet found the paths as if they had minds of their own, as if their toes could see the brambles and pine straw stretched out before them, freeing their dark, brooding eyes to stare straight ahead at the scores of men before them. They knew without so much as a glance behind them that others followed in their steps, and that all would gather at the place the white men called Sycamore Shoals for what could become the greatest meeting in their lifetimes.

The dawn seared the sky with an intense red as the sun broke from the earth and began to rise, burning off the morning dew and leaving the bodies to bask in the warmth as they converged.

The white men awaited them, their bodies clad in buckskin from deer shot on land that had once belonged to the natives, land they had long ago been driven from but to which many vowed to return. As the Indians slowed toward the entrance to the white men's village, a place they called Fort Watauga, their alert eyes noted the women were absent, sent to neighboring towns while the leaders gathered; or perhaps others remained inside their strange wood homes, occasionally venturing an inquisitive, fearful glance through partly drawn curtains.

The white men cautiously greeted them at the fort, gesturing toward the meeting house where red men and white gathered, telling those who understood the English language that the talks would begin as soon as they were assembled.

Noquali moved swiftly past these strange buildings that seemed to spring out of the ground overnight throughout their lands, steadily driving them from their own villages and further westward. The son of a Cherokee brave and a captured Shawnee squaw, he spent much of his time journeying between the villages now, listening to the growing debates concerning the encroaching white men and readying himself for the constant skirmishes that erupted between them. He was a young man who felt his destiny to become a great warrior, a man who had become increasingly impatient with the elders' talk of treaties and peace.

Fires blazed throughout the fort with whole carcasses of deer and boar clinging to great spits above the flames; meat that would be devoured at sunset, once the talks were done and decisions had been made.

As he approached the meeting hall, he glanced about him at the others. They had come from all directions—the Shawnee, the Delaware, and the Wyandot—but the treaty would officially occur between the white men and the Cherokee, who lay claim to the lands the newcomers wanted. In other times and on other days, he would have painted his face and gathered his weapons against these lesser tribes, but today the elders sought to set aside their centuries-old warfare and join together to negotiate as one.

Noquali could not recall a time when the white man had not been part of his life although he had grown from a young boy to manhood listening to his elders speak of those days. There had been in this great, vast land hundreds of tribal nations, stretching from river to river and from one mountain range to the other, nations that for centuries had coexisted, sometimes in uneasy friendship and often in war.

The ground itself belonged not to the living but to the spirits. Those entities whispered through the valleys and created the winds, made their lands fertile with crops, and sent animals fleet of foot and tender of flesh into their domain. The rivers and streams were the tongues of the spirits, sometimes lashing out in anger but often rolling gently with cool, crisp water to quench their thirst.

The native villages were erected on carefully chosen sites with proper respect paid to the spirits. But now those spirits were cast aside or defiled by these newcomers with their strange customs and wood forts. Many times Noquali had sat erect on his black stallion, peering from the crest of the mountains as the white men gathered in the valley below, claiming the land as their own as if it had never belonged to anyone else before them.

They came with different tongues, and those that spoke the language called French did not like those who spoke English, and they frequently clashed and conspired against each other, as the Cherokee and the Shawnee had done in these same lands.

Each sought alliances, but their promises wavered like the wind through the valley. Their treaties were of no value, their commitments useless, as time and again they forced the natives further from their ancestral homes.

And yet they were converging again to sign yet another treaty. Noquali's blood ran hot as he gathered with the others outside the meeting hall, his eyes brushing the surrounding terrain. The ones who called themselves the Watauga Settlers had agreed to remain east of the great mountain ranges, and yet here they were, squarely amidst them, encroaching once more on Cherokee lands. His nostrils flared as he watched the elders seated outside the meeting hall, befriending the white men as if all was well.

A tall man with thick black hair made his way to the center of the gathering and began to speak. He called himself James Robertson, but he spoke not with the tongue of the British but with a flatter tone, one the Cherokee had come to recognize as the settlers who fought against the British. As Noquali made his way closer to the tribal elders, he studied the angular shape of the white man's jaw, his erect, almost regal bearing, and his confident words.

It wasn't the first time Noquali had encountered this leader of white men. He had run across him time and again on the trails between the mountains and the fertile hills many moons west of this place. He had remembered him not for his willingness to trade and for his quest for peace but for his amazing eyes: they were blue, as vivid and fiery as the skies on a stormy summer evening. Noquali had to fight to keep from staring into those eyes, and he wondered what type of people grew eyes in blues and greens, the colors of the skies and the fertile, rolling valleys.

He lightly brushed the arm of another Cherokee. Their eyes met and they nodded in a silent greeting. He knew the pockmarked face well, as did all of the Indians who gathered here: it was Dragging Canoe.

He remained beside him, as they were kindred spirits: like Noquali, Dragging Canoe's father had also been of mixed Cherokee and Shawnee blood but his mother had been of the Natchez tribe. His face was pockmarked due to a curse the white men had brought with them, a curse that had killed many natives in their prime as well as children who had never known a full life. The curse had created fevers among them and painful pustules that left lifelong scars on those who survived. The warriors had been powerless against this curse that swept into their villages on a breath of wind, and so, too, had been the medicine men.

While the elders had sought peace with the newcomers, often abandoning land that rightly belonged to them, Dragging Canoe had become an increasingly vocal opponent to the white men's encroachment upon their territories. He was a fierce warrior, known in battle to be both fearless and merciless. He was well traveled and knew the English language as Noquali did; they also traded with the French, who used the lands for hunting and as furriers, often setting up stores in Indian villages, selling or trading trinkets the likes of which he'd never before laid eyes upon. They did not take away their land or drive them from their villages, and if Dragging Canoe and Noquali's urgings were followed, they would ally with the French.

But on this day, they both listened with growing trepidation that gave way to silent anger as their own elders sold land that had been in their families since the rise of the Great Spirit. They listened as this man with the blue eyes spoke of peace with the Cherokee and even of friendship. He held a paper high above his head for all to see, a paper he called a treaty that would give all of the Cherokee lands to the white man from the mountain ranges to the mighty river they called the Mississippi. Another man they called Henderson frequently interjected, smiling as he pointed and spoke of the paper they would call the Treaty of Sycamore Shoals.

And in return for the transfer of land, the white men agreed not to fight the Cherokee but to live in peace.

Noquali could feel his cheeks growing hot. His eyes burned as he glared at the white men, standing tall and proud as the Cherokee elders sat hunched and quiet as mice. It enraged him that their people had been led down this path of submission; that the lands their families had fought for and died for had come down to a piece of paper that amounted to surrender.

He ground his teeth and turned to leave in disgust when a strong voice stopped him. He watched as Dragging Canoe moved toward the center of the meeting, the Indians of all tribes silently parting as this great warrior passed by them.

Robertson and Henderson stopped speaking. Their eyes darted around the throngs of Indians, and several white men reached toward their guns. Instinctively, Noquali placed his hand on the handle of the long knife suspended from his waistband.

Robertson held up his hand and the white men appeared to relax, but Noquali remained at the ready as Dragging Canoe began to speak.

"The Great Spirit frowns upon this day," he said in a loud, clear voice, "and this lack of leadership of the Cherokee people." The elders refused to look Dragging Canoe in the eyes; a sign of disrespect, Noquali thought, further fueling his ire. "It was said when we lived east of the great mountains if we agreed to give up those lands to the white man, we could live in peace on the western side. And yet these men defy not only the treaty with the Cherokee but also the laws of their own men, which forbid them from settling here."

Richard Henderson answered in a calm voice, "Those laws are the King's laws, and we do not recognize the King of England as our leader. That they forbid us to live here is of no significance to us. We are free men."

"I have not met this king of which you speak. But I have seen the white men come to the shores of the great waters and promise not to advance. Then they push us further to the west until the mountains are against our backs, and they tell us everything from the mountains to the waters is now theirs. We have agreed time and again, placing our mark upon these papers you hold forth, to live in peace, to divide our lands between the red men and the white. And yet time and time again, the white man breaks their promises. Time and again, they push us further and further from our homes, the homes of our fathers."

Robertson stepped forward and opened his mouth to speak, but Dragging Canoe ignored him. He turned to the tribes gathered around them, inquiring, "What makes each of you believe—each of our elders believe—that this time will be any different? Now this paper tells us we must move further to the west, further than many of us have ever traveled, so these men can take our crops, can hunt the animals that are rightly ours, to live in the villages that we have lived and died to call our own."

He turned back to the elders. When he continued, his words came so viciously that he spat upon them. "I will not abide by this new treaty. Whole Indian Nations have melted away like snowballs in the sun before the white man's advance. They leave scarcely a name of our people except those wrongly recorded by their destroyers."

He paced in front of them. "Where are the Delaware?" he demanded, waving his hand at the handful of Delaware Indians interspersed throughout the crowd. "They have been reduced to a mere shadow of their former greatness. We had hoped the white men would not be willing to travel beyond the mountains. Now that hope is gone. They have passed the mountains, and have settled here, upon Cherokee land. Now they wish to have that usurpation sanctioned by this treaty."

He paused to glare at Henderson and Robertson before continuing, "When that is gained, the same encroaching spirit will lead them upon other Cherokee lands. New cessions will be asked until everything the Cherokees and their fathers have so long occupied will be demanded, and the remnant of the Ani Yvwiya, The Real People, once so great and formidable, will be compelled to seek refuge in some distant wilderness."

The crowds were beginning to mumble among themselves. Noquali was relieved that at least one Cherokee chief had the courage to say what many of them had felt for so long. Dragging Canoe continued, his vehemence growing, "There they will be permitted to stay only a short while, until they again behold the advancing banners of the same greedy host. And without any further retreat for the miserable Cherokee nation, the extinction of our race will be proclaimed."

A collective gasp ran through the crowd. Dragging Canoe glared at the white men before turning back to the Indians. "Should we not therefore run all risks, and incur all consequences, rather than to submit to further loss of our country?" Without waiting for a response, he turned and faced the elders again. "Such treaties may be alright for men who are too old to hunt or fight. As for me," he said, his eyes locking with Noquali's, "I have my young warriors about me. We will hold our land."

He strode to the edge of the circle. "I will not honor this treaty," he announced. "I swear to all those here and to all those we represent: the white man will never live in peace here. Let the rivers run red with their blood!"

# 1

## Virginia, 1779

Mary Neely sat on the floor at the top of the stairs, her swan-like neck arched forward as she strained to hear the men below.

The shadows grew long in the upstairs hallway as the sound of her younger brothers and sisters began to breathe in the rhythm of sleep; but Mary and her friend Hannah Stuart remained awake and alert. The two girls, both eighteen years old, looked more like sisters than friends: both were slight in stature with firm jaw lines and high cheekbones. Mary's hair was settling into a soft brunette after a summer of sun-streaked highlights, while Hannah's had more of a copper tone. They both had the mischievous light green eyes of the Scots-Irish, a becoming trait that was not lost on many.

They sat enraptured at the railing, huddled on the floor in their thin cotton gowns, their knees gathered beneath their chins and their arms wrapped around their ankles, watching and listening to the men below.

It was a meeting they had long anticipated, a culmination that had really begun a year earlier with a surprise visit from Colonel James Robertson, an old friend of Mary's father, Will, who delighted them with tales of his adventures in the west, of pristine wilderness and rolling hills there for the taking, of game so plentiful one only had to open the door and shoot without ever leaving the threshold. He spoke of a moon so large, he felt as if he could reach up and touch it; of waters so crisp and clear that livestock and men alike thrived upon it.

And in the weeks and months that followed, visits became more frequent; some from men Mary knew and others who were strangers. And along with the tales of adventure were new enticements for Pa to travel west to this new Eden.

He eventually acquiesced, leaving Mary's oldest brother Ike in charge of the joint operations of the family's cattle ranch and tobacco farm while he journeyed westward to see this new frontier with his own eyes. And upon his return, there were muffled conversations with Ma, discussions that went deep into the night when the children were presumed to be sleeping.

Mary lay awake those nights, listening to them and staring at the ceiling in their two-story home, catching bits of their conversation in between the breathing of her siblings, Jean and Beth, who shared her room. There were ten Neely children, ranging in age from Jean, the oldest at twenty-four to Jane, the youngest, who wasn't quite three; six girls and four boys living in a two-story home that was large by anyone's standards, living lives destined for success and wealth.

Now James Robertson was back, this time accompanied by several men, including Colonel John Donelson and a family friend, Tom Stuart. Neighbors from as far away as the Clinch River converged at the Neely house, mixing an autumn picnic with talk of more serious matters, matters concerning a migration westward.

"The cattle will be taken overland," Captain Robertson was saying as they gathered around a map. "I will be your guide, though Will Neely has been there often enough to assist me in the route. We'll leave in early December and arrive at Fort Nashborough before Christmas."

"Why not wait until spring?" Tom asked. At the sound of her father's voice, Hannah leaned forward and listened more intently.

"Indians," Pa said. His thick black hair caught the candlelight as he leaned toward the others. He was in his 40's but as fit as one half his age. He was an educated landowner who wasn't afraid of a hard day's work and had easily gained the respect of his fellowmen. "There are fewer attacks in the winter months," he was saying. "And with the leaves gone from the trees and the underbrush dead, we'll be able to see more of our route ahead."

"But the Indians," Tom pressed, "they have joined us in peace. Haven't the Cherokee sold their claim to the Cumberlands?"

"Yes," a tall man said, moving into the group.

"Captain John Blackmore," Hannah whispered to Mary. Her voice had a touch of awe in it.

Mary watched in fascination as the others parted to make room for him. He stood a full head taller than most of them. His shoulders were broad and he appeared fit enough to fell trees by himself. His hair was long and had a slight wave to it, and though it was black like her father's, it was coarser and wilder. His complexion was almost olive, and as he moved into the light cast by the candles, Mary was surprised to see that he was much younger than her father and most of the others.

"Richard Henderson convinced the Cherokee four years ago to sell their land," he was saying. "They use it as hunting grounds, and through our agreement they continue to frequent the area. We will live in peace among them."

"Then why should we fear Indian attacks?"

"One tribe refused to sign the agreement. Their leader, Dragging Canoe, still attacks the settlers moving westward. But there's no need to fear them; if we encounter them at all, it would only be in passing, as we will not be settling in their parts."

"Gentlemen," Captain Robertson interjected, "Captain Blackmore will not be accompanying us on the overland trip. Rather, he will lead the families from Fort Blackmore and the Clinch River region by water." He pointed at the map and waited for the others to follow the route he drew with his finger. "He will move along the Clinch River on flatboats, and will join up with John Donelson *here*, on the Tennessee River."

At the mention of his name, all eyes turned to Colonel Donelson. In contrast with Blackmore, he was shorter, his spine rounded and his physique slight; his hair had long ago turned gray and his face had a weathered, permanently woebegone expression. He was well respected, however, as a former member of the Virginia House of Burgesses and was treated as a senior statesman.

"We have flatboats being built as we speak," Donelson said in a rapid-fire voice. "Many of you here tonight will accompany me from Fort Patrick Henry…Captain Robertson's family will accompany my own on my boat, *The Adventure*, as well as Robert Cartwright and his family.

"Will, your family will also travel by boat; you will need to appoint someone to take charge of them."

"I will take charge."

Mary's eyes searched the floor below for the source of the voice. From the shadows in a corner of the room emerged her mother. She was the only female but as she marched into the center of the gathering, Mary knew she was a force to be reckoned with. She was as tall as Pa, and unlike Mary, she was big-boned and buxom. She had copper hair that could make her visible from a quarter mile away, and she had a habit of fixing her eyes upon a person as if daring them to disagree—and they usually didn't.

Colonel Donelson looked to Pa to interject but when he didn't, he cleared his throat. "Now, Maggie, you know we need a man's name."

"Why?" she demanded, crossing her arms in front of her. "You don't think I'm capable of managing my own family?"

Several men backed away while the others became acutely interested in their shoes or the flooring. Mary and Hannah leaned forward with growing excitement.

"That's not it," the Colonel said, forcing his most agreeable voice, "that's just the way it's done. You know that."

"Demanding a man's name is a silly custom concocted by a man."

"Just for now," Pa said, stepping forward and placing his hand on the small of her back, "let's use Ike's name. Just to keep things moving along here."

With the mention of his name, twenty-one year old Ike stepped forward. He was taller than Pa and more slightly built but he was solid. His black hair was cut short and he was clean-shaven. He walked with the air of a man accustomed to conquering hard work with ease, but his true love lay with law books. He stopped when he reached the Colonel. "I am up to the challenge," he said with confidence and pride.

"Good," Donelson said, pulling up a chair. A quill pen and inkwell were quickly brought to the table. *Isaac Neely*, he wrote on a piece of paper adjacent to the map.

Even from this distance, Mary knew Ma's lips were pursed and they had yet to hear the end of this matter.

"We will have to determine who else will begin the journey with me," Colonel Donelson was saying, "and who will accompany Captain Blackmore."

Hannah's father stepped forward. "My family and I will begin at the Clinch River with the Captain," he said.

Mary's and Hannah's eyes met. "You'll be with the Captain," Mary said conspiratorially. "He's young and handsome."

Hannah slapped at her. "Stop it, Mary Neely," she said with a wide grin. But when she returned to hugging her legs, she sighed deeply. "It's wonderful, isn't it?"

"Moving? I don't know. I'm going to miss it here." Mary's eyes followed the stairs to the room below, where the men were lined up to place their names on one list or the other. "George says his family won't be moving."

"George Spears?" Hannah asked. Her mouth turned downward. "He hasn't asked you for your hand yet?"

Mary shook her head. "Not yet," she said, "but I am sure it's only a matter of time." She eyed Captain Blackmore; his shoulders and broad back reminded her of George, though the latter had sandy hair and gray-green eyes, a testament to his German ancestry. His father, Old Man Spears, owned a tobacco farm nearby; Mary would miss hearing his thick accent.

"We're going to love it at Fort Nashborough," Hannah was saying. "It's going to be so exciting, traveling so far. And a riverboat journey, at that! Think of the adventures we'll be able to tell our grandchildren! The mountains we'll see, the people we'll meet... It's going to be Heaven on Earth, Mary Neely, I can feel it. I can feel it in my bones."

Mary watched her friend's face glowing with excitement. Despite her own reservations, she forced herself to smile. She wouldn't dare extinguish Hannah's enthusiasm, even if something was nagging at her soul, threatening to extinguish her own.

# 2

Pa left on a crisp fall day in early November when the trees were barren and the sky had turned a wintry gray-blue. It had been a bittersweet parting; there was an excitement in the air as their herd of three hundred cattle was readied to head toward Fort Patrick Henry, but Mary's heart was heavy with the months they would be apart.

"Let me go with you, Pa," she'd begged that morning. "I can help drive the cattle and cook for you, too."

He brushed a lock of hair from her brow and smoothed her hair. "You know you'll always be my favorite," he whispered.

"Please, Pa, let me go with you."

He smiled at her with that ready grin that brightened his entire face, but his eyes were somber. "River travel is easier," he said, "and safer. You'll cover much more ground in a boat than we will on land."

"But—"

"We'll be together on Christmas Day, Mary. I promise."

She waited until he said his good-byes to the rest of the family and to neighbors and friends who had come out on this chilly morn to see him off. Then she walked with him to his horse, a beautiful buckskin with a coat the color of a gold coin and a mane and tail as jet black as Pa's hair. She tightened his packs, though they were already tight, as he mounted.

"Be good," he said, gathering the reins in his hands. "Keep your head down."

"What does that mean?" she asked quizzically.

He didn't answer but looked at her briefly before turning the horse and clicking his heels. She watched in silence as he rode away with three able-bodied farm hands, their voices calling to the cattle dogs as they rode out of sight.

"Mary," a gentle voice interrupted her thoughts.

She turned to face George Spears. "George."

He took off his hat, though the wind had a sharp chill to it, and kneaded the brim in his beefy hands. "I know you'll miss your pa," he said at last.

"I wish I could have gone with him," she said wistfully. "I don't understand it; about three hundred people are to be in Captain Robertson's expedition. They'll need meals prepared and clothes washed…"

"He loves you, Mary," he said. "They'll have other cattle to herd, as well as sheep and other livestock. It won't be an easy trip."

"Hard work never put a scare in me," she said.

"Still," he said, his voice growing quieter, "it gives us more time together. I—I'm not relishing the thought of you being away from me, Mary."

"Oh?" she said, tilting her head coquettishly. "And what will you miss the most?"

He looked into her eyes for a long time. "Your voice," he said finally. "Your voice in the Sunday meetin', singin'. I've always loved the sound of your voice."

The noise of the men and the cattle faded to nothing more than a whisper on the wind. She pulled her shawl closer about her neck. "Will you join me there, George? At Fort Nashborough?"

A slow blush crept over his broad face. "I'll be joining you, Mary. You can count on it. Just as soon as I'm able, I aim to join the Virginia militia and head west to be near you."

"Pa says Fort Nashborough will be claimed as Virginia Territory, and somebody's already there to protect it."

"George Rogers Clark," George said. "He's been gathering up men in these parts, and I aim to join him. Might be next spring, after the tobacco is planted."

A sharp wind sent a chill up her spine and she shivered. She realized the others had already gone inside. "I best get with the others," she said. "Will you be joining us for supper?"

He walked with her toward the house. "I'll be back, Mary Neely, tonight and every night until you're gone. And I hope—" his voice came fast and low "—I hope the time creeps by for us so every minute feels like forever."

CASO

In the days after Pa left, the time flew faster than the birds heading south. Folks said the number of flocks heralded the approach of a lengthy, hard winter ahead. But Mary barely noticed them as the Neely house was abuzz with activity; they were up before dawn and climbed into bed exhausted at the end of long days. Ma acted like a general commanding the Neely clan, and her efficiency had a dramatic effect.

A flatboat, a boat the likes of which Mary had never seen before, was being built for them. It would become their home for the travel westward. She would lay eyes on it for the first time when they reached Fort Patrick Henry; to Ma's chagrin, it would not be until December, weeks beyond their original plans. It would contain a cabin half the size of their current home, so their days were filled with cleaning and clearing the house and paring down their belongings, taking only those things necessary to start their new life.

As November came to a close and December began, a sharp wind blew in from the north, bringing ice and snow. Mary lay awake at night, listening to the wind howling outside her window and watching the frost accumulate upon the panes. She huddled deeper under the down covers as the embers in the fireplace died away, shivering until morning when she arose and helped her sisters ignite it once again.

As Christmas approached, the snowdrifts rose as high as her knees, the bitter cold biting into her face as she made her way to the barn each morning to feed the chickens.

Folks began to remark that they had never seen a winter become this cold so early in the season. And try though she might, she couldn't help but wonder if she ought to listen to an urge rising up inside her, an urge to remain where she was. It didn't bode well, this unusually cold and bitter winter. It didn't bode well at all.

# 3

## December 22, 1779

Mary awakened in the semi-gloom before dawn. She'd been dreaming of her mattress stuffed with soft down, of sitting up and leisurely stretching before stepping onto the hardwood floor in a real house.

But as she awakened, she realized her nose was so numb that she feared it might have become frost-bitten. And when she burrowed her head beneath the cover, she found herself staring at her sister Jean's stocking feet. She rolled onto her back, knowing if she turned to her other side she would be staring at Beth's feet instead.

Her dreams were replaced with the reality of the crowded mattress on their first night aboard their flatboat. They had two mattresses in the confined area, upon which eleven people slept. In Mary's bed, seven females slumbered; Mary, two sisters and Ma with their heads at one end while three sisters slept with their heads at the opposite end. To afford them each more room, they were alternated with feet in between each head.

The boys fared slightly better; since there were only four of them, there were two headed one way and two headed the other. But though the youngest, Johnny, was only six years old, he had a tendency to turn sideways during the night, kicking his brothers in his sleep until they awakened and turned him right-side again.

But as cramped as they were, Mary did not relish the thought of climbing out from under the warm covers and facing the December frost.

Christmas was only three days away and they had yet to leave sight of Fort Patrick Henry.

They had arrived at the fort weeks ago, fully expecting their flatboat to be there awaiting them. Instead, they found dozens of families in disarray and the flatboats not yet built. They relied on the kind hearts and open doors of the people living at the fort that took them in and shared their meals, their beds, and the warmth of their fires. But as the days crept past, their living accommodations seemed to grow smaller and their hosts' patience shorter. Tempers flared as days turned into weeks. And as the weather turned ever more frigid, one couldn't go anywhere without hearing coughs that seemed to rattle inside weary chests and sniffles that turned into raging colds that passed from one to another like wildfire.

Mary joined the church choir and tried to settle into somewhat of a routine, as each of her brothers and sisters found meaningful activities to keep them occupied as time crawled by.

Letters were sent back and forth between Colonel Donelson and Captain Blackmore, and Mary took the opportunity to write to Hannah. She'd received her response only two days before; they were also without boats, and the treacherous cold had moved into Fort Blackmore as well. But in Hannah's perpetually positive manner, she was certain the delay would be to their advantage. She was still counting the days, though, that their glorious adventure would begin and as Mary had read her words, she could envision the gleam in her friend's eyes. It had been like a ray of sunshine amidst the growing squalor of their encampment.

The boats were readied only yesterday, and all their pent-up energy seemed to be spent at once as the fort became a flurry of activity. They excitedly packed their belongings and carried them to what would become their floating home.

Mary didn't think she would ever forget the look on Ma's face when she saw the boat for the first time. It wasn't half the size of their former home, as they'd been told; it wasn't even a fourth as large.

"It's barely larger than a raft," Ma had said, her voice quivering with apprehension.

"A raft is a dang sight bigger," Mary's brother Sam had declared.

Ma's lips were pursed and her brow furrowed as she inspected their temporary home. She was uncharacteristically quiet, something that wasn't lost on Mary.

Mary understood how the flatboat got its name; it was perfectly flat but for one room built in the middle of it. Under Ma's direction, they'd spent the day trying to pack and repack the single room with all their possessions, but in the end, they gave away or sold half of all they'd brought. It was many of the larger pieces that they were forced to unload: the couch overstuffed with duck down, the leather hand-sewn in Great Britain; the dining table that seated twelve; and all but two of the dining chairs. Then each Neely child from the oldest to the youngest had to select two of their personal items to give up. Mary selected her writing table, as it took up the most room, and the dainty chair that went with it. And as she watched it being carted away by its new owner, she reminded herself as her heart sank there would be other writing tables in her future, once they reached their own version of the Promised Land.

In the end, most of the room was packed tight with the food and belongings they would need for the trip. Only the area large enough for the two mattresses was set aside as living space for the entire Neely family on their river journey.

They'd spent the night within sight of the fort, their first night with eleven of them piled together upon two mattresses. And now, with the first light peeking around the edge of the small cabin door they called a hatch, they began to stir.

A man's voice called out in anger, followed by the shrill voice of a woman. Mary glanced across the room at her brothers just as Ike reached for his pistol.

They scrambled out of bed already fully clothed, converging on the hatch at the same time. Ma opened it, holding her gun close to her skirts. She stood for a brief moment, her head cocked and listening.

"It's the Jennings," she whispered. Her voice sounded as if she were in wonderment at the husband and wife arguing so loudly that their voices carried from one flatboat to the next.

Sam brushed past. "I'll be in the outhouse, makin' my own noises," he grumbled as he climbed down from the boat. Unlike his older brother Ike, his hair was long and had a tendency to look unkempt, the brown locks curling slightly as they went this way and that. He enjoyed hard work, driving cattle and breaking horses, and he'd been as disappointed as Mary that Pa had not taken him on the overland journey. Now he buttoned his suspenders and pulled them up as he headed toward the woods.

Mary stepped onto the slick deck, trying to steady herself even as she assisted the smallest Neely children. The voices from the next boat were growing louder and more insistent and despite herself, she found herself listening intently to their words.

"I'm not going," Mr. Jennings was saying. "That's that."

"Oh, yes, you are going," Mrs. Jennings screeched. "You're not throwing away our lives based on a silly little dream!"

"It wasn't a 'silly little dream'! It was a premonition, I tell you, an omen! We didn't reach Fort Nashborough—we were attacked, some of us were killed and others captured!"

Mrs. Jennings snorted loudly, and the Neely's mottled hound, Patches, began to bark. Ma immediately quieted him, and as Mary's eyes met hers, she realized Ma had been listening as intently as she.

"I've given up everything we had," Mrs. Jennings' voice was shrill. "My beautiful home, my servants, all of my fine clothes and furniture—my flower gardens, my carriage—everything! And now that it's all gone, you want me to turn back? And what, pray tell, would I go back *to*? Some other woman is in my house now! Someone else is riding my mare, someone else is wearing my clothes! You promised me more than I ever had here, if only I trusted you and went to Nashborough—"

"Mr. Jennings is in hell," Mary's brother Billy whispered hoarsely, "he's lost everything he owned but he still has his wife."

Mary rolled her eyes.

"Hush," Ma hissed.

"I'm asking you to trust me now," Mr. Jennings was saying. "Don't go! We don't have to—!"

"But, Daddy," Mary recognized the voice of Mr. Jennings' oldest daughter, Elizabeth, "I will have to go. My husband is arriving at Fort Nashborough any day now, along with Mr. Neely and Mr. Robertson—"

Mary glanced at Ma. At the sound of her husband's name, her face grew crimson. Mary wondered if she was sick with worry over Pa's fate and his overland journey.

"And I'm with child, Daddy," Elizabeth continued, "you know that! I have to go—I can't stay here without my husband, my dear Ephraim—and I want Momma to be with me when my time comes. I'll need her!"

The arguing continued unabated, but now others were beginning to emerge from their boats. And all were beginning to look not toward the Jennings boat, but toward the rear of the fleet.

A man bundled in layers of clothing and thick black boots was striding briskly along the shoreline, calling out to each boat and rapping on the side of the hulls. Ike rushed to the stern and listened as the man approached.

"We're taking off for the Cumberlands!" he called back to them.

Within the hour, the entire Neely clan was pushing away from shore. As far as Mary could see, there were flatboats filled with families, servants, dogs, and a few livestock, all moving out of sight of Fort Patrick Henry. Patches yipped gleefully as they pushed away; his barking was picked up by dogs in other boats as if they were speaking to one another. It made for a noisy but exciting start to their journey.

Each family had been compelled to appoint two members for flatboat training, and Ma and Ike had represented the Neely clan. Upon their return from class each day, they had instructed the others how to steer, push away from shore, and navigate the waters even while their boat stood perfectly still. On top of the cabin were two long poles called tillers—one that reached over the bow and the other extending over the stern. The one in the rear actually steered the boat but in the event they got turned around in the river, they could switch to the other side so the bow and the stern became interchangeable. Ike and Sam were at the top, which they called the bridge, and from their high vantage point, they could see down into the water.

Mary and Billy stood along one side with long poles, which they used to push the boat from shore and help guide it toward the center of the river where the current was strongest. Jean and Beth were on the opposite side, hopefully working in tandem with the others, while Ma remained at the bow.

This was Mary's first chance to actually churn the water with her pole, and she felt the excitement welling up in her throat as the vessel complied and began moving steadily westward.

She turned back toward the fort and watched as the Jennings boat cast off from shore, Mr. Jennings valiantly steering the boat toward the current. It had been a losing battle, Mary thought, fighting against two women. But as they moved further from the fort and from civilization itself, she hoped Mr. Jennings was wrong and his dream really hadn't been an omen of things to come.

# 4

## February 27, 1780

Mary couldn't remember when she'd ever been this cold as she made her way along a meandering path from makeshift outhouses to the boats, which were hopelessly locked by ice at the mouth of Cloud's Creek. They had managed to get far enough from Fort Patrick Henry to prevent the logical decision to turn back, but were now more than two months behind in their journey. Fort Nashborough felt like a million miles—and just as many years—away.

The trees were bent low with naked branches encapsulated in thick sheets of ice. As she slipped along the icy path, she found herself jumping each time a great branch cracked with the added weight. A moment later, it would hurtle to the forest floor with a great thud. What was more frightening was when the crack was followed by sheer silence; at such times, she would peer upward only to find the orphaned branch had become lodged within the limbs of other trees, perhaps to fall at a later time.

As she tried to hurry along the path, she felt irritated at how far they had placed the outhouses from the boats, although she knew in her heart it had made logical sense. But she felt isolated and vulnerable in this great, strange forest and she longed to be back among her family.

She heard another crack but she halted immediately, her heart thudding inside her chest with a growing viciousness. This one had come not from overhead but from the ground, as though someone had stepped on a piece of timber and broken it.

"Who goes there?" she called out.

A lone bird flew upward from the trees, its feathers pitiful in the biting cold and for a brief moment, she wondered how it would survive the winter. But in the next instant, she heard another crack and then another.

She turned, narrowing her eyes as if she could focus more easily past the gray trunks and inhospitable forest floor. "Who goes there?" she called again.

She spotted a head disappearing behind a tree and a flash of a long feather extending beyond it.

She turned back to the path and hurried along, her shoe soles too slick for the icy terrain, and she gasped as she almost tumbled into a tree. She heard more cracking sounds behind her and she turned to look even as she continued moving toward the shore. It was unmistakable now; the person was wearing a band of some sort with feathers protruding from it. She was unable to see the body, as it remained hidden behind the trees, but the headdress seemed to tilt this way and that as if it was mocking her.

Her feet moved faster now and she grabbed at the branches as she hastened along. In her growing urgency to reach her boat, the trees helped more than once to keep her from falling flat on her face. Her heart was thumping wildly and the terrain below began to swim before her.

She burst into a small clearing that overlooked the river. She could see the boats below, the people milling about and the shoreline dotted with fires in preparation for the evening meal. Gulping a great breath of frigid air, she filled her lungs and prepared to scream.

A figure jumped in front of her and for a moment, she could only see a flash of long, white feathers and a black robe covering the man from his shoulders to his ankles. But when her scream reached her lips, it was replaced with a shout: "Billy!"

Her younger brother doubled up with laughter.

Mary wanted to slap him. "What do you think you're doing?"

"I found this here set of feathers in the woods," he said, still roaring with laughter. "Scared you, huh?"

"You ought to be ashamed of yourself. What if I'd had a gun? I'd 've shot you, that's what." She pushed past him and continued down the path.

"I got you good," he chortled as he followed.

She stopped and stared at him. He'd turned thirteen years old at Fort Patrick Henry. He'd shot up at least a foot in the previous year and was almost as tall as Ike, but there the resemblance faded. His hair was sandy, turning blond in the summer months, and freckles scattered across his nose. He was gangly; either the clothes of a man hung on him as if his frame was barely larger than a skeleton, or the pants from the previous year stopped six inches before reaching his ankles. He didn't seem to care, though, and Mary began to wonder what he'd ever amount to.

She caught herself before she began a tongue lashing. It would do no good, she thought as she turned back. It would be better for her to simply save her breath.

When she broke through the trees, the wind felt as though it would slice her raw cheeks as it whipped across her skin. She pulled her shawl across her face in an effort to stave off the cold, but the material scraped across her dry, cracked lips, almost causing her to cry out with the pain.

She knew from the way the layers of clothes hung on her own petite frame, that she had lost weight—weight she couldn't afford to lose. Her mind turned quickly toward the evening's meal as she neared the boats.

Before their departure, Ma had carefully calculated plenty of food for their journey, and then they'd packed almost a third more—fruits and vegetables they'd canned themselves, sack cloths filled with grain, salt pork and cured meats. But with the incessant delays, they had been forced to ration or run the risk of running completely out of food. They had even stopped feeding Patches hush puppies—small bits of fried cornbread so called because they hushed the puppies so they could eat their own meals in peace—and began eating them themselves.

Without an extra layer of fat to keep her warm, she felt like a skeletal figure made entirely of ice. Her outer garments, like those of everyone around her, were constantly covered in hoarfrost, thawing only when they converged inside their tiny rooms to sleep. She knew once she saw her body again, she would be appalled at how emaciated she had become. But for now, her figure was hidden beneath layers of clothing that she'd rarely changed in the two months they'd been on the river; that would have required removing the clothes she had on, and she didn't dare bare her skin for fear of frostbite. The stench of dozens of bodies in the same circumstance as her own filled the air, along with the coughs and wheezes of so many unaccustomed to such hardship.

She reached the Neely boat and tried to warm her hands in front of the fire as her tired eyes roamed the shoreline, watching some of the servants tend to the livestock. A few of the servants were hired hands and freed black men but many others were slaves. Already, it was rumored that some of them were suffering from frostbite, as their hands were uncovered and their fingers exposed. One of Captain Hutchings' men was limping grotesquely, and Mary wondered if his foot had been injured.

She crossed the camp, her encounter with Billy all but forgotten. She kept the man in sight as she wandered past fires, children playing and women cooking. She caught a glimpse of 20-year-old Elizabeth Jennings Peyton as she made her way along the shore in the opposite direction. She was now heavy with child and waddled as she walked. Though she had been pregnant when they boarded her father's flatboat, everyone expected she would reach the Cumberlands before giving birth. But since the winter had set in with the hardest freeze and heaviest snows anyone could remember, it was now inevitable that she would give birth along the river. Mr. Jennings' dream had faded from most folks' minds as they mustered the strength they would need just to get through each day.

Mary said a quick prayer for Elizabeth. This was her first child, and according to the midwives on the journey, the first always took its time because the first had to blaze the trail. Elizabeth shared her small flatboat with six others—her parents, her brother Jonathan, Jr., two slaves—a man and a woman—and Obediah, a teenage friend of Jonathan's.

She reached Captain Hutchings' servant as he was leaving the flatboat. She held up her hand to stop him.

He halted immediately and dropped his eyes to the ground. It was impossible to tell how old he was; Mary suspected he might have been in his thirties but an unkind life had left its toll on him. He was thin as a rail and his spine was beginning to round outward as if he were carrying loaded buckets. "Yes, ma'am?" he asked politely.

"Simon," Mary said, "is there something the matter with your feet?"

"No, ma'am."

Mary hesitated. He continued peering at the ground and from the way in which he avoided her eyes, she knew her presence there made him uncomfortable. His skin was the color and texture of burlap and his forehead was deeply lined. He was dressed in cotton pants and a thin cotton shirt under a torn and dusty jacket. His shoes were worn thin and one of his toes protruded through a ragged hole.

She bent down and pulled his pants leg away from his shoe, gasping as she saw his blackened ankle.

"Simon," she said, "you have frostbite!"

"No, ma'am."

"I didn't ask you, I told you! Look at your ankle! Take that shoe off immediately. Let me see it."

Simon hesitated and Mary repeated her demand. Trying to balance on his opposite foot, he attempted to remove his shoe but it was swollen to such proportions that he was unable to dislodge it. "Please don't," he whimpered as he set his foot back down.

"What's going on here?"

Mary turned in the direction of the voice. "Captain Hutchings, this man has frostbite."

"Is that so, Simon?"

"No, sir."

"Look at his ankle," Mary said, motioning. "It's completely black." She pulled the pants leg up again. "There are blisters all over it. His foot is swollen and I'd be surprised if he can even feel it. You must tend to this man at once."

Captain Hutchings peered at her with small, sharp eyes; his expression was completely immobile. He was Colonel Donelson's son-in-law, having married his daughter Catherine twelve years earlier. Mary assumed he was about forty years old and she supposed she should have felt insolent speaking to him as she was less than half his age, but she didn't.

"You must get this man off his feet immediately." Mary motioned for one of the children nearby. "You! Get me some old rags and soak them in hot water. Don't dally about it." She turned back to one of the other servants. "And you! Carry this man to that fire yonder. He must get warmed straight away!"

The man looked at Mary and then at Captain Hutchings. The captain nodded, and Simon was picked up as though he weighed no more than a sack of potatoes and carried close to a nearby fire. Mary followed as the child returned with the rags.

After a great deal of effort, Mary and Captain Hutchings managed to pull the shoe off Simon's foot and they bandaged it with the warm cloths. Then they removed his other shoe and found his other foot was almost as black and decayed. Despite his protests, Mary peeled back the pants leg to his knees to reveal blackened, blistered skin. The stench was almost unbearable. After bandaging both feet and legs, she ordered two children to remain with him to keep the fire going and the rags hot.

She motioned for the captain to follow her as she moved away from the servant.

"I had no idea," he said when they were out of earshot.

"I suspect he was afraid to tell you." She took a deep breath. "He's going to lose both legs."

Captain Hutchings sucked in his breath.

"There's no helping it; he's too far gone. You must send for the doctor immediately and have his legs amputated."

The captain cupped his chin in his hand. "He won't be of any use without his legs," he murmured.

"Good God, his legs aren't of any use to him now! It's a miracle he could even manage to walk on them."

Captain Hutchings stared at Mary with cold eyes that seemed to pierce right through to her soul. She felt as if he was wondering who she was, to diagnose another's ailments, she who had no medical training? And who was she to demand care for another's servants?

Her eyes drifted past the captain and toward Simon. "But for the grace of God..." she began in a whisper.

"Yes," he said in a firm voice. "But for the grace of God."

# 5

Noquali sat atop the jet black stallion and studied the pitiful condition of the settlers below. The wind was stronger here on the crest and whipped past him with a bitterness and razor-like ferocity, but he did not appear to notice. His feet and legs were covered in beaver with the warmth of the fur on the inside, where it lay against his skin. Lapped over his beaver breeches was a long shirt made from buckskin. A full panther pelt completed his attire, its head perched atop his own head with its legs draped over his shoulders and around his hips. The black fur of the panther blended seamlessly with the horse, causing him to appear like some mythical creature rising out of the earth.

It had been more than four years since the signing of the treaty. Noquali had accompanied Dragging Canoe to the mountainous region and established a village they called Tsikamagi, along with leaders of other tribes who resisted the white man's invasion. Their members consisted primarily of Cherokee but also included a few Shawnee, Delaware and Wyandot who were determined to protect the land of their fathers and drive the white people back to the east, to the other side of the mountains.

The white men referred to Tsikamagi as Chickamauga and were now referring to those who fought with Dragging Canoe as Chickamauga Indians. It was ironic, Noquali thought, for the river that carried the same name meant "the river of death" and his people had become a serpent of death to the white men who ventured west of the mountains.

Indeed, they had fought the white invaders to the south and east, eventually establishing two additional villages: Dakwayi, which the white men referred to as Toqua; and Yunsayi to the south, which was also called Buffalo Town. They had established an alliance with the British, who were also fighting the settlers, as they had promised the Cherokee the full return of their land if they helped them defeat the Rebels. It was an uneasy alliance, as they'd learned the white men's word changed more quickly than the seasons, and so they'd also forged agreements with the French, who were more interested in trading with them than in acquiring their lands. And they'd needed traders, for they brought with them guns and ammunition.

The horse Noquali sat upon had been one of the spoils of war. They had become expert at watching the settlers and gauging their geographic progress westward, then attacking them when the time was right. As a result, they'd acquired many horses.

He leaned forward in his saddle, another acquisition from their attacks, and noted the dogs. They were a problem, as they would announce their presence and take away the element of surprise. But they had encountered dogs many times before, and they knew how to best approach. They had become expert at appearing from the shelter of the trees and mountains, mounting surprise attacks and raids that led to the capture of white women and the slaughter of white men, and they were growing rich with the spoils of war.

He watched a young man emerge from the forest. No doubt he was a settler, judging from his clothing, but he wore atop his head a band of feathers. Noquali felt his blood begin to boil. The ancestors of many of the tribes were buried in these parts, and he wondered if the man had robbed one of the burial sites. He supposed the rains might have washed away the top layers of soil upon the hilly area, thus exposing those precious items of the dead, but it was easier simply to hate them and to think the worst. It was, he thought, perhaps one of the things that kept the Chickamaugas fighting long after their neighboring brothers had surrendered their territories to the white man.

He narrowed his eyes. This group was larger than the others. They had grown accustomed to the trickle of settlers along the rivers; a flatboat here or a small group of canoes there. But this was different. He estimated over a hundred in this flotilla; women, children, men, and enough possessions to establish villages to the west. They were also traveling at the most treacherous time of the year, when the river often froze and game was less plentiful. Fish escaped to the bottom of the river to avoid the ice and crops at villages along their route had been harvested many months earlier.

Noquali would normally have been in one of the villages himself, staying warm by the fires and getting fat over the winter months. There were seldom battles raging between the settlers and the Indians during this time of year; it was too difficult to travel over icy and snow-covered terrain, especially through the mountain passes. Instead, they rested and bided their time until the spring thaws, when they would fight again.

But they had spies in many places, and several had recently returned from Fort Patrick Henry and Blackmore's Fort, further north, where they traded amicably with the settlers. Perhaps the white men thought they had joined their ranks and culture, as these Cherokee dressed more like the settlers than their blood brothers, spoke perfect English and understood well the ways of the white man. They traded furs and Indian jewelry for iron pots and leather boots, and when they left the forts and returned to the west, they brought with them news of two large fleets. It was said they would depart the two forts at nearly the same time with plans to meet along the way, carrying what would be the first large congregation of settlers to the land known as The Cumberlands.

And so Noquali sat atop his horse like a statue, studying the people below, counting them carefully, and assessing their strengths and weaknesses. They would not make it to The Cumberlands; he knew that, could feel that with the blood that coursed through him. If they annihilated this first group, it would be cutting the head off an enemy threatening their existence.

He heard a movement behind him but he did not turn his head. Instead, his eyes remained fixed on the people below while his sharp mind calculated the distance between himself and the visitor. He recognized the sound of the horse, the breathing of the man atop it, and before he came into view, he knew it was Archie Coody.

Archie was a half-breed. His father was a Scots-Irishman and his mother was a Cherokee squaw. He moved between the two worlds almost effortlessly, understanding them both. He'd served as an interpreter many times, but it seemed to Noquali that he embraced the life and the heritage of the Cherokee more than he ever identified with the white man. He had participated in many ambushes, sometimes helping to divide up the spoils and watch as the settlers were tortured; other times, he stepped in and purchased captives, saving them from sure death, and traded them later.

He was a large man; his skin was darker than the white man's but not quite the complexion of the Cherokee. His eyes were as green as the meadows on a spring day, and his hair often gained red streaks during the summer months when the sun bore down mercilessly upon their heads.

As he came alongside Noquali, though, his head was covered with the head of a large black bear, the pelt reaching around his large body just as Noquali wore the panther's pelt. His eyes were also fixed on the people below and the two sat in silence for a long while before speaking.

"The ice is breaking downstream," Archie said at last.

Noquali nodded. "Then they will be leaving soon."

"The Shoals are shallow."

"Shallow enough for the boats to be grounded?"

"Possibly. Especially the larger ones." Archie gestured toward two boats taking up the rear. "They have too much on those boats; they will be weighed down at the Shoals."

Noquali watched as a woman heavy with child painstakingly climbed aboard one of the boats. Then he gently clicked his heels against the stallion's side and turned his back to the shore. "Then we will see them downstream," he said, tipping his head forward in a farewell gesture.

He was moving down the mountainside when Archie called out to him. "Will you be needing help?"

"You are always welcome to join us," Noquali answered without turning back, "and always welcome to partake in the spoils."

# 6

The following morning dawned cold and bleak but as reports from scouts filtered back to them, the camp came alive with excitement. They had discovered ice breaking up in the river ahead, clearing the way for their journey to truly begin at long last. A buzz went through the camp as everyone scurried to complete the morning's chores but finally they were underway.

All but the smallest of the Neelys remained outside the cabin, helping to keep the flatboat in the center of the river with the tiller and long poles. They quickly learned if they were not in cadence, the boat would spin in all directions and Mary had to admit it was rather comical to see some of the settlers trying valiantly to steer their boats while they gyrated in the water. The group was comprised of farmers, ranchers, lawyers, doctors, surveyors, and opportunists—but sailors, they most definitely were not.

Directly in front of them was Captain Hutchings' boat. While he stood on deck and studied their surroundings, his servants navigated the river—all but Simon, who sat just outside the single room huddled in a blanket and stared at the wake left behind.

He had refused to allow the doctor to amputate his legs. And although the captain could have ordered it, he did not. Mary wondered if they both were under the delusion that he could recover, and she worried that their inability to stop the frostbite's progression would cost the man his life.

The hard reality, she knew, was a servant was worthless without the use of his limbs and Simon would be no exception. Perhaps the man thought he could give the illusion that his condition was only temporary. As Mary continued working with the pole, she glanced in his direction. Though he looked increasingly sickly, she reassured herself that at least he was off his feet and under a blanket. After all, the captain's wife, Catherine, was partly responsible for his well-being and she occasionally checked on him, as did their small son, Christopher.

The Jennings were in the rear, having gotten off to a slower start than the others due to Elizabeth's condition. Mary tried to spot them, but it was impossible with the long line of flatboats and canoes.

The river wound like a serpent around increasingly higher mountains and Mary found herself staring upward at the towering Clinch Mountain as they floated past. The mountain's ridgeline stretched as far as the eye could see in one continuous, ice-encrusted path that made her marvel.

She figured there were twenty flatboats in their party in addition to the canoes that made their way up and down the vessels, making sure all was well and carrying news and instructions from one family to the next. And somewhere out there beyond Clinch Mountain were another ten or so vessels that included Hannah Stuart and her family. She found herself wanting to move faster, to get further downriver, until they reached the point where the rivers collided and the two expeditions would be united. She could see Hannah's dimpled smile and hear her distinct laughter which always sounded like a medley of bells... And then her mind wandered to George and as the miles were left behind her, she found herself missing his broad shoulders, his ready smile and his gentle touch.

"Is all well?"

Mary was jolted back to the present as one of the men rowed past in a canoe.

"Yes!" Ike shouted from the bridge above Mary. "And how is everyone behind us?"

"Fair," came the response. "Mrs. Peyton had some false labor this morning, and she's resting now. Several have got the croup."

Mary groaned. The croup could spread through the boats like wildfire, which meant those who were sick would have to be quarantined. They certainly could not afford any more delays, she thought, even if she had to paddle her way to Fort Nashborough alone!

"Taking a break," Ike said as he climbed down the ladder from the bridge to the deck. He stretched his legs and Mary wondered if the winds were more vicious on the bridge, and if he was trying to keep the cold from stiffening his bones. A book stuck out of his coat pocket; he was never without one, she thought. Especially his law books. He seemed most content when he was lost within their pages.

She wiped her brow and marveled at the perspiration that accumulated in the cold of winter. As she looked at the sky, she realized the sun was high and hotter than it had been in days past. It must be noon, she thought.

A movement caught her eye and she followed it. It looked to be a bald eagle and a large one at that. As it soared high above them, she estimated its wingspan at nearly six feet across. In awe, she followed its fluid movement as it climbed ever higher, and she found herself wishing she were a bird. If she could only soar like that, she thought, she could be in Fort Nashborough within days!

As it crested the mountain, she gasped. A row of Indians stood along the top of the mountain, their feathers stark against the noon sky.

"What is it?" Ike asked, coming alongside her.

Mary glanced at him before turning back toward the mountain. Her heart was pounding so rapidly that her chest hurt. "Indians—" she began, and then stopped.

There was nothing along the ridgeline.

"Where?" He shielded his eyes from the sun's glare and peered at the mountain.

She pointed. "They were right there."

"Where?"

She pointed. "Right along there."

He stared for a long moment and then shook his head. "There's nothing there, Mary."

"I know I saw them!"

"You're spooking yourself. You're listening to Billy's wild Indian stories late at night, and you're imagining things."

"Now, now," Ma said, joining them. She stared at the ridgeline long after Ike went to the stern. "Don't frighten the children, Mary."

Mary nodded silently and returned to her pole duty. But try as she might, she couldn't get them out of her mind. They were watching them; she was convinced of that. And even now as they floated westward, they were out there, watching them still.

# 7

It was late afternoon when Mary noticed the water had become sandy. When she stopped to look over the side, she was alarmed to see it had grown progressively shallower. As she hurriedly looked to the inhabitants in the boats in front of her, she found they too had noticed the change and were becoming increasingly alarmed.

Ike called out from the bridge to slow the vessel as they began to bottleneck. Amid the frantic shouts from the Neely boat and the one behind them, they hurried to extend their poles between them to prevent the vessels from colliding while Ike attempted to steer the boat out of harm's way.

Mary, Ma and Beth hurried to the bow to keep a proper distance from Captain Hutchings' boat. As Mary stared in front of her, she noticed Simon's pant legs were almost busting at the seams, and she realized his legs were beginning to swell to grotesque proportions. He was slumped on deck, and not even the sudden halt of the boats managed to awaken him. It was just as well, she thought with a sinking heart; as long as he's fainted he won't feel the pain.

She looked beyond them to Colonel Donelson's boat at the front of the line. She watched in horror as it hit the bottom of the river with a grinding noise. The boat just behind it rammed into it, pushing it deeper into the shallows. She watched as the inhabitants staggered across the deck amid screams and cries, trying to prevent themselves from being hurled overboard.

As the boats swirled in the waters, the men tried valiantly to steer them toward deeper water. A series of encouraging shouts sprang forth from the other boats. Sam and Billy rested their poles, each taking off their hats and shouting at the top of their lungs as if they were watching a horse race. Billy put two fingers in his mouth and whistled as loudly as he could, as if the mere sound could give the others the strength to reach deeper water.

But they came to an abrupt stop. From the movements of the men on board Colonel Donelson's boat, *The Adventure*, Mary could tell they were peering over the sides of the boat at the river bottom upon which their vessels were stranded.

Now silenced, Billy and Sam returned their caps to their heads and watched with growing seriousness.

Mary realized she had been holding her breath; she expelled it now as she watched the two boats attempt to cast off from the shoals. Several of the men jumped overboard in water up to their shoulders, diving beneath the surface to inspect the damage. The boats behind them were stacking up and several were beginning to drift in the deeper waters behind them.

The minutes crept past and then an hour. The winds began to tear through the valley, sending a chill up Mary's spine. She shivered and pulled her collar higher in an effort to protect her neck, but her clothing did precious little to defend her from the bitter cold.

She realized with a sinking heart they could not reach the far shores and the safety of the land, as the center of the river where they were currently stranded consisted of the deepest water. By the time the sun began to set, they were hopelessly locked together in the middle, stopped in their tracks by the two boats that now stretched sideways across the sandbar that had arisen like an iceberg to block their path.

The stunned silence was replaced with men's voices as they discussed their dire predicament, the cries of small children who were getting hungrier and colder, and the women determined to care for their families even if they remained in the middle of the river.

As Mary glanced upward at the mountain range surrounding them, she saw a single horse standing parallel with the ridgeline, its rider blending seamlessly with the animal and casting a dark silhouette in stark contrast to the snow-covered mountain.

"Ike!" Mary called out as her throat constricted, causing her voice to sound more like a hoarse whisper.

He knelt down on the bridge so he could hear her better, but her eyes had not wavered from the mountain. As he followed her gaze, he jumped back up to his full height and called out to the men in canoes.

"Indians!" Ike shouted, turning and pointing.

But before the men could turn to look, the horse and rider were gone, replaced by the sinking sun.

"We ought to go up there," Sam said, grabbing a musket as he came alongside Mary.

"And do what?"

"I ain't plannin' on sittin' here 'til I get a special invitation to a scalpin'," he said, his jaw squared. He straightened his spine as he spoke, causing him to appear more mature than his years. "I say we go on up there and kick some—"

"That's enough of that talk," Ma interjected as she joined them.

Sam fell silent but his face was dark and his eyes didn't waver from the mountaintop.

"You need to hold your temper," Ma said.

"Temper ain't got nothin' to do with it," Sam said. "It's survival, pure and simple. Them or us."

"We're just passing through," Ma said. "We're of no threat to them—"

"Can't say the same about them, now can we?"

She fell silent. Just when Mary thought the subject had been dropped, she spoke in a low, quiet voice. "Don't be so quick to run into a fight, Sam. You'll live longer if you don't fashion yourself as a rip-roaring Indian fighter."

Ma moved off, leaving them to the setting sun and their own turbulent thoughts.

CB8O

Mary tossed and turned throughout the night. Each time she closed her eyes, she envisioned the Indians rushing down the mountain and attacking them in their sleep, even though each boat was tasked with providing night watchmen.

Ma's face had been white and taut as she instructed Ike and Jean to guard their boat until midnight while the others attempted to sleep. Jean was the eldest at twenty-four and was most comfortable playing the role of surrogate mother. Her hair was copper like Ma's and she had the same physical stature, but in temperament they were polar opposites. She was soft spoken and genteel, always ready to lend a nurturing hand in changing diapers or mending clothes or caring for a sick child. But she was decidedly uncomfortable guarding a boat.

At midnight, Ma arranged to take over for Jean so she could lie in bed and comfort the children. Beth, who was two years younger than Jean, was chosen to help her until dawn. Sam decided to remain awake and alert with both shifts.

Every half hour, Mary heard the men in canoes calling out to the watchmen before drifting past to the next boat in line. And though the sound of their voices was immediately reassuring, as they drifted past, the fear of an Indian attack filled the void they left until the voices were heard again.

Mary felt the mattress shift in the middle of the night as Beth and Ma dragged themselves out of the warm bed. She felt guilty for remaining under the covers as the hatch opened to the biting wind that whistled around the cabin. When the hatch closed once more, she knew her job would come soon enough; before the first rays of dawn, she would be responsible for preparing the morning's meal and readying the smallest children for the new day.

Not one of the Neelys complained, though Mary knew the combination of sleep deprivation and cold would take their toll. All of them were accustomed to chores, but Mary couldn't help but marvel at how luxurious their lives seemed back east compared with their present situation. She could only hope their arrival in the Cumberlands would make their journey worth the effort.

As the darkest hours of the night descended upon them, she continued to hear calls up and down the fleet. This time, the men in canoes seemed to have been replaced with a constant hum from boat to boat. It began with Donelson's boat; the watchman on duty called out that all was well. The call was picked up by the next boat and then the next, until all of them were accounted for. This went on throughout the long night amid the constant barking of the dogs. She was grateful that fortune had placed them in the middle of the line of vessels; it would have to be particularly unnerving, she thought, to be out in front like the Donelsons or bringing up the rear like the Jennings. As she finally drifted off to sleep, she dreamt of Indians attacking. And with each wave of attack, the boats drifted further and further apart until they could no longer protect themselves and each other.

As her nightmare continued, she roused herself from slumber. She lay there for a long time, wanting to stop the cycle of tossing, turning, and nightmares, but not wanting to leave the relative comfort of the warm bed. Finally, she stumbled to her feet and wrapped herself in heavier clothing. As she opened the hatch to their one-room cabin, she could already hear the activity just outside their flatboat. Though dawn was barely beginning to peek through the mountain passes, the men were already surveying their circumstances and planning a strategy to extricate their vessels with a renewed sense of urgency.

The tense morning hours dragged on. It was mid-morning before *The Adventure* was broken loose from her sandy perch, and in the end it was not the efforts of the men but the welcome appearance of rising water that dislodged it. Two more had become stuck as well, one belonging to the Boyd family and the other to the Rounsifers. In an effort to lighten the load, the inhabitants of both boats swam or climbed to the boats behind them while many of the men pushed and strained to free them from their moorings.

When at last they broke through, a loud whoop was sounded that picked up like a wave at the front and carried through to the last boat, upon which Elizabeth Jennings Peyton was rumored to be close to birthing.

Mary felt the excitement in the air as they began moving again. Ike and Sam clambered aboard, their clothes weighed down with ice crystals after their swim from *The Adventure* to the Neely boat. Under Ma's insistence, they were rushed to the cabin where they removed the clothes before the cloth became stuck to their skin, and replaced them with layers of fresh dry clothing.

As they rejoined the others, Mary heard a soft voice beside her. "May I steer the boat?"

Mary glanced down at her sister Meg. Only eight years old, she had been babysitting her youngest sister, Jane, who was barely three. It would have seemed like a simple job if only Jane had been more sedentary, but poor Meg had been forced to run after her all over the boat throughout every waking hour. Nap times had been frustrating, to say the least, as Meg had attempted to hold her down and force her into slumber. And Jane was having none of it.

Now Mary smoothed Meg's silky blond hair. "Aren't you tired?" she asked.

Meg nodded toward Jane, who had finally fallen asleep on the deck. "I'd like to do something else."

"I understand, honey," Mary said softly. "Stand in front of me, and we'll steer together."

With Meg leaning against her, Mary positioned her hands on the pole between her own.

"Sing to me, Mary," Meg said, her voice small and hushed against the rhythmic sound of the pole moving through the water.

Mary began to sing her favorite church hymn, her voice quiet and halting. But as they floated along, her voice gained confidence and clarity as her melody floated across the waters.

They stood together as the minutes crept past, occasionally moving the pole to prevent their vessel from drifting too far from the river's center. Meg hadn't stood with her long before Mary felt a heavy weight against her thighs. Looking down, she realized her little sister had fallen asleep standing up, her tiny hands still grasping the pole.

# 8

As Noquali entered the council house, the icy wind that piled the snow against the sturdy wood building gave way to the warmth from a huge fire pit. He walked straight toward it under the attentive eyes of a dozen Cherokee who parted for him as he strode past. Reaching the pit, he knelt and spread his bare hands over the flames, relishing in the warmth that spread through his limbs. The frost that had formed on his lashes melted into teardrops that ran down his cheeks.

This was a sacred fire, a fire that would never be extinguished as long as his people remained in the village. Its flames were used to light the fires for every family's dwelling in the village; stacks of wood were kept dry at the edge of the council house, carefully tended by women who now stood a few yards away intently watching him.

Noquali was in the Chickamauga Indian village known as Running Water. It consisted of more than one hundred one-room log cabins with dirt floors and real wood shingles on the roofs, a style they had learned from the white men. It was also the home of Dragging Canoe and as such, it served as the tribal council place for the band of Indians that included the Cherokee, Shawnee and Delaware. They had even been joined by many Creek, Choctaw, and British subjects and further to the west, the Chickasaw were joining their ranks. Several Shawnee warriors had also established homes at Running Water, including Tecumseh and his brothers, Cheeseekau and Tenskwatawa, and their father, Shawnee Warrior.

Word was sent of his arrival, and he was soon joined by another warrior and John Rogers, a white trader. After greeting one another like long-lost brothers, a meal of bear was brought before them.

"You have news," Dragging Canoe said as he grabbed a haunch of bear meat and carefully pulled a mouth-sized portion from it.

"Yes," Noquali said. "There are two groups coming from the east through the mountain passes. One fleet comes by way of the Pellissippi—the river the white men call the Clinch River," he added, glancing at John.

Dragging Canoe nodded. "And the other?"

"The others are on the Hogohegee, the one they call the Holston River."

They chewed in silence for a moment before Dragging Canoe asked, "Where will they meet?"

"In four moons, perhaps five, without interference they may reach Danda'ganu'."

He nodded. As they ate in silence, Noquali pictured Danda'ganu' in his mind's eye, the name for two mountains that faced one another across the river the white men called the Tennessee, after the Indian village Tanase. Danda'ganu' meant 'two looking at one another'; since the beginning of time, the two mountains had served as giant watchtowers overlooking the great river. They had once sheltered two Cherokee villages, but now the villages were empty, the people scattered, and all that remained were the burned-out shells of buildings the white men had torched. It tugged at Noquali's heart to think of the once-vibrant centers of Cherokee life and he bit angrily into the bear meat.

After their towns were destroyed, they had moved further westward, establishing Running Water as well as five other villages with about forty homes in each: Nickajack, where John Rogers made his home; Long Island Town, just south of them; Lookout Mountain Town, just east of the great mountain; and Crow Town, where Dragging Canoe's son, Young Canoe, lived. Crow Town was the largest of the five and the furthest south.

But the fifth village, Tuskegee Island Town, was in the most strategic location for attacks along the river.

As if reading his mind, Dragging Canoe mused, "Do we strike them as they lay cut off from each other?"

"We strike when the opportunity presents itself," Noquali answered.

"You have learned well."

"I have only spoken the words I've heard you speak many times before."

"How many warriors will you need?"

"We have counted three hundred men, women and children."

"Fifty warriors? One hundred?"

"Fifty. We will pass through the lower Cherokee towns; we will gather more warriors there. Then we will separate, each converging on a separate fleet. Each will strike when the Great Spirit has provided us the opportunity."

Dragging Canoe nodded. "It is our land and our hearts are pure. The Great Spirit will surely smile upon us and help us to push the invaders back across the mountains." He stood and wiped his lips.

Noquali finished eating and stood beside him. "Then you want them pushed back only?"

He smirked. "Let the river run red with their blood. Kill as many as you wish; capture the rest." He turned to make his way through the council house. He stopped when he reached the entranceway and turned to gaze at Noquali. "Allow one to get past you. One to tell the tale of our bravery; one to carry the warning back to the others."

At that, he disappeared through the door into swirling snows that seemed to swallow his imposing figure. Noquali drank of crisp water from a large bowl on a communal table. Then he wiped his mouth with the back of his hand and nodded to the squaws that he was finished. They quickly removed the crumbs from their meals.

He felt hot under the weight of the panther pelt and he stepped to the entrance of the council building. He watched the rising wind, noted its direction, and felt the biting cold on his cheeks. Then he raised the panther's head atop his own and disappeared as Dragging Canoe had, into the white, clean snow that twisted and danced through the village.

# 9

Mary's joints ached as though they belonged to an old woman. The winter air was dry and left her skin painfully cracked; a condition the strong winds aggravated. The day had crawled by as the boats continued their westward journey with each mile looking numbingly like the one before.

But at least they were moving.

They had made good progress today, partly due to Colonel Donelson's decision to keep moving. The men had noticed the presence of Indians watching from the mountain range and he was intent on moving past as quickly as possible. They were instructed to remain in the middle of the river, which meant staying away from the shoreline regardless of their wants or needs. It resulted in a grueling time as the hours ticked by; time spent standing in the bitter cold and wind or in the stuffy, rank confines of the flatboat cabin that served as stockroom, bedroom, and makeshift outhouse.

Mary found herself staring at the terrain beyond the river banks, watching every tree and every movement, no matter how slight. A giant buzzard burst forth from a thicket, and she jumped, her heart beginning to beat wildly.

"You okay, Mary?"

She placed her hand around her neck and fought to calm her nerves. "I reckon so, Ike. It's just my imagination trying to get the best of me."

He rested on his haunches on the bridge above her and followed her gaze toward the shore. "I wouldn't say that. Not no more."

She peered at him out of the corner of her eye. "What do you mean?"

"They've been followin' us," he said quietly. He glanced around as if making sure they were not overheard.

"Who are they?"

He shrugged. "Don't know. But this is Dragging Canoe's territory."

She looked back at the shore. "I don't know anything about Dragging Canoe."

"Colonel Donelson gave us an earful... He leads a Cherokee tribe, but his mama was a Natchez Indian and his papa was part Shawnee. If you ever hear of Shawnee afoot, Mary, you run the other way as fast as you can, you hear?"

She nodded.

"The Shawnee, they're vicious. They'll torture and kill you. Dragging Canoe, he's got that Shawnee blood in him and he's out to kill all us settlers. It's said he got his name cuz he was so intent on joinin' up with warriors when he was a young'un that he was found draggin' a canoe down to the riverbanks..."

Mary stood in silence for awhile before she asked, "Why does he hate us so?"

"The Colonel told us when the Cherokee made peace with us settlers, he disagreed. Thought the Cherokee ought to keep their land and kill the white men who crossed into it. He formed his own band and settled somewheres along the Chickamauga River. They're known as the Chickamaugas now, and from what I hear, they roam these parts just lookin' for white men to kill and white women to capture." He spit into the waters. "If I ever see him, Mary Neely, I aim to kill him."

She gazed upward at him. He'd been clean-shaven when they'd left home but now, like most of the men, he'd grown a thick beard. "You're sounding like Sam now," she said, "and that's not like you."

"Extreme times call for extreme measures," he said quietly.

"How will you know it's him?" she asked, watching the current beneath them.

"His face is all pock-marked like. He had small pox when he was a young'un and it scarred his face forever. I'll know him when I see him."

"What do you think we'll find when we get to the Cumberlands?"

"Civilization," he said with a wry chuckle. "I aim to get some land and be a gentleman farmer like Pa... Maybe do some surveyin'. And I'd like to practice law."

As Ike stared into the tree line, Mary watched the current with growing curiosity. "Ike," she said after a long moment, "have you noticed we're moving faster?"

He glanced at her before looking down at the river. Then without a word, he rose and turned to stare across the bow.

Mary moved toward the front of the boat, shading her eyes against the setting sun in an attempt to see beyond the vessels in front of her.

They were fourth in line; *The Adventure* led the way, followed by Mr. Boyd's flatboat. Captain Hutchings' boat was behind the Boyds, but Simon was nowhere in sight. Mary supposed he had been taken into the shelter to get him out of the frigid air. Mr. Rounsifer's flatboat, once freed from the shoals that morning, had dropped back behind them.

A man in a canoe was trying to maintain a constant position as the flatboats drifted past. Ike and Mary moved to the side nearest him and watched him as he shouted across to Captain Hutchings.

As they drew nearer, Ike recognized him. "He's one of the scouts," he said to Mary. Then he shouted, "What do you know?"

"There's an island up ahead," he shouted back. "Aim for it; we're puttin' in there for the night. Stay away from the far shores."

Ike barely had a chance to nod before they were past him, the boat picking up speed as the terrain began to slope. "Rapids," he said. Then, "Mary, quick, get ready to go over!"

Mary cried out for Meg. "Get the children inside, Meg, now!"

Without hesitation, Meg herded six-year-old Johnny and Baby Jane into the room as Ma rushed to the bow.

"Don't let them out," Mary said as she began to pull the hatch to, "until I come and get you, you hear?"

"Are we gonna die?"

"No, but you're in for a ride," Mary said. "Stay away from those boxes; you don't want anything to fall on you." She closed the hatch and said a quick prayer as she made her way to the side of the boat. Without planning it, she realized Ma was at the bow with her pole ready; Beth and Jean were on the opposite side of the boat across from Mary; and Billy and Martha were at the stern. Sam remained on the bridge with the tiller as Ike shouted instructions.

The river roiled and tumbled now while the family fought to keep a safe distance from Captain Hutchings' boat. They became airborne before slamming back into the water and they scrambled to turn the bow toward the west just as they hit another swell.

The water sprayed and spit over the side of the boat. They began to slip and slide as they fought ever harder to keep from falling overboard. They heard shouts behind them as each family followed their precarious path, and Mary thought fleetingly of Elizabeth Jennings Peyton, plummeting over these rapids. It might be enough to bring on the baby, she thought. God help her.

As the boat lurched, she realized there were rocks projecting from the water and she screamed for Ike. When he turned to face her, his face was pale and his eyes wide. She pointed toward the rocks, and without hesitation, he began shouting for them to steer the boat toward starboard.

"Which way's starboard?" Billy shouted.

"North!" Ike yelled. "To the right, to the right!"

It was more easily said than done as they struggled to keep from ramming into the rocks. When they avoided a boulder on the left, they found another on their right, and they pitched and listed with growing intensity.

With rising panic, she realized rapids appeared just before a waterfall. As the river flowed ever faster, she wondered how they would ever survive. Surely the scout would have told them if there were falls up ahead, she thought.

They crested a great rush of water and she caught a fleeting glimpse of the river below and of an island that rose up in the center. *The Adventure* was heading toward it at great speed, and Mary watched as all hands tried to slow their vessels as they approached it. In turn, shouts went up to the boats behind, ordering them to slow. The command was impossible to follow. The river had become violent, and they were losing their battle against it.

"Steer to port! Steer to port!"

"Speak English, Ike!" Sam's bellowing voice erupted.

"Left! Left!" he shouted. "Hard left!"

The cry went up from boat to boat, and Mary realized the rapids continued on the starboard side, while the looming island stopped its progression on the port side.

*The Adventure* was the first to strike the island, and it struck with such force that Mary caught her breath. Before she could recover from the shock, Ike and Ma were shouting for them to steer clear of the boats in front of them. They frantically maneuvered further to port until they were swept onto a sandbar and stopped at the edge of the island.

One by one, the boats behind them piled up. Some were able to stop in time while others slammed into the shoreline or other boats. There were shouts from every side as crates fell and supplies were scattered through the water.

"Is anyone hurt?" The cry came up. "Is anyone hurt?"

Mary rushed to the hatch and threw it open. Meg knelt in the center of a mattress, each of her arms cradling the younger children. Her eyes were as wide as saucers, her fear mirrored in each of the younger children's faces.

Johnny had both hands wrapped around a pistol, his small fingers barely large enough to keep a grip on it.

"Give me that," Mary said, grabbing the pistol. "What do you think you're doing?"

"I'm gonna fight the Injuns!"

"That's what you think," she retorted. "You're more likely to shoot your sisters with it. Don't do that again."

She returned the pistol to its rightful place beside the cabin hatch and surveyed the damage. The supplies had tumbled from the other side of the room, but the children were safe.

Mary knelt in front of them.

"Are we alright?" Meg asked, her chin trembling.

"You're alright," Mary said, hugging them. "Everybody's alright."

She realized her voice was stronger and more confident than she felt as she hugged the children ever tighter.

# 10

The campfires glowed in the early darkness, the red and orange flames vibrant against the stark winter terrain. They'd spent the waning hours rearranging the boxes to ensure they were more secure in the event they hit more rapids. The Neely boat had fared well compared to some of the others. Donelson's boat had been damaged and lost various items in the water, some of which was recovered and some which was broken beyond use. Several men had pitched in to repair the damaged vessel and inspect others, finally declaring each in turn seaworthy.

The women had conferred about their evening meal, comparing the lists of food each had left. In the end, they had put many of their rations together—a few potatoes here, canned vegetables there, some salt pork and small chunks of ham, to make a stew that was divided between several smaller pots.

It was enough to prevent them from starving but not enough for anyone to feel comfortably full. Now the women were busy directing the older children in cleaning up while the men began to gather along the shoreline.

Mary made her way to Elizabeth Jennings Peyton, who was resting with her back against a tree. Her eyes were closed but she opened them as Mary approached.

"How are you doing?" Mary asked, kneeling beside her.

"The baby's kicking," she answered, smiling weakly.

Mary placed her hand on Elizabeth's belly and felt the strong, steady kicks. "It's a boy," she declared softly.

"I hope so. Ephraim wants a son so badly. We've picked out a name for him already; he'll be Ephraim, Jr., of course." Her nose was pinched and she tried to reposition herself to get more comfortable.

"You know why his kicks are hurting more?"

"Cause he's bigger?"

Mary shook her head. "Cause he's turning around. His feet are up here." She pointed high on Elizabeth's belly. "It won't be much longer now."

"How do you know these things, Mary?"

Mary nodded toward Ma, who was supervising the clean-up activities. "Been through it six times with Ma," she said, "plus lots of neighbors."

Elizabeth's face shone. "I'm so excited, Mary. We have such grand plans for him. He's going to be a lawyer. They need them where we're going, you know."

"Yes, I suppose they do."

"Ephraim and I already decided he'll go back east for his schooling, once he's old enough. He's going to be a statesman." She rolled her hands over her bulging belly. "I talk to him all the time. I know that's silly, but I do. I tell him how thankful we are to have him, how much me and his daddy want him, and how we'll just do everything in the world for him."

"He's lucky to have you and Ephraim as parents."

"I hope he thinks he's lucky," she continued, her voice rapid and filled with pride, "cause I'll devote my life to him and making sure he grows up fit as a fiddle and as smart as—why, as Thomas Jefferson himself."

A droplet of water fell on Mary's cheek and she wiped it away. She stood and then reached her hands toward Elizabeth. "It's starting to rain," she said. "Let me help you up."

Elizabeth laughed. "Mary Neely, you can't weigh more than a sapling. If I grabbed your arms, I'd pull you right down on top of me."

"I'm stronger than you think. Try me."

Mary braced her feet against the protruding tree roots as Elizabeth grabbed her arms.

"Don't let me fall," Elizabeth admonished. "I can't injure the baby."

"You won't fall."

The larger woman rocked back and forth a couple of times, her belly rolling like a ball as she tried to gain momentum. Then grasping Mary's arms tightly, she came to her feet as Mary helped to steady her.

A torrent of rain swept over them and Elizabeth teetered quickly over to the Jennings boat to find cover while Mary rushed back to her family. The women were shouting at the children now, some to hurry and clean the pots and others to herd them under cover.

Mary helped to return the cooking pot to their boat just as the wind swept the rain sideways, pelting them with droplets that turned to sleet. Mary's face stung as she helped Jean gather the smaller children into the boat's tiny cabin.

They sat on the mattresses in the waning light. After a long moment of silence, Ike spoke.

"Colonel Donelson told us to stay in the middle of the river, no matter what." His voice was grave.

"That's what we've been doing, isn't it?" Ma asked. "It's where the current is strongest."

Ike's eyes remained fixed on the weather. "There's another reason." When he turned to face them, his eyes looked pale and sharp against the darkness. "We're goin' deeper into Indian Territory. Seems there's a white man who travels freely among the Indians; name's Simon Girty. He don't like settlers; heard tell he's a loyalist."

"What has that got to do with us?" Ma asked.

Baby Jane grew restless and Mary plopped her onto her knees and bounced her as Ike continued.

"He's taught the Indians to run along the shoreline and call out to folks movin' down the river. Sometimes they act all friendly-like; other times, they send white captives out callin' for help." His voice was as hushed as if he were telling a ghost story around a campfire. "If you steer toward shore, they'll wait 'til you get close enough and then hoards of Indians will come from nowhere and attack." He looked at each of the Neelys in turn.

"They aim to kill. Or capture. And if they capture you, you'll wish you was dead."

"Ain't nobody gonna capture a Neely," Sam said, puffing out his chest.

Ma sucked in her breath. "How many guns do we have?"

"Three pistols. Four muskets."

"And I got my own musket that Pa gave me," Sam said.

"Keep them loaded," Ma said brusquely. "They're to stay beside the door at all times, ready to fire. At the first sign of trouble, Sam, Ike, me and Billy will grab the muskets."

"That leaves one," Mary said. "I can shoot as well as you."

Ma nodded. "Jean, you and Beth get the rest of the children inside this cabin, hunkered down. Keep the pistols close at hand. If the Indians get to the cabin…"

Johnny began to tear up, and Ma ruffled his hair. "Now, now, son, there's nothing to fear."

"I ain't afeared," Johnny said, wiping the tear from his eye. "Sam's gonna teach me to shoot, and I'm gonna fight the Injuns."

"Lord help us." She got to her feet quickly and crossed to the cabin hatch in two steps. "Ike, you'll stand watch with me. In a few hours, it'll be your turn, Mary, along with Sam. The rest of you go to sleep. Tomorrow'll be another busy day."

With that, she grabbed a musket and passed it to Ike. Once they were through the hatch, they closed it behind them, plunging them into darkness.

# 11

N oquali reached Tuskegee Island Town two days later. He had been slowed by a great storm that swept down from the northwest, alternately dumping a foot of snow, several inches of ice, and then freezing rain upon the land. As the temperatures rose and the ice began to melt, the terrain was slippery and hazardous and horses struggled to maintain their hold on the sloping, treacherous mountains.

He had been joined by warriors from each village he passed. In a time of war, they would have fasted, danced, and contemplated their upcoming battle for as much as four days; but that would not be necessary now. They did not anticipate any great battle. These were settlers moving unawares along the river with their women and their children; there had been no sightings of soldiers accompanying them.

By the time he reached Tuskegee Island Town, he knew if they did not find the opportunity to mount a surprise attack on the settlers on the Pellissippi and Hogohegee Rivers, they would organize one here.

He made his way through the village to the home of Bloody Fellow, a young Cherokee brave who had sworn, along with Dragging Canoe and many other chieftains, to drive the white men from Cherokee lands. He was now the Chief in Tuskegee Island Town and his cooperation would be necessary for Noquali to commence an attack from this vantage point.

Like the other Indians in the village, Bloody Fellow lived in a log cabin. His wife greeted him at the door and beckoned him to sit at the wood table while she warmed some kanohena, a traditional Cherokee liquid made from hominy. It was bitter but its warmth was welcome on this frigid day and the two men sat in silence for a moment while Noquali grew warm by the fireplace.

"We estimate as many as three hundred on the Pellissippi and Hogohegee," Noquali said.

Bloody Fellow nodded. His head was shaved except for one jet black lock that reached from the top of his head past his shoulders. Now the lock glistened in the light cast by the flames. "Yes; we have been tracking them... Archie Coody told me you have been watching them as well, and you have been to see Dragging Canoe."

"I have his permission to attack."

"Where?"

Noquali shrugged. "Wherever we can." He sipped the hot liquid.

"Perhaps the best spot is at The Whirl."

Noquali nodded his agreement. The Whirl was also known as The Boiling Pot, as it consisted of a dangerous whirlpool in the Tennessee River that was known to suck men and small vessels right under the water, never to be seen again. The river itself was treacherous, even on the best of days; it was wild and untamed, the currents tricky and often rotating, with shoals rising unexpectedly in the middle of the river where the waters should have been the deepest. But The Whirl was one of the toughest, most hazardous spots one could encounter. The cliffs were high on either side of it, allowing the Indians to watch from above as unsuspecting travelers floated toward it. The currents would become faster and then their vessels would begin to rotate. If they attempted to outrun the Indians attacking from the shore, the current would sweep them around again, right into their hands. And if they tried to remain in the very center of the river, where they had been told it was safest, they would instead be sucked right into the mouth of the whirlpool, where they would drown and their boats would become nothing more than splinters.

It was not luck but by design that Bloody Fellow chose this location for Tuskegee Island Town. It overlooked the entrance to The Whirl; travelers who tried to avoid it by turning around and paddling upstream could easily be cut off. Ironically, the best way to reach the village was by water, but the Indians knew how best to navigate the river to avoid the tricky currents and The Whirl itself. Noquali had arrived by a more hazardous route through the narrow, sharply curving mountain pass—a route that also shielded them from attack by the settlers, as very few of them could manage to find the path and even fewer managed to remain on it.

"They travel with John Donelson," Noquali said.

"Donelson?" Bloody Fellow rubbed his chin thoughtfully. "He usually goes overland, far north of here."

"John Rogers, the white trader, traded at Patrick Henry's Fort on the Pellissippi. He says this is Donelson's first trip by water. He intends to take his people to the fort they are building in the Cumberlands."

"They cannot be allowed to reach the Cumberlands."

"I agree, as does Dragging Canoe. If this group arrives in the Cumberlands, hundreds—perhaps even thousands—of white men will be riding this river. And if they dare to traverse the rivers in the dead of winter, there will surely be a steady flow of them when spring arrives."

"If we allow that to happen, they would destroy these villages as they destroyed Chickamauga, Chilhowee, Chota and Tanasi."

"Chota is being rebuilt."

"Yes. And I pray to the Great Spirit that the others will be, as well." He slapped the tops of his thighs. "And we must do everything in our power to protect our villages from further ruin."

"That is my intention."

"Have you been to the other new villages? A lot of Creeks are moving in with us and joining our forces against the invaders."

"Which villages do you refer to?"

"Creek Crossing, Creek Path, Will's Town, and Doublehead's Town."

"Ah, Doublehead," Noquali said. The name was familiar; the Cherokee Chief Doublehead had been given his name because he adopted one position when he was with the white men and quite another when he was with his own people. He also had a reputation as one of the fiercest and most merciless warriors, preferring to torture his captives in lieu of a quick death. "If Doublehead can join us here before the settlers arrive at The Whirl, his participation would be most appreciated."

"I will send word to him at once."

Noquali rose. "Thank you for the drink."

"Will you be remaining in Tuskegee Island Town?" Before Noquali could respond, Bloody Fellow added, "The woman known as Jo-leigh is here."

Noquali's head jerked toward him. Embarrassed, he looked away. "She is?" he murmured.

"At the edge of the village. She escaped Chickamauga."

"Her family—?"

"The rest of her family was murdered."

"Was she injured?"

"Her injuries have healed. But she yearns for you. She asks each person who comes through the village if they have seen you."

His heart began beating erratically and his cheeks felt flush. "She is at the edge of town, you say?"

Bloody Fellow opened the door. Even the blast of cold air could not cool Noquali's cheeks. He pointed toward the cliffs. "There," he said. "Go to her. She will be expecting you."

# 12

## March 2, 1780

The rain had continued for two days, the frigid droplets stinging as they hit Mary's chapped face. The trip had become so harsh and demanding that the Neely family was forced to work in shifts as they continued down the Holston River, and she found herself counting the minutes until her shift was over. The wind and rain was coming from the west, which meant they were heading directly into it; in order to keep the boat in the center of the river, it took constant diligence as they faced the storm's onslaught head-on.

The current grew stronger and the boat rolled and tumbled on the waves until it was all she could do to keep her balance. Ike stood above her on the bridge and as Mary glanced up, she noticed he was having difficulty remaining on his feet and specks of snow littered his beard. Billy, who was using the tiller on the bridge, was not faring any better.

"Mary!"

She barely heard Ike's voice through the maelstrom.

"Get two more hands!"

She tried to rush toward the cabin but the tossing of the boat forced her to move in uneven lurches. She found herself slipping and sliding in one direction only to be forced into the opposite direction with the next wave. When she reached the hatch, she had to place her pole on the deck and pull with both hands in order to open it. When she did, she found the rest of her family staring at her from the mattresses.

"Two more hands!" she shouted, the wind taking her breath away. "Two more—"

It was as if her breath had been sucked from her, but as she fought to shout once more, Sam rushed past her. The rain hit them with a vengeance and they tumbled into each other, trying to regain their footing as the vessel pitched.

Ma pushed her whole weight against the hatch to close it as Mary tried to return to her post. She knew her mother was bone-tired; she'd been up most of the night, helping to keep watch, and had worked more than her share throughout this exhausting day.

Mary's clothing felt weighted down by the mountain of water falling upon her and she realized as she returned to the bow that she was walking as stiffly as if she were plowing a snowdrift with her body.

The flatboats were not meant for this type of travel, she thought as she fought with the others to maintain control. At best, it might have floated down a leisurely river, allowing the current to move it forward. But these waves pummeled it mercilessly. She could hear a sound akin to wood cracking; terrified, she could only watch as the waves swept them swiftly through the rising waters and closer to the boats in front of them.

"Starboard! Starboard!"

The cry came up from Mary's left, and without pausing to think, she tried to steer toward the right but her pole was useless in the vicious waters. She hoped and prayed the tiller was more effective. Somewhere in the back of her mind, she registered something looming up ahead, a bend of some sort, but she was too intent on steering the boat to pause.

"Turn her! Turn her!"

Ike's voice was rising now in desperation. They were pushing with all their might toward the right. Then there were four more hands on deck, and they were all desperately trying to turn the boat sideways in the water if they had to, just to keep it from moving left.

Beth was beside Mary as she began to slip on the soaked deck. Mary reached out to prevent her fall when she caught sight of a land mass jutting out from shore, directly in their path. *The Adventure* narrowly skimmed its outermost shore, then two more boats rammed together as they each fought to distance themselves from the island.

"Turn! Turn!"

Ike's voice brought her back to the present, and she grabbed Beth as they all frantically tried to turn the boat. They found themselves unable to stop, the wooden vessel riding the waves like a toy boat. They were approaching the boat in front of them with gathering speed, so close Mary could see the panic on their faces that mirrored their own as the Neelys swept past them, barely missing the edge of their boat.

They were moving farther to the right now, closer to shore, and up ahead they could see *The Adventure* putting in to shore.

They can't stop there, Mary thought anxiously. We'll all pile on top of them!

"Starboard!" Ike called out once again, his voice fading into the wind as Mary heard a loud crack beside them. They all watched as the Henry boat, unable to turn, rammed into the point of the island.

Sam dropped his pole and headed toward the port side as Ike called out to him.

"Get back here!" he yelled.

The Henry family was tumbling into the waters, the current pushing their bodies through the waves as though they were nothing more than dolls. Mr. Henry's head bobbed above the water only to be sucked under with the next wave.

Sam stopped, his face contorted in confusion. "They need help!" he yelled back through the wind.

"No!" Ike ordered with such force that Sam slipped and slid toward starboard once more.

As they rounded the island and came out on the other side, Mary glanced back. The Henrys were scrambling to shore, one by one, as their boat began to list in the violent waters.

Mary bit her lip as she looked at Ike. Pa would never have let them fend for themselves, she thought. Her rising anger was quickly replaced with fear as she realized they were not yet safe themselves. They fought the current as they were swept downstream sideways, their valiant efforts to reach the far shore feeling like nothing more than wishful thinking.

When at last they approached land, another kind of terror set in: that of ramming the land as the Henrys had and losing everything. It took all of their power and might to land; as they careened past *The Adventure*, she could see the faces of the inhabitants, their mouths open as if shouting, but she couldn't hear their words amid the wind and the waves.

When at last they came ashore, it was with a sudden jolt that took Mary's breath from her and caused the entire Neely family to tumble off their feet. As they scrambled to regain their footing, Mary realized they had stopped completely; the bow was pointing upwards from the shore where it had settled.

Before she could come to her feet, Ike rushed past her, grabbing Sam by his coat collar.

"Don't you ever do that again!" he yelled.

Ma was beside her two sons in an instant, but to Mary's surprise, she did not pull Ike off his younger brother.

"They needed help!" Sam pushed back. "I've never seen a Neely that wouldn't come to another's aid!"

Ike pointed his finger in Sam's face and fought to regain his composure. "You can't do that, Sam." He turned toward the others. "None of you can do that."

He ran his hand through his hair. Mary watched quietly as water dripped from his drenched locks. "I'm responsible for each and every one of you," he said. He glanced at Ma. "Even you. And I can't lose one of you 'cause you jumped into the river after somebody else."

He looked beyond them. Mary was almost afraid to move, but she cut her eyes in the same direction. Mr. Henry had resurfaced, and the entire family was trying to save their possessions as their ship sank ever deeper.

"I need y'all to listen to me, and listen good. When we're in the middle of savin' our own lives and our own boat, don't you worry about anybody else's, you hear? It's tough out here and it's gonna get tougher, and there's gonna come a time when each man may have to save hisself. And if I have y'all jumpin' off this boat goin' after somebody else, it might be our boat that can't be controlled, and our lives that might be lost."

Sam watched the other boats as they passed the Henrys, desperately trying to save themselves from the same fate as they steered toward the same shoreline the Neelys had crashed into.

"When it's all over," he said quietly, "when it's all over... we'll go back to help. If we can."

# 13

They did go back to help; Sam, Ike, and Billy, along with more than a dozen men from various boats. Mary sat on the opposite shore and watched them as the Henry boat listed dangerously in the water. While two men dove under and inspected the damage, the others began a line that reached from the boat's cabin to the island shore. One by one, their possessions were handed off from one to the other, until they were left in a pitiful pile on land.

Mary wrapped her arm around Meg as they watched. The young girl was silent; too silent, Mary thought. She often heard the child crying softly into the wool blanket in the deep of night, when she should have been sleeping, and her eyes were as large as saucers with deep blue rings forming underneath. Or maybe her eyes only appeared larger, Mary thought, because she had lost so much weight. They all had lost weight; they all were exhausted and the hunger never seemed to be sated.

Ma stood behind them, bouncing Baby Jane on her hip. She'd turned three years old back in December while they were near freezing at Reedy's Creek, but Mary couldn't remember now whether they'd even taken notice of her birthday. Jane had developed a cough from deep in her chest. She never seemed to rest and it took a combined effort to keep her out of harm's way, though Mary couldn't for the life of her understand how she could have so much energy on so little food. She often noticed Jean coaxing her to eat, but although they were all half-starved, she didn't show signs of a healthy appetite.

Now Mary instinctively reached out to tighten the bow on Jane's cap. She smoothed her thin, fine golden locks as she pushed them under the crocheted cap.

Out of the corner of her eye, she noticed Elizabeth Peyton and her mother making their way toward them with a half dozen women.

"Maggie," Mrs. Jennings said as they drew near, "Colonel Donelson says we're to cook supper here and stay the night. All of our provisions are low…"

"It makes perfect sense to combine our food," Ma said without hesitation. "Mary, come with me."

Mary rose and brushed the dirt off her clothes.

"May I come, too?" Meg asked.

"Of course you can, sweetheart," Mary said as she followed Ma.

They met in the darkening cabin. Ma handed Baby Jane to Meg.

"Mary, our food is running low," Ma whispered.

Mary studied her in the waning light. She was only in her early forties, but she had aged during the months since they'd left home. There were bags forming under her eyes from a lack of sleep, and her forehead, once smooth and white, was now weathered and furrowed. Her copper hair showed graying at the temples now; it was pulled back into a smooth bun that hid its length. Her clothes were kept neat, although they were mottled with dirt and river water. Her shoulders were wide and strong, and though she had lost weight during their journey, she still struck a formidable presence.

"What are we going to do?" Mrs. Jennings whispered from the doorway. "There are so many of us to feed—"

"We'll find what provisions each boat carries, and what they can contribute to a soup," Ma said. She opened two of the wood crates and pulled out some potatoes and onions that had seen better days. "A soup can be anything and everything. We'll meet outside my boat here, and whatever we have, we'll cook together."

While Mrs. Jennings conferred with the other women, Elizabeth was sent back to the Jennings boat to haul the large black pot to the Neely site. Two more pots joined them, and

Mary was soon put to work with her sisters and friends gathering wood.

The shore was flat only for a short distance before it began angling up toward the base of a cliff. There were few trees in the area and what ones there were, were too green and wet, making them unsuitable for firewood. They wandered the length of the shore where the boats had been tied up before finding enough sticks and aged wood to start fires for all the pots.

The youngest children were tasked with gathering kindling. Meg carried some in her outstretched skirt and as they walked along the shore, Mary couldn't help but glance upward at the cliff's ridgeline. They had been so careful to stay in the center of the river, she thought, and now here they were, lined up along the shore like a row of sitting ducks. But unlike the ducks, they couldn't fly away in an instant; their boats were cumbersome and precious time would be needed to push them from shore.

She shivered despite herself.

"What is it, Mary?" Meg asked. "Are you sick?"

"No," she said, looking at her with what she hoped was a reassuring smile. "Just a bit of wind must have found me."

They reached the pots and arranged the wood and kindling. Before long, they had the fires started, their efforts sending up clouds of smoke from the shore.

The Jennings women returned with Mrs. Harrison, Mrs. Donelson, Mrs. Robertson, and several other ladies. Between them, they counted enough potatoes, onions, carrots, and beans to feed a group half as large.

"We have more," Mrs. Robertson said apologetically, "but we don't know what we might need later…"

"Of course," Ma said, taking charge. "This will be just fine. Just chop the vegetables into very small pieces. We have some fatback we can add to the mix to give it some flavoring. Does anyone have any flour or cornmeal?"

"I have a little," Mrs. Donelson said.

"If each of us brings just enough for our own families, we can make some biscuits or cornbread to go with the soup. It will be just fine," Ma repeated.

They busied themselves with hauling water from the river and chopping the vegetables. Mary peered at the men across the river while she worked; there was no doubt now the Henry boat would soon sink. That meant the Henrys' belongings would be divided among the other boats for passage, and the family would be separated according to the amount of room available on the remaining boats. A few more days like this, Mary thought, and we might be walking when we reach Fort Nashborough.

As nighttime fell upon them, the delicious scent of vegetable soup wafted through the camp. Soon, the men were back and lined up at the pots with bowls in hand.

"Where's the meat?" Mrs. Harrison's teenage son, Reuben, demanded.

Ma spoke up. "There is no meat for tonight's supper. There are plenty of vegetables and you'll feel full." She plopped a thin slice of cornbread on the edge of his bowl. "And good hardy bread to go with it."

"No meat?" His jaw went slack and his brows furrowed as he glared at his mother.

Mrs. Harrison shook her head. "It's all we have," she said quietly. "We must ration our supplies."

"No meat?" Reuben's voice rose.

"Move along," Ma said, ladling out enough soup for the person behind him.

He stepped forward a few paces but then stopped abruptly. Turning around, he looked at them with a smirk. "A real man needs meat," he declared.

"Run along, Reuben," Ma said, "and when you're a real man, you'll get some."

He said something under his breath as his face reddened in anger, but one of the older men stepped between Reuben and Ma. "You're no match for her," Mary heard the older man say.

She turned back to the soup kettles, helping to serve food to the younger Neely children. When at last the children and the men were fed, the women divided the remaining food among themselves. It was precious little, and as Mary sat along the bank, she resolved to eat it as slowly as possible to make it last longer. She hoped her stomach would begin to feel full with the combination of the soup water and cornbread but when she scraped the bowl clean, she felt as if she hadn't eaten at all.

CRSO

"Has anyone seen Reuben Harrison?"

Mary had just finished washing the last kettle in the frigid waters of the Holston River when she heard the voice approaching. She turned back toward land, where she barely made out Reuben's sister making her way past the boats. The fires had long ago died down; they'd decided not to keep them burning through the night, as they were in Chickamauga Territory. Mary had wondered at the decision, since there were twenty boats lined up along the shore that would be impossible to miss, but she had remained silent. She assumed Colonel Donelson had been this way before and as the leader of their group, his word was law.

"Last time I saw him was at supper," Mary said.

"It's the last time any of us saw him," his sister replied. She stopped within a few feet of Mary. She was only a teenager and the bulk of warm clothing she wore weighed down her slim frame; her shoulders were rounded and she walked with a tired and resigned step.

Ike approached them.

"We think he went hunting," she continued. "He kept complaining about the lack of meat."

Ike looked behind them at the cliffs. They were dark and foreboding. The trees along the ridgeline waved in the growing wind. They could play tricks on a person's eye, Mary thought as she followed his gaze; they almost looked like Indians lining up against the night sky.

With pursed lips, Ike marched away from them and toward some of the other men. Soon, they were studying the cliffs as well. Within a few minutes, the camp was abuzz with Reuben's disappearance. Colonel Donelson was livid, repeating his orders to everyone there that it was essential they remain together. Their only hope for survival was in their numbers.

The men conferred for several long minutes. Mr. Harrison wanted to go in search of his son, and several others were willing to join him. But Colonel Donelson held them back, arguing that Indians could be afoot. Indians could see better in the darkness than white men, and they would know this terrain like the backs of their hands. Mr. Harrison, in contrast, would be stumbling through the darkness and could get lost or injured.

After a spirited debate, it was decided they would fire six shots over the course of the next hour, spaced several minutes apart. If Reuben had lost his way, the sound of gunshots should lead him back to the group.

∽⟐∼

Mary lay in bed and stared at Jean's stocking feet. Ma, Billy, and Beth were on watch until midnight. Then Ike, Jean and Martha would take over. Mary and Sam would relieve them before dawn.

Ike was coiled near the outer wall, tilting a book so he could read by the muted moonlight that found its way through the cracks between the logs. He seemed oblivious to Sam and Johnny talking about Injuns and fighting. Closer to Mary, Jean's voice murmured softly as she told a nighttime story to Meg and Baby Jane. Martha was already fast asleep.

The sound of the third gunshot reached her ears. She closed her eyes. Her muscles ached from the exertions of the day; it seemed like such a long time ago when she was standing on the deck, fighting to keep the boat from striking the sandbar or overturning in the river's current. But as much as she tried to sleep, she could only toss and turn in the gloom of the cabin. Each time she closed her eyes, she envisioned Indians sweeping down the cliff side toward them, their tomahawks at the ready. With each shot that sounded, she wondered if they were leading the Indians directly to their camp.

As sleep began to sweep over her, she wondered tiredly if they had Reuben at that very moment. If they had him, she thought, a quick death would be merciful. She had heard so many stories of their savagery that to be captured would be the worst thing that could possibly befall a person.

The last shot echoed through the cliffs and across the waters and the night grew still. As she drifted off to sleep, she wondered if Reuben Harrison would bring death to them all.

# 14

The men met at dawn. Mary accompanied Ma and Ike to Colonel Donelson's boat, where a heated debate was already underway.

Everyone except the Harrisons appeared incensed that Reuben would have rebelliously defied the Colonel's orders and strike off on his own. Mr. and Mrs. Harrison were grief-stricken and fearing the worst had happened to him. And Colonel Donelson used the opportunity to stress how important it was that they all remain together. They were all hungry and men more active than Reuben had gone without meat for many days as well, but it was important that they move quickly through Chickamauga Territory before letting down their guard.

There were those who wanted to continue on their journey, arguing that too much time had been lost already.

Mrs. Harrison tried to appeal to their humanity with her teary pleas. "To leave poor Reuben behind would certainly mean capture or death," she cried. "He would have no resources to keep him alive once his ammunition ran out—"

"And I checked our supply," her husband interjected, "and he didn't bring much. And not a one of you here has heard any shots since his disappearance. If he had gone out hunting, as everyone has presumed, wouldn't he have found game nearby and attempted to shoot it?"

"It could be a trap," Mr. Jennings said. "There may be savages watching us now. Reuben might have wandered from the camp and been captured immediately, and they might be waiting in ambush if we mount a search party."

"Or he might have been injured," Captain Hutchings argued. "He might be just beyond earshot with a broken leg or a fallen boulder across him, waiting for help to arrive. Can any of us live with ourselves if we don't at least make an attempt to find him?"

"It makes no sense," another said. "We're told to stay in the center of the river and post watchmen at each boat throughout the day and night. Then we camp here, not knowing how close we might be to an Indian village. This delay on shore could mean the death of us all."

Mary was relieved that someone had vocalized what she had feared throughout her fitful night's sleep. She stole a glance at Ma; she was looking straight ahead, her thin lips pursed and her eyes flashing.

"We cannot in good conscience leave him," Colonel Donelson said, moving into the center of the group. "We'll make teams of six men each. Each team will search for an hour at a time, until he's found. The others will guard the boats here."

"I hope they find him alive," Ma said under her breath, "so I can wring that boy's neck."

Having seen Ma kill many a chicken with one swift twist of the wrist, Mary wondered if it might serve Reuben Harrison better to remain missing.

&#x6388;

As the search parties rotated in shifts, the women took advantage of the delay to catch up on housekeeping chores. Clothes were washed on the boulders that jutted away from the south shore and then hung on lines hastily stretched from one boat to the next. Several women pulled their mattresses from the close confines of the cabins to air them in the cold, crisp breeze. Others took the time to perform inventories of their foodstuffs and conferred with women of neighboring boats on upcoming menus that would help to stretch their remaining provisions.

Mary spent the morning washing clothes with her sisters and watching little Johnny marching up and down the shoreline alongside their boat. Sam had located a long, straight tree branch, which he'd begun whittling into something that might eventually resemble a musket. And when Sam was called away to do his part in searching for Reuben, Johnny had seized his new trophy and was marching with great seriousness with the makeshift barrel resting against his small shoulder. He occasionally stopped and, placing one hand over his brow to shield his eyes from an imaginary sun, he appeared to be searching for the enemy. Not finding any, he would resume his solemn march.

Upon returning to the cabin at noon, Mary found Ma had pulled out a number of wooden crates and was combining their remaining foodstuff into fewer boxes to lighten their load.

Ten children and Ma go through a lot of food, Mary thought when she eyed what remained. She couldn't help but wonder what they would do when the food ran out.

As if in response, Ma said, "Mary, check with the Jennings, Robertsons and Donelsons to find out what they have left. Perhaps we can combine our meals again tonight."

As Mary turned to go, she noticed Ma's drawn and worried face. It was so uncharacteristic of her not to maintain a controlled, forceful presence. "Are you alright, Ma?" she asked.

She looked at Mary with resignation. "We should have arrived three months ago," she said quietly. "We had plenty of food to get us through the trip, had things gone according to plan." She straightened her back and took a deep breath. "But there's no sense in thinking about what might have been. We'll make it through this." As if in an afterthought, she added, "We'll have to."

Sam joined Mary as she made her way along the shore toward Mrs. Jennings' boat.

"No sign of Reuben, I take it?" Mary asked.

He chortled. "He might be stew right now."

"That's awful to say!"

"There is all sorts of game out there, Mary," he said as they walked. "I came this close—" he held up his hand in front of his face "—this close—to a buck. Turned around, and there he was.

Wasn't afeared 'a me or nothin'. Like he hadn't never seen a man before."

"I reckon he might not have," Mary said. "So where is he?"

"I was too shocked to shoot," he said. "But it won't happen again, I guarantee you that."

"I hope not," Mary teased. "We need the vittles." As if responding to the mention of food, her stomach growled. "See what I mean?"

As they reached the Jennings' boat, the sound of two gunshots reached their ears, followed by silence. Sam spotted Ike and they both took off running toward the woods.

"Sam!" Mary called.

"No need to worry!" he yelled over his shoulder. "Ain't Injuns or there'd be more noise!"

Reluctantly, Mary turned back toward the Jennings boat. She met Mrs. Jennings on deck; she had discovered a box of preserves they had canned late last summer. If they planned things right, the sweet fruit could be an unexpected delicacy enjoyed with their morning biscuits.

"It will have to be rationed," Mrs. Jennings stressed, "no more than a spoonful apiece. We just don't know how long it will have to last…"

Mary realized upon further inspection that although the preserves would be well received, the Jennings were running dangerously low on other food. The carrots were limp and their potatoes were turning mushy and were filled with eyes, which could be poisonous. It was determined they would make another soup as they had the previous night, combined with other vegetables the other families could afford to add.

"How is Elizabeth?" she asked.

Mrs. Jennings began to beam. "It won't be long now, Mary. Go see her. I know she'd enjoy a visit from you."

Mary found her on a mattress in the darkened cabin. "Are you sleeping?" she whispered tentatively.

"No, Mary," she said, waving her in. "I'm so glad you came. I've just been lying here, holding my belly." She laughed.

"Your ma said it won't be much longer."

"I'm feeling pains. They're not regular yet, but I can tell I'm getting near."

"Your ma is real excited."

"We're *all* excited," she said. "I've been thinking about what you said, about it being a boy and all. And I know you're right. I can feel it. Ephraim is going to be so happy to have a son."

Mary realized they should have already been at Fort Nashborough by now, and Ephraim should have been pacing outside their home while the midwives helped with the birthing. Instead, they were separated by hundreds of miles. She was sure the thought was not lost on Elizabeth, but she smiled and said, "Men always want a son right off, don't they?"

"And my pa is even excited. I can't wait to get there, Mary, and see the look on Ephraim's face the first time he holds him. He'll be named Ephraim, Jr., did I tell you that?"

Mary felt her forehead. She was clammy and hot, though it was cold in the cabin. "Are you eating right, Elizabeth? You're eating for two, you know."

"I'm eating what I can," she said. "Things are different out here, Mary. I think of all the food I would have had back home…"

"I know. I try not to think of that, though."

"We'll soon be at Nashborough, and then everything will be alright. We're going to build a house and Ephraim is going to farm. I'm going to have the best vegetable garden. And Little Ephraim, he's going to help out his daddy and maybe we'll get a school started there. A future lawyer needs good schooling." She giggled. "Silly me. They probably already have schools."

A pain gripped her and she rolled onto her side and moaned. Mary felt her belly. The baby had moved lower and the kicks were into Elizabeth's upper rib cage.

"How often are they?"

"They're not regular yet. I'm to tell my ma when they are."

"You get some rest, Elizabeth, and I'll be back to check on you. You need anything?"

She shook her head and closed her eyes. "All I need is a healthy baby boy resting in my arms," she whispered.

"He'll be here before you know it," Mary said.

Elizabeth didn't respond and Mary moved toward the hatch. She had just closed it shut behind her when she heard a series of whoops from the people along the beach. Thinking it was Reuben, she rushed off the boat and toward the woods, where the latest search team was emerging.

But instead of Reuben stepping onto the shore, the men dragged two large bucks and deposited them beside the nearest boat.

"Supper!" Sam proclaimed with a broad grin.

Mary was elated. Real meat! The shore was abuzz with activity. There would be more than enough meat to add to the soups; none of it would go to waste.

She hurried back to their own boat to tell Ma of their good fortune. Halfway there, she passed Captain Hutchings' boat. Seeing the Captain on deck, she called out, "How is Simon?"

He shook his head.

Mary stopped and waited for him to continue. When he didn't, she climbed aboard the boat. "Where is he?"

He motioned toward the cabin. "Better not go in there," he cautioned.

Mary brushed past him and opened the cabin hatch. A horrible stench swept over her, and she grabbed her apron and held it over her mouth and nose. Her eyes watered as she stepped over the threshold, and she hesitated as she tried to adjust to the blackness.

As the winter sun crept through the doorway, she was able to make out a large room divided in half by a series of hanging blankets. One side was hidden from view; on the other, she made out supply crates and a dim figure lying on a bed of straw in front of them. "Simon?" she said as she drew near.

Catherine parted the blankets and emerged from the other side of the room. Simon did not answer but lay quietly, his eyes fixed straight ahead.

For a moment, Mary thought he was dead. She placed her hand upon him and waited for his lungs to expand his chest. When it didn't, she reached for his wrist. His pulse was weak.

Simon drew in a sudden, raspy breath.

As if in answer to her thoughts, Catherine said quietly, "It won't be long now, Mary."

She pulled the coarse, moth-eaten blanket from his lower legs. Even in the darkness, she could see his ankles swollen to grotesque proportions. Her eyes followed his gangrenous legs past his knees and to his upper thighs, where his pants were bulging at the seams.

She covered him with the blanket and felt his forehead. It was cold. Too cold, she thought, for a living being. She spoke to him softly for a few moments, but he did not respond. Finally, she left, not knowing if he'd even known she'd been there. Catherine followed her onto the deck and closed the hatch behind them. Captain Hutchings was standing at the edge of the boat, watching the men skin the two bucks.

"It's too late to save him," she said quietly.

He nodded.

"Why didn't you have the doctor amputate his legs?"

Captain Hutchings took a deep breath. "We're going to a new frontier, Mary Neely, one in which every man must be fit, capable of providing for himself and his family—or, in Simon's case, for his masters. What would he have done without legs? He would have been but another mouth to feed, a drain on our resources. Better that he die here and quickly, than spend decades as half a man."

Mary fought back tears. "I'm going to fetch the doctor," she said. "It's the right thing to do."

He looked away from the men below and fixed his gaze on Mary. She was aware of Catherine standing just at her elbow, but she remained silent. After a moment, he nodded.

She left the boat with a heavy heart as she went in search of the doctor. There would be fresh meat for the living, but in Simon's case, it wouldn't make any difference.

# 15

Noquali sat in the sturdy wooden chair and stared at the flames that leapt inside the wide fireplace. In his mind's eye, he was reliving the evening just two days before when he first stepped foot into this cabin. It was a memory that he knew would be etched on his mind forever.

He had gone straight from Bloody Fellow's cabin to the one at the edge of the cliffs overlooking the river. He had raised his hand to knock but the door had slid open, revealing one room perhaps eight feet deep and fifteen feet wide. A small bed was pressed against one side, and a wood table had dominated the opposite side. The air had appeared golden from the light cast by several candles' flames. The fireplace had been roaring as it was now, enveloping the cabin with a warmth that welcomed him inside and out of reach from the storm's ferocity.

She had been standing with her back to the door and at the sound of it opening, she had turned toward him.

She was a tall woman, almost as tall as he; her lithe figure was cloaked in a long-sleeved buckskin dress that reached below her knees. Her ankles were alluring, her slender feet in moccasins in which the fur had been turned inward against the skin but which were rolled outward at the tops nearest her ankles.

Her hair was the color of a raven, appearing almost blue-black in the candlelight. It was straight and coarse and cascaded over her shoulders, framing her figure. His eyes had moved upward to her face and he stepped inside, closing the door behind him. The howling wind subsided inside the solid structure, and all he could hear was her breathing, shallow and soft, and the fervent beat of his own heart against his chest, which now almost heaved with his own breathing.

As his eyes moved upward, he took in her long, graceful neck, her firm jaw line and her high cheekbones. Her brows were gently arching and black. Her eyes gazed upon him wordlessly and as he stepped around the table and moved closer to her, he saw the only clue that she had French blood coursing through her veins: her hazel eyes.

As he came toward her, he could see the pain in those eyes; though she stood stoically, her chin high, the eyes betrayed the wounds deep inside. They were haunting, and he knew they would continue to haunt him even when the time would come for them to separate once more.

He laid his rifle against the table to free his hands. Before his arms could reach her, she flew into him, burying her head against his thick panther pelt, the sobs coming quickly, furiously, as if she had saved every tear for the moment she laid eyes upon him again.

And he had stood there in the luminosity of the flames and held his brother's wife as she cried.

☙❧

He heard her stirring behind him as she formed corn pone on the thick wood table and he watched as she stepped around him and dropped them into a kettle seasoned with fat that hung above the flames. He continued gazing at her in silence as she cooked his meal.

It wasn't until she had placed the fried corn pone, hominy and thick slabs of venison in front of him that she eased into a chair opposite him and silently nodded.

As they began to eat, he felt a catch in his throat but he knew he had no choice but to discuss the very thing that would be the most difficult.

"Your father, Crooked Walk…"

"He is dead," she said quietly, her eyes downcast. She gazed for a moment at her plate filled with food before raising her head to meet his eyes. "When the white men came, he was sitting at the door to our cabin. You know he was not able to stand without difficulty."

Noquali nodded. Crooked Walk had arrived at his name as a young warrior; he had been shot in the back near his spine. Though the medicine man had been able to remove the round, it had left him with an unsteady gait. Unable to fight with the others and unable to hunt, he had become a sage. Tribal members had gathered around him during times of stress—a gathering blizzard, a summer drought, or the appearance of Europeans, and he would tell them what he had dreamed and what their futures held.

He had foretold of a family arriving near their Indian village almost twenty years ago; a man, his wife, and a son barely able to crawl. They would come by river, he predicted, and they would foretell of others coming with them, others who could not be trusted; others who would mount attacks against them and drive them from their lands.

And when the family had approached, the warriors had been waiting. They captured them easily, as they'd traveled alone; the man had argued vehemently that they were traders and wanted to live in peace. But he had been British at a time when the British had seized Cherokee hunting grounds and had driven the natives from the land of their fathers. So in retaliation, they had burned him alive at a stake erected in the center of the village.

Crooked Walk had taken his wife as his own. She was French and went by the name of Apollina—"Gift from Apollo"—until Crooked Walk had discovered its meaning. Then he had renamed her in a Cherokee ceremony and called her Gift from Great Spirit. She had embraced the Cherokee people, becoming a good wife to Crooked Walk, and had provided him with one child—a daughter they named Jo-leigh.

"They killed him as he struggled to rise," Jo-leigh was saying now. "I saw him fall as I ran through the village…"

"And your mother?"

"They dragged her out of our home by her hair. She screamed to them that she was French, but they called her an Indian lover..." Her voice faded and she picked through her food. "They killed her. They slit her throat—" she motioned with her slender hand "—and as she lay bleeding, they cut off her arms and legs."

Noquali turned his head, his teeth clenched. The white men knew what this would mean: that the beautiful woman would spend eternity without the use of her limbs. Finally, he turned back. Jo-leigh had continued shoving her food from side to side on her plate but had not taken a single bite.

"How is it, you were able to escape?"

Her moist hazel eyes met his. "When they came, I was picking winterberries. I was near the ponds when I heard the first gunfire. I ran to the edge of the village and saw my father and mother killed. I ran."

He remained silent, his eyes fixed on hers.

"I ran with the others, through the woods, through the ponds. I ran even when I heard the horses behind us, when I saw those in front and beside me fall. I ran into the brushes until the thickets made it too difficult for them to follow me." A tear formed at the inner corner of her eye, but she brushed it away. She rolled the sleeve of her buckskin dress upward, above her elbow. "I did not know until later that I had been shot."

He reached for her hand, cupping it in his own. He stared for a long moment at her disfigured elbow, the poorly healed wound and the awkward bend of her arm. Then he unrolled her sleeve back to her wrist as if hiding the affected limb could somehow repair it.

"You know we have been launching attacks on the white men," he said at last.

"Yes."

"And we are killing them, just as they killed those in our village."

"Yes."

"For every Cherokee they kill or maim, we shall kill ten of them. It is no longer enough for us to drive them from our lands, the lands of our fathers. Now it is crucial that we slaughter them."

"And Holds-the-Moon—"

Noquali tightened his grip on Jo-leigh at the mention of his brother's name. He closed his eyes as though he could banish the image of his brother's dying breath, but it remained, as he knew it would always remain. When he opened his eyes once more, she was looking at him with an odd mix of emotions—pain, sadness, and something else, something tender, something loving.

"Holds-the-Moon was a brave warrior," he said at last. The words were hoarse and barely above a whisper. "He fought well and killed many of the invaders. But we were overwhelmed..." He looked at her arm, now hidden by the buckskin, and felt a wave of guilt sweep over him. He should have had at least a wound to show that he fought bravely as well, but he didn't. He had only the words of the others who fought alongside them, and suddenly, that no longer seemed adequate.

"I am alone now," Jo-leigh said.

"You are not alone."

Her lower lip quivered, and he touched it gently with his forefinger. "You will always have me," he whispered.

"Will I?"

He wanted to sweep her into his arms, to press his lips against her black hair, to kiss away the tears that appeared to be on the verge of erupting from her. He had loved her, even as his brother had loved her, but in the end she had chosen Holds-the-Moon, and in the end he knew he could never love another the way he loved her.

He relaxed his hold on her hand and cleared his throat. "And you have another."

She opened her mouth, but he silenced her. "A brother," he said.

She laughed cynically. "I have no brother."

"Yes. When your mother was captured, she was married—"

"Her husband was killed," she interjected. "And she married my father."

"Yes. But at the time of her capture, she had a child, a son."

"He was also killed."

He leaned back in his chair but he didn't let go of her hand. Her hand felt cold now, although the flames in the fireplace continued to rage. "I met a trader during my travels," he said, "who was there when your mother was captured. He remembers the day. The boy was barely more than an infant. One of the women had recently lost her son and adopted him."

She looked away from him and he knew she was weighing his words. It was a common custom for each captive to be adopted, killed or enslaved. It depended upon the mood of the conquerors at the time, or upon the behavior of the captives, or sometimes both.

"Where is he now?" she asked.

"I will see him shortly. He comes with a small band of Shawnee; he will help us repel the invaders."

"Shawnee?"

Noquali nodded. "His father is a Shawnee chieftain. His mother is part Shawnee, part Cherokee. They wander now that their lands to the east have been seized, and today they are traveling here to push back the invaders and eventually to return to their homes."

"What is his name?" she asked.

"He travels easily between the tribes and the white men, often serving as an interpreter. His name is White Messenger." He rose from the table and reluctantly dropped her hand from his. "And now I must go. My men await me."

She followed him to the door and helped him place the panther pelt over his clothes. He placed his hand on the door but stepped back without opening it. Then he took a quick step forward and pulled her into his arms. He breathed in the scent of her hair and her skin, and he placed his mouth against her ear. "You will see me again, Jo-leigh. I promise that you will see me again."

# 16

They spotted the Indians shortly after dawn. Their movements were almost imperceptible at first; they looked like nothing more than another evergreen swaying in the wind. But as the weak winter sun rose, the woods across the river came alive. Mary watched in growing horror as they moved from trunk to trunk in an orchestrated mass movement parallel to their camp.

Like a disturbed beehive, the camp was abuzz with barking dogs and preparations to cast off. Reuben still had not returned but Colonel Donelson made an instant and autocratic decision: there would be no more search parties. The call went out from boat to boat to prepare to launch immediately.

Mary and the others helped Ma push the boat off the shore and into the water, where they were instructed to wait until *The Adventure* had moved past them. One by one, the boats joined them and swayed with the current in the frigid wind.

And now they sat, impatiently waiting for *The Adventure* to cast off, but Donelson was embroiled in an emotional discussion on shore.

Mrs. Harrison was pleading for Donelson not to leave Reuben behind. Especially with the Indians just across the water, it would mean death to their son.

Mary heard the Colonel's answer as the wind carried his voice: "I cannot risk losing every man, woman and child, Mrs. Harrison. And that is precisely what I would be doing if we were not to depart immediately. Reuben is in God's hands now. There is nothing more we can do."

He began to climb onto his boat, which the others had pushed to the edge of the water, but Mr. Harrison stepped in front of him. Mary couldn't hear what he was saying, but she concluded that he was arguing against leaving their son behind. Mrs. Harrison stood beside him, wringing her hands and sobbing.

Then Donelson climbed aboard *The Adventure* and maneuvered into position. As they made their way past the Neely boat, Mary chose a spot near the stern and prepared to shove off with her pole. Beth, Jean and Ma were in positions along the sides while Ike and Sam remained on the bridge.

Patches barked as the boat moved past them, as if he understood their journey was resuming and he was anxious to get underway. The barks were picked up from one boat to the next until they filled the air.

Mary watched as Mr. Harrison untied a canoe from his flatboat. Mrs. Harrison rushed into the cabin and carried out a few items, which he stashed in the small vessel. Then he dragged the canoe onto the shore and returned to push off the Harrison boat as his wife began to cry anew, her body wracked with her distress.

Two men joined Mr. Harrison after pushing off their respective boats. Mary watched as the Harrison vessel moved past them, followed by the others, one by one. The Henrys, having lost their flatboat, were now separated among the other vessels, along with their possessions.

The Jennings boat was the last to move into the water, and Mr. Jennings waved at Ike to move out before him. In tandem, the Neelys began to push toward the center of the river, where the current swept them westward behind the others.

As they moved further from the shore that had been their home for the past two days, Mary eyed the Indians on the opposite shore. They were watching them. They did not attempt to follow them; they had no boats and they did not run along the shore keeping pace with them. They simply watched, but it was their utter silence and their manner of moving in waves almost like a perfectly timed military unit, that caused a lump to form in Mary's throat.

There were no women among them and no children, as far as she could tell; only men who stood in buckskin and furs. They watched them depart from the safety of the woods' perimeter, standing tall with long barreled rifles and spears at their sides.

The Jennings were behind them now and the current was causing them to gain speed.

As they moved further and further away, she caught a glimpse of the wooden boxes Ma had unloaded when combining their remaining food. They were stacked near the wood line. Mary didn't know why, but she suddenly felt a wave of sadness sweep over her, as if she were leaving her home behind her. The Henry boat was heavy with water, one end entirely sunk while the other end rose out of the water angling toward the sky. Then she saw the small canoe with Mr. Harrison and the other two men take to the water. They rowed in the opposite direction, heading eastward.

Reuben's folly might have sealed their fate, Mary thought as they passed out of sight. God be with them.

&#x6384;

An hour later, the sound of men's voices reached her ears above the melee of the children playing. As she looked ahead, she caught sight of a scout in a canoe, calling out to each boat that passed. Upon hearing his news, a shout of glee went up from each family.

Mary moved to the side of the boat where she could be within earshot.

"What do you know?" Ike called out from the bridge.

"Clinch River Company," he said. "We encountered their scouts overnight. They're only a day from us, at most!"

The Neelys simultaneously cheered. Mary's spirits felt lighter than they had since their voyage began. Finally, after all these months, she would see her friend Hannah again. She thought of her friend's sparkling eyes and dimpled smile, of her ability to see the good in everyone and in everything that happened. She knew that Hannah would be beside herself with joy at the prospect of joining Donelson's fleet.

As the miles swept past, Mary daydreamed about their reunion. They could ride together, she thought excitedly, sometimes on the Neely boat and sometimes on the Stuart boat. In the evenings after their meals, they could compare their experiences on their river journeys, and share their dreams for their futures. Things would be entirely different when Hannah joined them, Mary thought. They would be fresher, more exciting, and more fulfilling.

Without thinking, she pushed harder on the pole to speed their journey. And as she looked at the boats in front of them and the Jennings boat behind them, she realized they, too, were moving with a fresh urgency.

CB&O

At mid-morning, a call went up from *The Adventure*. It was picked up from one boat to the next. Ike shouted the message over Mary's head from the bridge, relaying it to the Jennings behind them: Reuben Harrison had been found.

The boats slowed and a murmur began of astonishment and relief that quickly turned to anger.

He was sitting on a large boulder that protruded from the shoreline. He appeared to have wandered along the shore moving steadily westward for the past two days, as the settlers had delayed their own journey to search for him further east.

Ben Belew, a settler in one of the boats ahead of them, pulled to shore and yelled for him to jump aboard.

Reuben appeared to take his time, as if his newfound freedom had made him a man, until Mr. Belew shouted at him with poorly concealed impatience. Reuben quickened his step as he waded into the water, climbing aboard as the crew readied to help him onto the deck.

As the Neely boat swept past them, Ma stood at the side and glared at the young man. Mary knew she wasn't one to stand for impudence, and wondered if Reuben knew just how lucky he was not to have been picked up by Maggie Neely.

# 17

They reached the Tennessee River a short time later. As each boat left the Holston, the inhabitants cheered; but as the Neely boat slipped into the Tennessee, Mary found herself looking back at the river that had been her home for so many weeks and wondering if she would ever lay eyes on it again.

They stopped at mid-afternoon. After picking up Reuben, two men decided to return to their last camp in an effort to find Mr. Harrison and the men who had remained with him. With Colonel Donelson's consent, they left by canoe. Mary watched them as they rowed out of sight, the canoe remaining close to the shore where the crosscurrent could speed their journey.

The children, under the watchful eyes of several parents, scoured the woods for kindling while the older children hauled wood from fallen trees. It seemed a never-ending cycle of life on the river followed by the ever-increasing challenge of making their food last longer and go a little bit further.

Reuben insisted he had killed a rabbit and eaten it whole the previous night, but from the way he devoured the corn pone his mother gave him, Mary thought his story unlikely. His disappearance, though, had generated a debate about their need for food.

As Mary began chopping the vegetables the women had contributed for another soup, the men gathered around Colonel Donelson. Ike and Ma were there and Mary longed to be with them. Beth and Jean, her older sisters, didn't care much for those discussions, preferring to use their time to sew or cook or tend to the smallest Neely children. In contrast, Mary could feel herself pulled into her mother's strong footsteps. She watched her now as she gathered with the men and discussed their growing concern with food.

"This isn't a matter of wanting a little more food to add fat to our bones," she was saying, her voice carrying over the sound of the children. People listened when she spoke, and now the men turned their full attention to her. "This is a matter of survival. We are dangerously low on our provisions and we are not yet halfway to Fort Nashborough. What is to become of us, if we run out of food?"

Colonel Donelson appeared to be choosing his words carefully. "We've reached Chickamauga Territory; the most dangerous part of the voyage. We must press on until we have passed through their lands."

One man pointed at the surrounding woods. "I can see deer from here," he said. "Last night's venison made the difference in how many were fed. We have enough left over for tonight's meal but no more. What would be the harm in shooting a few more deer while we wait for Harrison to rejoin us?"

Donelson's eyes scoured the terrain. "It's too dangerous," he said. "If one comes down to the water to drink, we could consider firing off one good shot. But we must presume there are Indians about, and to wander through the woods could mean stumbling into an ambush. Even firing one shot along the riverbank could alert them to our position... We must remain diligent."

"I'm tired of running scared," another man argued. "We've been seeing Injuns all along. And we have yet to be fired upon. What would be the harm in trading with them? Perhaps swapping a blanket for some corn or trinkets for bear meat."

"I've heard tell there's an Indian village a few days west of here—"

"You won't be stoppin' at that village."

The man's voice was deep and gravelly and rung with authority. Mary finished chopping and dumped the vegetables into the kettle of water, then seized the opportunity to move toward the group.

He was a tall man with dark brown hair and piercing blue eyes. He was dressed in a well-worn buckskin jacket and breeches; and where most of the settlers were bundled inside layers of clothing, he seemed content without so much as an overcoat. And unlike the others who wore boots fashioned back east, he wore moccasins with leggings. A knife in a leather sheath hung from his belt and he carried a rifle, powder horn and shot bag as well as a possibles bag. Mary recognized him as one of the scouts who traveled miles ahead of them and brought back reports which Donelson consumed with great interest. His name was Jedediah Cobb, better known as Jed.

"That village belongs to the Chickamaugas," he was saying.

"Chickamaugas are nothing more than Cherokee. And many of us have traded with the Cherokee in the east."

"That's where you're wrong, my friend," Jed answered. "The Cherokee no longer accept them. Dragging Canoe refused to make peace with the settlers; he has declared his allegiance to the British. And even here, in the wilderness, we remain at war with Great Britain."

"But surely we can trade—"

"They will not trade with you. They will take what they want from you, and then scalp you and take your women. To stop at their village would be suicide."

A hush descended upon the crowd. Finally, in the quiet, Ma asked, "Then what are we to do for food?"

Jed stepped back, deferring to Donelson, who said with renewed vigor in his voice, "The Clinch River Company under Captain Blackmore is no more than a day away. They should have more provisions than we do, more than enough for us to reach Nashborough."

No one asked what would happen if they did not have the needed provisions, a fact that was not lost upon Mary. She made her way back to the kettle, catching Ma's eye as she left. From her mother's expression, she knew it had not been intended for her to overhear their conversation. But as she returned to the kettle and picked up her spoon to stir the soup, she knew they were in dire straits.

Two women were making their way from one soup pot to the next, carefully rationing the rest of the venison. The handful of meat that was deposited in the Neely kettle was the same amount her father used to eat in one sitting. Now it must feed Ma and ten children, as well as two other families. The carrots and potatoes were in sad shape and the last of the canned beans had been divided into three meals.

When they lined up for their meal that evening, Mary carefully ladled two bits of potato, two carrot slices, a single green bean, and a chunk of meat into each bowl, along with a generous scoop of broth. She tried to console herself with the contents of the liquid, as yesterday they had boiled the bones of the deer, creating a venison-flavored soup stock that was rationed among the families. They used the jars they'd once carried fruits and vegetables they'd canned in, but which were now empty, to hold the precious broth.

Beth stood behind her, handing out a biscuit to each person in line. As they'd made their way further from home, the biscuits had become smaller and smaller, and tonight they were no more than a single bite, a bite Mary knew they must relish for they didn't know what tomorrow might bring.

# 18

They cast off from shore before sunrise as the assigned watchmen spotted smoke from campfires a short distance away. Not knowing if they were friends or hostile Indians, Donelson gave the order to move out before breakfast.

It was a rainy, dreary day. But as Mary stood on deck and worked her pole in tandem with the others, she barely felt the frigid drops weighing down her clothes and dripping from her head. She was going to see Hannah today.

The river grew increasingly choppy, causing her to stand with her feet far apart to maintain her balance. Baby Jane was dry retching; her stomach, like theirs, was empty. It took all of the older Neelys to keep the flatboat from turning sideways in the water, so little Meg remained in the cabin, keeping Baby Jane and Johnny calm, a job they all realized was almost more than Meg could handle.

The morning was filled with memories for Mary: memories of the playroom in their old home, of the wooden rocking horse Pa had made with his own hands and which had been left behind for lack of space. Of the pack of hounds that could be heard baying through the night; hounds that had all been left behind, except for poor Patches, who huddled in between boxes in the cabin in a feeble attempt to stop sliding as the boat pitched. Memories, too, of the large fireplace in the kitchen and the bowls filled with fresh-picked berries; of canning beans and tomatoes and creamed corn.

Seeing Hannah again would allow her to relive those times. Seeing her face and hearing her ready laughter would remind her of happier times, simpler times. Tonight, if the rain subsided, perhaps they could sleep on the deck, as she knew they would keep the rest of the family awake with their all-night whisperings. There would be so much to catch up on; she couldn't wait to compare stories from their journeys, to talk about the things they'd seen... And now, from tomorrow onward, to experience the rest of the journey together.

She thought of George Spears and wondered if he missed her. Perhaps even now he was preparing for his own voyage west. No, she thought, he was going to wait until the crops were planted. By the time she saw him again, she would be settled in her new home.

The miles swept past and the river grew calmer and the long string of boats in front of her and behind her became a monotonous blur.

CB80

They passed the Clinch River around noon. All eyes were on the mouth of the river as they swept past, searching for signs of the Blackmore party. They continued for some distance before whoops came up from the last flatboat and all eyes turned back upriver as Captain Blackmore's boat came into view.

He stood at the bow like a pirate, Mary thought, with his thick black hair wild and unruly in the wind and the rain, his clothing soaked and clinging against his broad chest.

The whoops and yells were picked up and grew like a wave from one boat to the next and all who could afford to put down their poles took off their hats and waved them in greeting.

Colonel Donelson called out to the first boat behind him and through the shouting and whistles, his command was picked up and repeated down the line: they would stop for the night at the first suitable shoreline.

It seemed as if it took forever for him to select a spot, as Mary peered behind her and tried to spot the Stuart family. There were perhaps ten boats in Blackmore's group; joining with Donelson's party, it would swell their group to thirty boats. As the river wound around the bends, she realized she could not spot the last of the boats.

She called out to the boat behind them, asking about the Stuarts, and the call was picked up and carried from boat to boat. But to her chagrin, it stopped when it reached Captain Blackmore, and no return answer was forthcoming.

Finally, Ike shouted to them that Donelson was stopping up ahead. The boats slowed and maneuvered, some better than others, until they were all coming ashore.

Mary helped to pull their boat onto the shoreline and tie it up to keep it from drifting, a feat that required seven of the children pulling and straining alongside Ma. Mary pulled impatiently, her eyes darting from boat to boat as some passed her to dock just west of them and others stopped short of Donelson's boat.

When at last they were secured, Mary glimpsed furtively at Ma.

"Go ahead," she said, "but hurry back, Mary. There are chores to be done."

Mary rushed to the boats behind her, excitedly glancing at each one as she went past. Some of the families she knew and others she didn't, but none of the boats contained the Stuarts. Puzzled, she reached the end of the line and stared east at the river, now empty.

She walked back up the shore as people began greeting each other, the women hugging old friends while the men slapped each other on the backs. She passed the Jennings boat, where Elizabeth could be spotted just inside the cabin doorway on the mattress, groaning. She passed Catherine Hutchings and her son Christopher; Captain Hutchings was nearby directing the servants as they secured his boat. No one had seen the Stuarts.

She reached the last boat and stopped. Turning, she looked down the shoreline at the hoards of people departing from their boats, at the kettles already being placed in preparation for dinner, at the tents some were setting up along the woods' edge.

She walked back down the line, her footsteps growing heavier. She stopped for a brief moment at the Neely boat. Ma, Beth and Jean were setting up their soup kettle.

Ma opened her mouth to speak but stopped as she caught sight of the disappointment on Mary's face. Her eyes mirrored Mary's concern and she instantly turned and looked toward the other boats.

Without speaking, Mary continued to the boat at the far eastern end. Surely, Hannah would be looking for me, she thought. She'd envisioned her jumping off her boat and running toward her—and now, as she walked ever more slowly along the beach, passing by the same boats she'd walked past only moments before, it was dawning on her that Hannah wasn't there.

Captain Blackmore was standing on the shore near the bow of his boat, calling instructions to his crew.

"Captain Blackmore, sir," Mary said, stopping to stand beside him.

He glanced at her. "Hello there, Miss—?"

"Mary. Mary Neely."

"Ah, Will Neely's Mary?"

"Yes, sir."

He pulled a horn from his vest. Turning away from the group, he blew it, its sound wafting forlornly over the water.

"Sir?"

He had cocked his head as if he were listening. "Yes?" he said without looking at her.

"The Stuart family. Where are they?"

His eyes blinked suddenly and he turned to face her. "Mary Neely," he said as if her name were just beginning to register with him, "you're Hannah Stuart's friend, aren't you?"

"Yes, sir."

He stood there staring down at her, his eyes black and unblinking. He looked even larger to her up close.

In the distance, they heard a responding horn.

"That would be the Stuart boat," he said. "The whole family has contracted small pox."

"What?" Mary whispered in disbelief.

"They've been quarantined for the safety of the others." As if in an afterthought, he said, "You might be able to see their boat if you were to wander along the shore, but I must warn you, small pox is highly infectious and you are forbidden from going near them. The disease could wipe out our entire fleet."

"But if it could wipe out the entire fleet," Mary said, her voice strained, "what does that say for the Stuarts?"

"They're in God's hands now." Captain Blackmore looked beyond her, his eyes lighting up in recognition of Colonel Donelson. As he moved away from her, she remained in place for a long time, staring east as the sun sank lower behind her.

# 19

Noquali found Archie Coody at a campsite overlooking the Tennessee River. The snow, for the most part, had melted down to a thick crust that crunched as his horse walked across it. He stopped at the edge of the woods and dismounted, leaving his stallion to forage through the snow in search of old grass.

Archie stood and joined him at the cliffs. They stared toward the east for a long moment in silence. The sky was so pale, it was almost white. The trees were stark and forlorn; many of them had lost their leaves and now stood naked against the bitter winds; others contained brown, withered leaves that had long ago died and were waiting for new spring foliage to push them off the branches. Only a few deep green trees hinted at the evergreens that were used to shield the Indians from sight. And below the bleak sky and the dreary mountainous terrain were the rushing waters of the Tennessee River, its constant movement the only reason it had not frozen over.

"Donelson has passed the Clinch River," Archie said.

"Then he is on the Tennessee."

"Yes."

"They are making slow progress."

"They were stopped for a time on the Holston River; a foolish boy wandered from their camp and they spent a lot of time searchin' for him." He paused to chew on a wad of tobacco.

"What has become of the boy?"

"We watched him for a time… He headed west as Donelson's men searched east." He chuckled and shook his head.

"And?"

"A few wanted to capture him; kill him where he stood or take him back to Tuskegee Island Town."

Noquali waited in silence as Archie spit before continuing.

"He came close to some of our camps, but turned back toward shore. He spent the night lookin' for food, but didn't find none. We decided to remain hidden, so as not to alert the other white men."

"That is good."

"Have you any word from Bloody Fellow?"

"Yes. I bring with me about a hundred warriors. They will spread out between The Whirl and the white men and attack when they have the opportunity." Noquali peered upriver but saw no sign of the settlers. "What about the second group?"

"They joined Donelson around noon."

"Where are they now?"

"Camped."

He nodded. "Let them get deeper into our territories. By then, we will have spread out so they cannot outrun us."

Archie spit again. "Come, Brother," he said, gesturing toward the campfire behind them. "Kilt a wild turkey this mornin' and it ought to be finished cookin' shortly. You'll be joinin' me for supper?"

Noquali felt Archie moving away from the cliffs and back toward the campsite. He could hear a pot rattling as he moved it around and the scent of wood smoke and cooked meat wafted toward his nostrils. But he remained at his vantage point as the wind whistled through the trees and across the panther fur, staring at the river below and thinking.

# 20

With Donelson's and Blackmore's consent, Mary set up a cooking pot that was visible to the Stuart's boat. By calling back and forth to Mr. Stuart, who was the only one outside the flatboat's cabin, she made it known she was prepared to cook their meal.

"How is everyone?" she shouted.

"Fair to middlin'," he answered.

"How is Hannah?"

There was a delay in his response and Mary found herself holding her breath.

"We're all down with the small pox," he answered finally.

"Are you bad off?"

"It's small pox."

She swallowed. "Can Hannah step outside?"

He looked toward the cabin. His shoulders seemed more rounded than Mary remembered them. "She can't get out of bed," he called to Mary. "Best you stay a good distance from us."

"Do you need anything?"

"Food," he answered without hesitation. "And if there's a doctor in your party, we're in need of one."

"I'll make you some food now," she answered, "and I'll get the doctor straight-away."

Ma arrived just as Mary was double-checking the fire under the pot. Silently, she handed some tiny biscuits to her, which Mary placed beside the kettle.

Ma remained there for a long moment, simply staring at the Stuart boat. Mr. Stuart had returned to the cabin and now their vessel was so quiet, it appeared deserted. Not even a dog was about.

"Did you see anyone?" she asked at last.

"Only Mr. Stuart."

"No one else?"

"No, ma'am."

As Ma's eyes continued to search the boat for inhabitants, Mary couldn't help but think of the times the Stuarts and the Neelys had spent together. Ma and Pa had known Tom Stuart and his wife Sarah ever since Mary could remember. They were about the same ages—all were in their forties.

"But for the grace of God…" Ma said at last, her voice fading in the bitter air.

CঞEO

The next morning, Mary left a basket of biscuits that combined were no larger than two hands and their final half jar of fruit preserves. With Sam's help, she carried the empty cook pot from the previous night back toward the Neely boat. Then she strolled along shore, finally stopping at Captain Hutchings' boat. Catherine and her son Christopher were nowhere to be found, so Mary continued into their cabin.

There was more light today than the previous time Mary had ventured aboard, and now she was able to see that their cabin had been divided into two areas: one for the Hutchings' small family of three, and the other side for their servants. The Hutchings' side was roomy with a full size bed and a trundle bed for Christopher, a small dresser and a table and chair that appeared to be used as a writing desk. It looked spacious to her in comparison with the smaller Neely quarters.

The other half was markedly different. This one appeared to be a stockroom and contained everything from their furniture to cooking utensils. In the center of the room, straw was strewn; it might have been thick when their journey began, but it had long ago been packed down by use. It was clear to Mary the servants slept upon the straw and now several threadbare blankets were rolled up and pushed to the far edge.

Simon's almost lifeless body had been pushed as far out of the way as possible. He lay on his back with a thin blanket covering most of his body, but she noted his feet stuck out from under the too-short material. She found the doctor at Simon's side, checking his pulse.

"How is he?" she asked.

He shook his head. "It's only a matter of time."

"Is there nothing we can do for him?"

He stood and gathered his black bag. "Pray for his soul," he said as he left.

Mary followed him from the cabin onto the deck of Captain Hutchings' boat. "The Stuart family—"

"You haven't been to their boat, have you, child?" He stopped and peered at her over his square spectacles. He was white-haired and stooped, but as Mary looked at him, she wondered if he appeared older than his actual years.

"No, sir… Colonel Donelson gave me permission to cook for them, and leave it a distance from their boat. Mr. Stuart called to me and asked for a doctor."

A resigned chuckle escaped from him. "I can't help them. There is no medicine," he said as he descended to the ground, "even if we were in the best hospital in Philadelphia, there is nothing that can be done for them."

Mary hurried to catch up with him. His stride was fast and long, and he appeared to be anxious to have their conversation end. "But if there's nothing that can be done, what is to become of them?"

They reached *The Adventure* and the doctor hesitated. "They're in God's hands, child," he said, echoing Captain Blackmore's sentiments from the previous day. "In a proper hospital, one in two might die. Survivors could be blinded or crippled. Out here—out here, the odds are considerably worse."

Before Mary could respond, he climbed aboard Colonel Donelson's boat. She stood for a long moment, staring at the sand along the shore, thinking of Hannah and the suffering she was going through at this very moment.

"Their throats will be filled with boils," he said.

Mary looked up. The doctor was standing at the edge of the boat, peering down at her.

"Warm liquids will help them. Their food should be soft and moist. Don't give them anything they'd have to chew… They'll have high fevers and probably chills. During the worst of it, they'll be blinded."

"If they're all sick, who will move their boat? What if they're too ill to eat on their own?"

"We can't help them, child. There's not a one of us on this journey who have had the disease and lived to tell the tale. Only those who survive it can be around it without fear of contracting it again.

"All you can do is what you've already done." He turned to go, but a moment later, he was back. "And, child—you mustn't touch anything they've touched, do you understand? Everything they use—beds, blankets, clothing, cups—they can all spread the disease."

With a heavy heart, Mary left *The Adventure*. When she reached the Neely boat, Ma was leaving as Mary began to climb aboard.

"Elizabeth Peyton is in labor," she said. "I'll be riding with the Jennings today." She stopped and looked at Mary with her large green eyes. "We must be strong, Mary."

"Yes, ma'am," she said automatically. She felt as if she were in a bad dream. She barely heard her brothers and sisters as they prepared to launch. *The Adventure* was already gone and one by one, the others were pushing off and heading west.

Ike waited until Mr. Jennings gave him the signal before departing. As they made their way into the center of the Tennessee River, Captain Blackmore blew the horn, the signal to the Stuarts that the fleet was leaving.

A long moment later, an answering horn reached their ears.

Mary wondered as she watched the five eldest children maneuver their boat how the Stuarts could possibly launch with

all aboard suffering… and how they could possibly keep up with
the rest of them.

CႨ૪Ꭷ

They stopped twice. *The Adventure* had moved far ahead of
the rest of the fleet and Donelson had decided to stop at mid-
morning until the rest of the boats had caught up with him.
When the scouts reported the Stuarts were within a half mile of
their boats, they took off again.

They stopped for the night along the shoreline, a shore that
Mary thought was beginning to look exactly like all the others.
As they prepared their suppers, word spread through the camp
that Simon had died.

# 21

## March 7, 1780

They buried Simon in a shallow grave facing east toward the home he once knew. The ground was frozen; the men had labored the night before to dig a proper grave but the ground was so hard they'd decided to stop when it was barely three feet deep.

The service was conducted before dawn. It was brief; too brief, Mary thought, for at the end of the service, she did not know any more about poor Simon than she had before, which was precious little. She didn't know if he had ever loved, had ever married, had fathered children. She wondered if he had family members still alive, and if they would ever know what fate had befallen him.

As they laid him to rest in the blanket he'd been wrapped in over the past few days, Mary began to sing. It was soft at first and plaintive, but by the second verse she seemed to have found her voice and the words tumbled out and drifted on the frigid wind. The others joined in sending up a chorus of voices that was a tribute to Simon, a tribute Mary hoped he heard as his spirit looked down upon them.

The wind rose from the west, threatening to slice through their clothes, and the iciness Mary felt only served to focus her thoughts on Simon's frozen feet and the frostbite that had claimed his life. It was early March and the winds should have been milder and the temperatures warmer, but they were neither. Instead, they were harbingers of an extended winter, of bitter cold, and perhaps, Mary thought, of the hardships they were yet to endure.

They stood with their backs to the west and as they sang, the faintest red ribbon appeared on the distant horizon. As the men tossed the last shovels of sod on top of Simon's grave and tamped it down, the crowd began to disburse and ready themselves for another day's journey.

Mary made her way toward the rear of the fleet, where the Jennings and Neely boats waited. She climbed aboard the Jennings boat to check on Elizabeth before the boats were ready to launch.

The Jennings boat was smaller than the Neely's but instead of the eleven passengers on the Neely boat, it had only seven. They consisted of Mr. and Mrs. Jennings, Elizabeth, her younger teenage brother, Jonathan, Jr.; Obediah, a young man who was traveling alone to the western territories, and two Negro servants, a male and a female.

As Mary climbed aboard, the four men were readying the boat to cast off. She passed by them and opened the door to the cabin, where Elizabeth lay moaning.

There were three women assisting her in childbirth: Mrs. Jennings, Ma, and Mary's eldest sister, Jean. As the muted light reached them, Ma broke away and met Mary at the door.

"Is anything the matter?" she asked.

"No, ma'am. Just checking on Elizabeth."

"This one's a slow one." She shook her head. "The poor girl is in a lot of pain, but the baby doesn't seem ready to enter this world yet."

"We'll be casting off soon."

"Jean and I will stay with the Jennings. I hope before this day is out, she'll have her baby in her arms."

Mary closed the door behind her and left the boat as the men prepared to push it from shore. Her brothers and sisters were waiting for her, and soon after she climbed aboard the Neely boat, they cast off.

Captain Blackmore blew his horn from some distance in front of them, having waited until the Neelys and Jennings were adrift before alerting the Stuarts to their departure.

CRISSO

The river was wider here and the mountains had gradually
faded to gently sloping hills that did little to stop the wind from
rolling in from the southwest, directly into their path. The river
tumbled like waves on the open sea but instead of propelling
them forward as it had in previous days, it fought them vigorously
with each mile they traveled.

Mary's arms felt heavy and sore from the constant exertion
of trying to keep the boat from turning about. Beth, Martha,
and Billy all worked alongside her, silent except for their
occasional grunts and groans as they fought the waves. Ike's voice
rang out constantly from the bridge, warning of obstacles to
avoid in the water, but soon his voice began to blend with the
sound of the waves and the wind.

Theirs was one of the larger vessels, a fact Mary hadn't
considered until she looked ahead at the long line of boats. Each
was engulfed in its own desperate struggle; the smaller boats
pitched and roiled like leaves in the wind. The waves crashed
over the sides of the vessels, creating slippery and often icy
conditions that only increased the hazards of their perilous
voyage.

It was as if the earth were opening up, Mary thought, and
attempting to swallow them.

She looked behind her at the Jennings boat and the four
who fought to keep it upright: two grown men and two teenage
boys. She recognized Jonathan, Jr. alongside his father and the
servant they'd employed as long as she could remember. The
fourth man, she didn't recognize at all; she was told he was about
eighteen years old and traveling alone, and she wondered about
his family and their circumstances. The men's feet were set wide
apart to keep their balance as their boat turned in one direction
and then another as they drifted farther from the group.

It had to be the worst conditions under which to have a
baby, Mary thought. For the labor to last for so long and to be in
such pain, only to be pitched about in turbulent waters in the
final hours. She worried about Ma and Jean on board the boat,

helping Elizabeth along in her labor while being tumbled about inside that dark, dank cabin.

The hatch to the Neely cabin burst open and Meg straddled her legs from one frame to the other to keep from falling onto the deck. "Johnny keeps throwing up!" she yelled at the top of her lungs, but her voice was almost carried away by the heavy winds.

"I'll tend to him!" Mary barely heard Martha's voice as she brushed past her like a drunken sailor. She was only sixteen years old; her figure was short and slight, her long blond hair hanging in wet folds about her face and shoulders. She was the quietest one in the Neely family, preferring to spend her hours watching the sky and the changing terrain as it passed her by, deep in her thoughts. On calm days, she worked tirelessly on a quilt, which was to be the first item in her hope chest.

Now as she moved past Mary, she saw how gray her face appeared and she knew the waves were taking their toll upon her as well. Martha slipped and slid toward the cabin, pushing Meg inside and closing the door behind her.

In front of them, one of the smaller vessels listed dangerously and through the heavy winds, they heard a collective scream from those on board as all hands rushed to the opposite side to right it. Mary held her breath as the vessel hit the waves with a vengeance and the sound of cracking wood reached her ears.

She wondered how on earth the Stuarts would be able to fight the rising winds. But to stop, even for a day, would separate them further from the rest of the group, and Mary was at a loss to figure out how they could survive by themselves. She strained to find them behind her; through the fog, she figured less than a mile of the river was visible behind her. But they were nowhere to be seen.

❦

They stopped in the early afternoon. The boats limped onto the shoreline one by one, the inhabitants weak and exhausted.

When the Neely boat reached land, Mary's legs were shaking so badly from her exertions that she doubted she could remain standing long enough to secure the boat. Beth dropped to her knees on the opposite side, her head slung over the side of the vessel. Ahead of her, she saw one person after the other assuming the same position.

The Jennings boat was slow in joining them; by the time they were nearing shore, Captain Blackmore was at the Neely bow. Mary had seen him stop at one boat after another and motion behind him, and now she moved toward the bow to stand just below the bridge.

"There's an abandoned Indian village through those woods," he yelled up to them. "We're camping there for the night. Secure your boat and join me there."

Somehow she gathered the strength to work alongside the other Neelys to properly secure the boat and gather the supplies they would need for a night's lodging and food. Her excitement mounted as they climbed from the boat and she assisted the youngest children. The aches in her arms that made them feel like dead weights, the pain in her calves from hours of fighting the raging waves, and the frigid cold that turned strands of hair to icicles, meant nothing to her now.

She was going to see her first Indian village.

# 22

The woods were eerily silent as they made their way to the village. Mary found herself jumping at each tree that swayed in the wind, at each branch that shifted as a fellow traveler pushed through. Her heart began beating so strongly that she felt it pulsing in her neck and despite the cold, perspiration erupted on her forehead.

A falcon broke through the trees, screeching as it circled overhead, and several women gasped in alarm at the sudden noise. Mary could feel her temples throbbing and she quickened her pace lest she become separated from the rest of the group.

She carried an armload of food and cooking utensils. Meg was close behind her, her small hands grabbing Mary's skirt so tightly that she could sense the child's fear. It was the first time since leaving Fort Patrick Henry that they had ventured this far from their vessels. After so many weeks of constant vigilance and reminders to remain in the center of the river, she questioned the logic of moving so far inland and further from the security of their only means of escape.

Then the woods ended abruptly and she found herself at a massive clearing.

When she first glimpsed the structures in the village, she wondered if they had stumbled upon a white man's settlement. The buildings were made of wood and appeared as sturdy and permanent as anything she'd seen in the east. There were dozens of them; some appeared small enough to house only four or five people, while others appeared large enough to be communal buildings.

Colonel Donelson assigned each of the families to buildings set close together; close enough, Mary hoped, to protect one another in the event of an attack.

Dusk had not yet descended and they used the last of the daylight to inspect the building that would be their home for the night. She was surprised to discover an elaborate room built into the ground; in the center of the room was a fireplace, now cold, the black ashes still staining the ground. Low wooden benches were arranged around it.

"Colonel Donelson said these are beds," Ike said, pointing at the benches.

"Did he?" Ma wandered around the room and eyed the benches. "Then we'll start a fire and spread our blankets on the benches."

"Can I sleep with you, Mary?"

Mary glanced down at Meg. "Of course you can," she said. "You're not afraid, are you?"

Meg nodded. "I'm afraid of the Indians."

"There's nothin' to be afeared of," Sam said. "Ike and me will stay awake to protect you."

"And me, too!" Johnny said, brandishing his wooden musket.

Mary winked. "And they *will* protect you," she reassured Meg. "Now help me get a fire started while Jean and Beth get a cookpot going outside. I'm hungry; aren't you?"

&#9702;&#9702;&#9702;

The men assembled around the campfire after supper as the women gathered the cooking utensils to clean them. Under the watchful eye of two men appointed to guard them, a few women and children made their way to the river to wash the pots, plates, and spoons.

Mary stayed behind and added wood to the fires. She caught Ma's eye; the older woman peered at her with the knowledge that her daughter was loitering and for a moment, Mary was afraid she would tell her to leave. But surprisingly, she remained silent and Mary made her way toward the edge of the campsite and into the shadows, where she could listen to the men speak.

"How do we know the Indians won't return?" Captain Hutchings asked.

Jed Cobb made his way toward the center, his attire making him appear as if he were completely comfortable in the wilderness. He rested the butt of his rifle on the ground and placed his hands over the end of the barrel with the ease of a preacher at a lecturn.

"The Cherokee abandoned this place years ago," he said in his raspy, authoritative voice. "The Chickamaugas lived here once... but you see they ain't here now."

"They are still in the area," Mr. Boyd pointed out. The men seemed to lean forward in unison, their faces peering at the tall man who appeared so confident.

"Gentlemen," Colonel Donelson said, "many of you have met Mr. Cobb. He is our lead scout and is very familiar with this area."

"Oh, the Chickamaugas, they're still in these parts," Jed answered. "But they ain't returnin' here. 'Bout this time last year, we was warned by friendly Injuns Draggin' Canoe was plannin' on attackin' settlers near the Tennessee and Holston Rivers— this very place where we now stand. Colonel Robertson ordered a counterattack against the Chickamaugas—burned eleven towns along this here river. Much of this one here was burned, but more important, we cut off their food."

"I heard," one man said, "they retaliated against the settlers, killing the men and capturing their women and children. And that Dragging Canoe vowed he would not stop fighting but would rise again and again to attack any white man along these waters."

"He ain't gonna attack us here," Jed answered confidently.

"How do you know this?" Captain Hutchings demanded.

"He attacks further downriver."

"Downriver?" Mr. Boyd said. "Then we must pass him on our way to the Cumberland?"

"Yep."

Mary felt the hairs begin to stiffen on the back of her neck.

After the murmuring that rose among the men subsided, Jed continued. "We should be approachin' Tuskegee Island in the mornin'. That's where the Chickamaugas are. And I need you to listen up good: stay in the middle of the river. Avoid the shore—no matter what happens."

Colonel Donelson joined him and addressed the men. "You've heard me speak of a white man who was captured by Indians when he was a boy. His name is Simon Girty."

A collective whisper began at the mention of his name.

"He fancies hisself more Injun than white man," Jed announced. "He taught the Injuns to make captives run along the shore, callin' to boats for help. If you aim toward land, those Injuns'll wait 'til you're within strikin' distance. Then they'll ambush you and slit your throats—or make you wish they had."

"Are you askin' us to turn a blind eye to captives beggin' us for help?"

Mary was surprised to hear Sam's voice. He stepped forward from the shadows. He appeared so young, she thought, in comparison with the other men. And yet there was something mature about him beyond his years, something she couldn't quite put her finger on.

"You ain't got the slightest chance of rescuin' nobody," Jed answered. "Your life depends on ignorin' 'em. Stay away from land and move quick as lightnin' and you might just live. Turn toward shore, and your fate lies in the hands o' the Injuns. You'll be captured, tortured, or kilt."

"Do we know for certain they will attempt to ambush us?" Donelson asked.

"As certain as you see me standin' here. In these parts, theys only two kinds of pilgrims: them that is ready and them that's dead."

"How can one be prepared for an ambush?" Mr. Boyd asked.

"Tomorrow, we move quickly," Donelson said. "Keep your vessels in the strongest current and do whatever is in your power to move as swiftly as possible."

"No matter what you see, no matter what you hear," Jed added, "keep on a'movin'. Do not stop. You hear? No matter what."

"And what if one of the boats gets into trouble?" Sam asked.

Mary caught a glimpse of Ike; he remained silent but his jaw squared and she thought she caught a flash in his eyes.

"There are more o' them than us," Jed answered. "Save your own hide and them that's on your own boat. You go back, and you'll just end up dyin' right alongside 'em."

Ike appeared to relax at Jed's words but Sam just shook his head.

The men continued to discuss their strategy for moving past the hostile Indians, but their voices became nothing more than a buzz in Mary's brain. Her thoughts were focused on the Stuart family, who were half a mile away from their group. As they sat around the campfire in the company of others, Hannah and her family remained quarantined on their small boat. She wondered if anyone would tell them of the danger that lurked ahead. And she wondered if their sickness would prevent them from remaining close enough to the rest of the fleet to afford them at least a small degree of security.

She shook her head, as if to rid it of bad thoughts. They would all make it through, she thought. They had to.

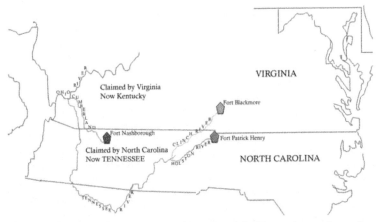

Mary Neely began her journey at Fort Patrick Henry, located on the Holston River near present-day Kingsport, TN. The Stuarts began at Fort Blackmore on the Clinch River near present-day Gate City, VA. In 1780, the Holston River joined the Tennessee River at present-day Lenoir City, TN. The Clinch River joined the Tennessee near present-day Kingston, TN. When the Donelson Party reached the Tennessee, they were 601 miles from the Ohio River. The Cumberland and Ohio Rivers join near present-day Paducah, Kentucky.

Flatboats varied in size. They consisted of a flat-bottom boat and a cabin with a hatch facing the stern. Some cabins had windows. Tillers were used on top of the cabin, called the bridge, to steer the boat. Additional poles were used at the sides, front and rear as needed. These boats are not built for whitewater rapids like those the Donelson Party encountered. Artwork by Bonnie Watson.

In 1780, the Tennessee River wound its way through the wilderness. It was known for treacherous rapids, whirlpools and shoals. In the 1930s, the Tennessee Valley Authority rerouted the river, creating a series of lakes and dams. Many of the Indian villages are now completely submerged.

There were plenty of places along the route where the Chickamauga Indians could ambush the Donelson Party. The pictures on this page were taken near present-day Florence and Muscle Shoals, AL. Many thanks to Barbara Broach and Milly Wright, who served as guides.

The Neelys settled at Neely's Bend along the Cumberland River near Nashville, TN. They operated Neely's Salt Lick, now known as Larkin's Sulfur Spring. It would be the site of William's death and Mary's capture by Shawnee warriors.

The Neely family built this home in the spring of 1780. The original dwelling had a dogtrot where the three windows are shown above. The first floor was completely underground and was used as an Indian escape room in the event of an attack. Gutters, new windows and roofing, plumbing and electricity were added in the 1960's. It is now located in Clarksville, TN.

This is the only known authenticated picture of Mary Neely. It was taken between 1830 and 1850 and has been handed down through Mary's descendents. It is reprinted here with the permission of descendent Tom Robertson. Forensics expert Barbara Condrey of the Chesterfield, VA Police Department regressed the picture to show what Mary would have looked like in 1780.

# 23

## March 8, 1780

The scream pierced through the still night air and echoed through the valley. As if acting with one thought, the women in the cramped quarters of the Jennings' temporary lodging tried to calm Elizabeth as she wrestled with giving birth.

Mary placed a flat piece of bark between her teeth. "Bite down on it!" she directed, helping to pull her into a semi-reclining position. As the labor pains began anew, Mary worked alongside Jean to keep the exhausted woman in a position to help speed the delivery as Ma and Mrs. Jennings worked near her lower body.

It had been a difficult night. Ma had been called to Elizabeth's side almost before they'd lain down to sleep, and she had sent for Jean and Mary soon after. The doctor had arrived during the night to examine her, declaring all that was needed now was for nature to take its course. So the women had rallied around Elizabeth as mid-wives, offering support, encouragement and instructions.

Their work had been complicated with the additional responsibility of keeping Elizabeth quiet. As darkness set in, the Indian village took on an eerie quality; though the moon rose high above them, it only served to cast subdued fingers of light through the treetops, causing everything else to appear as purple shadows that moved as the trees danced in the wind. Most of the log homes were burned-out shells; in the darkness of night, they appeared as misshapen figures scattered among them. Even the owls appeared to give the village a wide berth, leaving it so quiet that the slightest sound streamed past the houses and echoed through the valley.

Men were stationed at the boats near the river and circling the village, and Ike, Billy and Sam did their duty as sentries in two-hour intervals. Yet as Mary and Jean took turns hauling water from the river during Elizabeth's labor, Mary couldn't shake the feeling of vulnerability. She wished they had remained on the river, constantly moving while Elizabeth gave birth, even though she knew it was not practical. The waters were too treacherous to navigate in the dark.

Elizabeth moaned once more in a prolonged expression of her agony before collapsing into Mary's and Jean's arms.

"It's a boy!" Mrs. Jennings exclaimed.

Mary busied herself with wiping down Elizabeth's forehead. Despite the crisp, late-winter night, the cabin was stifling and Elizabeth was drenched in perspiration. The fire had been allowed to die down as the women's feverish activity had provided more warmth in the close confines than anyone needed.

Ma wrapped the baby in a blanket and called to Mary. "Clean him up," Ma directed as she handed him to her. Her voice was curt but Mary glimpsed her eyes growing moist as she reluctantly handed him over. As soon as Mary had him in her arms, Ma returned to Elizabeth to finish tending to her.

Mary dipped a rag into a bucket of water and gently began cleaning little Ephraim Peyton, Jr. It would have been appropriate for the baby to cry out with all the capacity his lungs could muster, but Mary found herself trying to comfort him in an effort to keep him quiet. She couldn't imagine a more exposed place to give birth than an Indian village after the savages had been spotted watching them for several days now, or a more defenseless creature than little Ephraim.

He had a shock of black hair on his little head that curled gently as Mary wiped it. His eyes were puffy and heavy lines under them showed the strain his birth had taken throughout this long night. When he opened his eyes, he seemed to focus on Mary and she found her chest welling up with love and a yearning to protect him. In the candlelight, she couldn't quite identify the color of his eyes, though they were light; gray, she thought, or perhaps blue.

He was a large baby, maybe all of seven pounds, but now, resting in her arms, his hands appeared so tiny, his feet so small. She carried him to Elizabeth, who was lying down, her arms outstretched for her first glimpse of her son. Mary laid him gently into his mother's waiting arms.

A wave of exhaustion swept over her and she caught Ma's eyes.

"You did good," Ma whispered, resting her hand on Mary's shoulder. "This was the toughest labor I've ever seen... Go get some rest now, child."

Mary nodded silently and picked up her coat from a chair beside the door. But as she opened the heavy wood door, she welcomed the blast of cold air as she realized she, too, was drenched in sweat.

Her legs felt heavy as she made her way from the Jennings' lodgings. She hesitated and tried to remember which cabin the Neelys had been assigned to. As she studied the huts that appeared almost identical to one another, she realized the sun was rising. The horizon was so pale, it gave no hint of blue sky or yellow rays, but appeared like an anemic watercolor painting.

John Donelson was conferring with Jed Cobb. As Mary moved past them, she realized the colonel was fully clothed as if he was ready to start another day. Jed appeared rumpled, as though he had been up all night.

Doors began to open and slowly, people began to wander outside. Talk began of starting breakfast. Though Mary felt the now-familiar pangs of hunger, she wanted sleep more than anything else. When Ike stepped out of a cabin, she made an instant turn toward it, her pace quickening as the thought of a warm place to sleep beckoned to her.

"Gather your things!" Colonel Donelson ordered, making his way through the village. "Return to the boats! We're leaving immediately!"

Word spread through the cabins like wildfire: the scouts had spotted Indians during the night, and they were headed straight toward them.

Mary stopped at the door to the cabin. Ike's expression mirrored her own: he, too, had been awake through the night and was in desperate need of rest. The images of Ma, Mrs. Jennings and Jean raced through her mind. And of Elizabeth, who had been in a difficult labor for nearly twenty-four hours… and of little Ephraim, just born into this world and already having to be swaddled and carried to a boat, where he would spend his first day of life.

# 24

Noquali sat upon his stallion at the crest of the mountain, his back erect and his chin raised as he peered through the trees below. A band of Indians, mostly Cherokee but interspersed with Shawnee and Creek, were making their way down the mountain toward the river. They moved fluidly, their faces painted in black and red. And though the sun was weak and they were well shielded by the wilderness, he knew each was well-armed with rifles, pistols, arrows and knives.

He watched the river swirling and cascading over the boulders and shoals, obstacles that would serve them well in their attack. There was no sign of the settlers on the river, but he had not expected them, either; he knew it would take some time for them to depart the Indian village he held so sacredly in his heart, and return to the river.

He felt a movement behind him. Without turning, he knew from the horse's hooves and the man's breathing that it was Archie Coody.

Archie joined him for a brief moment, their eyes focused on the stream of braves that weaved their way around the trees and rock they knew so well, their line appearing like an undulating serpent making its way to the water.

"It is time," Archie said. His breath caused a puff of vapor as it hit the cold morning air. Noquali watched it rise and dissipate.

"Yes," he said, turning his stallion toward the footpath that meandered to the river. "It is time."

# 25

It was close to mid-morning before the fleet was back on the river. Mary learned that directing hundreds of men, women, and children to leave immediately was easier said than done, and she wondered what would have happened if an Indian attack had been imminent. It occurred to her that one more stop like the previous night could mean the settlers might find themselves in a life-or-death situation.

She was beginning to hate the water. Before departing Fort Patrick Henry, she carried a romanticized notion of sitting on the deck, leisurely watching the untamed wilderness pass by as she wrote letters to George or perhaps a bit of poetry. She knew Beth had carried the same idea; she was engaged to George's brother, Jacob, and Mary often heard her pen scratching late into the night as she wrote letters to him in a sturdy journal. She supposed at some point Jacob would be joining her in the Cumberlands—perhaps with George—and Beth would give him the journal to read all her letters at once.

But now as they both struggled with the rest of the family to maintain control over the flatboat, they had become too busy to read or write during those long hours on deck. And sadly, they were either too busy to pay much attention to the beauty that surrounded them, or too exhausted to care.

When Mary did look beyond the waters, it was in search of an Indian presence. The stress was becoming unbearable. She could see in the lines of Ma's face and of her sisters that the strain was taking its toll on them as well. Even Billy had discarded his trickster ways and had become far less jovial.

She faced the south on the port side, helping with one of the poles to keep the flatboat in the center of the river. Sam was on one side of her and Ma was on the other. Martha, Jean and Beth were on the opposite side, while Ike and Billy remained on the bridge with Ike facing the bow and Billy with the tiller that reached over the stern.

She glanced beyond Sam at the boats behind her. The Jennings had taken the longest to depart. Elizabeth had been so drained that Mrs. Jennings had begged Colonel Donelson to be allowed to remain through the morning, but he was adamantly opposed to the idea. He told them bluntly it could mean certain death or capture. He had assigned a strapping young man to carry Elizabeth to their boat if needed, though, but in the end Elizabeth walked with little Ephraim in her arms.

She hadn't looked well, Mary thought as she strained to see their boat behind them. Her face had been pasty and pinched and she had walked haltingly. She hoped Mrs. Jennings had been able to make her comfortable in their tiny boat's cabin and perhaps even now she was asleep on the mattress with Ephraim beside her.

Ma had offered to ride with them, but Mrs. Jennings had told her it wouldn't be necessary.

Colonel Donelson had instructed them to fire a shot in the air when they departed, to alert the Stuarts who had come ashore a half mile below them. It had been almost half an hour before Mary heard the shot ring out, which could mean the Jennings were as much as a mile behind them, and the Stuarts at least half a mile further.

They had been too rushed this morning for Mary to check on her friend Hannah, and now she wondered how those on her boat were faring. There were twenty-eight of them in all, which included Hannah's entire family, servants and other couples or singles who had not warranted a boat of their own. She hoped some of them were well enough now to tend to the others. She tried to convince herself that Hannah would be well soon; well enough for them to ride part of the journey together, but her heart wasn't persuaded.

As Mary turned back around, she spotted the scouts' canoe making its way from *The Adventure* to each boat in turn.

"A Cherokee village is up thar," Jed called out to them. "Stay in the middle of the river. Do not—ya hear me, *do not*—go ashore on the south side!"

"We'll stay in the middle!" Ike called back.

As Jed remained steady in the river and waited for the next boat to pass him by, all eyes were on the south side where Indians were gathering on the shore. Some were dressed in furs, which made them appear otherworldly with huge claws extending at the ends of their hands or heads of animals perched upon their own heads. Others wore red and black paint that made them appear like demonic creatures, with spears in place of tridents.

Mary shivered at the sight of them. "There must be dozens of them," she said, her voice involuntarily dropping to a hoarse whisper.

"My God," Ma said. Then she quickly turned around. "Martha," she called, "make sure the children stay inside the cabin." Then she turned to Sam. "Get three of the muskets. Leave one behind for Martha. Mary, at the first sign of trouble, get to the cabin door."

"Yes, ma'am." Mary knew what her mother was inferring: she would have to be the last line of defense for the youngest Neely children. She moved closer to the cabin as Martha finished herding the children inside and closed the door.

Sam handed a musket to Ma and another to Ike on the bridge. They were all loaded, and they stood on the port side with their weapons by their sides. Sam had his musket at the ready, as it always was, and was standing with his legs apart for a firmer foothold on the moving vessel. Jean and Beth were handed pistols, which they tucked into their skirt pockets to keep their hands free to navigate the boat.

As the boats drew closer, the Indians began running along the riverbank. At first Mary couldn't make out what they were saying. But as the Neely boat began moving past, she caught several words.

"We are friends!" one of them yelled.

"Come ashore!"

"We have food for you!"

"We trade!"

Some of them had armloads of furs, which they held up as if they were attempting to sell them. Two Indians dragged a large buck carcass onto the shore. Pointing at it, they called out, "We have food! Come! Eat with us!"

Mary glanced at the boats behind them. The others appeared to be doing exactly as the Neelys had; they were prepared with their weapons, but they stood idly watching them as the river's current swept them past. Rueben Harrison appeared to be arguing with his mother, perhaps wanting to go ashore and trade for meat.

Now the Indians were beginning to run along the shoreline, trying to keep up with the fleet. They were joined by others until several dozen raced along the river's bank.

"There are no women," Mary said. Her voice was hoarse as if her throat was constricted and she realized her mouth had become perfectly dry. The coat that had kept her barely warm enough now seemed to weigh a ton, and she fought the urge to loosen or remove it.

"And no children," Beth whispered.

Mary felt the skin on the back of her neck as if a cold wind had suddenly blown upon it. There was something odd about groups of men running along the shore, trying to cajole them into stopping. She squinted as if the action could improve her eyesight. They were young, she realized, perhaps as young as teenagers and the oldest ones might have been in their thirties, at most. There were no elders, no women, and no children. Just men. Men of fighting age.

The boats ahead of them were slowing.

"What are they doing?" Ma said, the panic in her voice reflecting Mary's own inner turmoil.

There was a commotion aboard *The Adventure* and as all boats began coming to a controlled stop, all eyes were turned to Colonel Donelson.

Donelson, his son Johnny and John Caffrey were untying a canoe that was affixed to the side of their flatboat. Mary could hear Jed calling out to them to continue moving downstream, but Donelson waved him off.

Mary frantically tried to keep her eyes on the Indians on shore while she also attempted to watch the Donelsons. The whoops from the Indians had grown stronger with enticements of friendship, corn and hominy, medicines and meat.

Behind her, another commotion was brewing as Rueben tried to untie the Harrison canoe. Mr. Harrison had his hands full as he struggled to keep Rueben aboard.

"Keep moving," Ma yelled up to Ike.

Ike's eyes flitted over the water. "I can't. I can't move past *The Adventure*."

"Then get to the north shore."

Ike directed the others to navigate further from the Indians and toward the north shore. As they moved away from the rest of the fleet, Mary noticed others had begun moving as well, until several of them were converging close to the north shore.

*The Adventure* remained in the middle of the river but now the canoe was lowered to the water.

"Where are they going?" Ma said to no one in particular as Johnny and Mr. Caffrey climbed into the canoe and began paddling toward the Indians.

"It's suicide," Ike said. His voice was so venomous that Mary turned her face upward to look at him. His cheeks were deep red and his eyes were narrowed. "What's the use in keepin' us to the middle of the river, when they're goin' ashore at the first temptation?"

As Mary turned back around, she noticed another movement on the far shore. Further downstream, three men were readying a canoe. They almost appeared like mythical creatures, she thought at first. Then she realized they were dressed from head to toe in animal skins. A very large man seemed even larger with a full bear skin sprawled across his back, the head resting across his own head almost like a hood, the arms somehow affixed to his sleeves and leggings. Two smaller but lither men were dressed similarly: one in a sleek black skin and another in a tawny one.

As Johnny and Mr. Caffrey began paddling toward the Indians on the south shore, the three furred men cast off toward them. As they neared one another toward the center of the river, Mary realized the one in black was sporting a panther skin; she became mesmerized by it. It was the largest cat she had ever laid eyes upon.

They called out to Johnny and Mr. Caffrey, apparently convincing them to stop paddling until they caught up with them. They halted in the center and fought the river's current until the three strange men caught up with them. The one with the bear skin pushed the head off his own, revealing brown hair.

"A white man," Ike declared.

The commotion grew behind them as Rueben tried anew to untie his canoe and join them.

But as Mary turned her attention back to the canoes in the center of the river, she realized Johnny and Mr. Caffrey were returning to *The Adventure*. And the three men were following them.

They reached *The Adventure* and all five men were assisted aboard. Then Donelson called out to Jed, who had been waiting on their port side. Jed responded by paddling toward the boats stopped along the north side, calling out to them to continue downriver.

As Mary assisted the others in moving back to the strong current in the middle of the river, she glanced behind her. Rueben had successfully launched the Harrison canoe and he and his friend Obediah were paddling toward *The Adventure*.

"The fools," Ike said.

Mary took up a spot at the stern as Billy used the tiller to guide the boat back toward the center of the river and the stronger current. She watched the Indians as they stopped shouting along the shore, but they continued to move like a growing wave along the riverbank, staying up with the fleet. In the distance, she saw the Jennings boat; it seemed small now in the vastness of the river. She felt confident they could see the rest of the fleet and they would know to keep moving.

And like a spot on the horizon no larger than a bird, she saw the Stuart boat limping along behind them.

# 26

Noquali helped to secure the canoe to the flatboat and then waited patiently as Archie boarded. A hand was extended over the side. Noquali studied it briefly before grasping onto it and climbing aboard. It was a white man's hand, small compared to his own, calloused, cut and parched. It was the hand of a rich man, he decided, a man unaccustomed to manual labor. He had seen too many hands like this one; too many men unprepared for the treacherous waters and untamed wilderness.

"Colonel John Donelson," one man said, extending his hand to Archie.

"Archie Coody," he responded, shaking his hand vigorously.

"My son Johnny," Colonel Donelson continued, gesturing toward the young man who had assisted Noquali on board, "and Mr. Caffrey."

"Pleased to meet you," he answered without introducing Noquali or two additional Cherokee who boarded the ship.

"We'd be pleased if you'd join us for a cup of tea or perhaps a meal," Colonel Donelson said.

As he spoke, several men moved a table and chairs onto the deck. He motioned for them to sit as he directed a woman Noquali presumed to be his wife, to prepare some food.

Noquali remained silent as he sat at the table. Archie and Donelson were engaged in a pleasant conversation as if they were old friends.

"Is the weather always this bad this time of year?" Donelson was asking.

"Worst winter I've ever heard tell of," Archie answered. "Longest one, too. Where you folks headed?"

Noquali watched the women as they poured water into a battered tea kettle before placing it over the flames of a makeshift fire pit on deck. They appeared to be conferring; one had a worried look on her face as they disappeared into a large cabin, only to emerge a moment later with a tray of food. They placed the tray on the table; the younger woman smiled nervously as she arranged china plates in front of each person. His eyes moved slowly, methodically around the table. Donelson and Mr. Caffrey were on one side while Archie, Noquali, and the other Cherokee—Swift Feet and Night Owl—sat in the remaining chairs.

"We're not stopping in this territory," Donelson was saying, "and we'd appreciate it if you'd let any natives know this. We come as friends, and we are only traveling through."

"Through to where?" Archie asked.

"Fort Nashborough."

"Don't reckon I've ever heard of a fort named Nashborough."

"It's in the Cumberlands, west of here. It's not a military fort, but a fort for settlers moving out west. You know, until they get settled."

Noquali watched as the women placed small biscuits on each plate. He admired the china without yet touching it; it was a pretty pattern and one didn't see too much china out here in the mountains. The teacups were placed alongside them, tiny little cups that probably held no more than a few swallows, he decided. He wondered if his finger would make it through the delicate handle and then decided it would not.

"I was hoping," Donelson was saying, "that you'd be able to tell me what to expect in the rivers ahead, being more familiar with this territory than I."

"Have you never been this way before?" Archie asked as the young woman poured an opaque liquid into each cup.

"No; it's my first trip by water."

"What route are you planning on taking?"

"We're following the Tennessee until we reach the Ohio; then we're taking the Ohio to the Cumberland River."

"Heading further west?"

"No; by the time we reach the Cumberland, we'll be west of the fort. We intend to turn back eastward." He directed his son to bring a map, which they laid out on the table. Noquali studied the hand-drawn map with its crude river markings. He knew these lands; he knew each stream and tributary, each footpath and each town. As he looked at the drawing, he saw only six lines depicting rivers and none illustrating any of the other bodies of water they would encounter.

His eyes rested on Donelson's hand as his finger traced their voyage. Like his son's, it was small, almost fragile. And it was peeling with the dry, cracked skin of one exposed to nature's elements. Instinctively, he glanced at his own hands resting on the table, hands that were strong and capable and moisturized with bear fat.

As Archie continued chatting, Noquali's eyes wandered back to Donelson, taking in his worn, stained clothes. These were pioneers who had experienced much hardship already, he thought as his eyes moved upward to Donelson's face. It was lined and weathered; his cheekbones were high and gaunt. His collar was a bit too large for his neck, as though he had recently lost weight. There were dark circles under his eyes, and as Noquali began to study the others surrounding them, he realized they all had the same pinched, unhealthy look.

He had seen that look all too often among the travelers. They came from the lands on the other side of the mountains, where the wilderness had been replaced with farmland, where hunting had given way to raising livestock, and where a burgeoning population enabled them to trade or buy whatever they wanted—even dainty china cups. They reached these lands and they were often woefully unprepared for the hardships, the unforgiving landscape, and the brutality. Their fate would depend on their ability to adapt.

"Please eat," Donelson said, holding the tray of biscuits out to them. Archie took one and Donelson offered the tray to

Noquali and to the other Cherokees in turn. They each took one, followed by spoonfuls of sweetened fruit from jars.

As Night Owl heaped his plate with the sweet fruit, Noquali heard a faint sigh beside him. Turning, he noted the sad expression on the young girl's face as she wistfully watched the Indian eat. They are starving, he thought as he observed her eyes watching every morsel that was consumed. They are starving and they have brought out the best foods for us.

He bit into the biscuit. It was hard and stale. He dipped the remaining biscuit into the tea to soften it but it remained tough and almost inedible.

Donelson's wife carried a tray of meat to the table and placed it before them. Smiling, she said, "Please, help yourselves to the food."

As the tray was passed to each Indian, Noquali noticed the meat was fatty and he wondered if this was all they had. As they ate, he began to notice that the white men barely touched the food; it was clearly meant to feed their guests.

"There are only a couple of Indian villages along this route," Archie was saying. "They are Cherokee and they are friendly. They signed the treaty."

Noquali avoided looking at the other two Indians.

"Who are these young men?" Archie asked, pointing at a canoe that contained two undisciplined teenagers who were circling *The Adventure.*

Donelson scowled. "Every group has one or two young men who have difficulty with maturity, don't they?" he said. His words seemed to have been chosen to allay their concern, but his expression continued to show annoyance with the young men.

Noquali watched them with growing interest. They both carried rifles and they were focused on the Indians who continued to run along the shore, keeping pace with the boats.

"They will not harm your people," Donelson said as if reading their minds, "they are cocky, yes; but not foolhardy. None of us mean your people harm…" He turned back to Archie. "You are a white man?"

It was a question rather than a statement and Archie's eyes widened momentarily before he answered, "My pappy was Scots-

Irish. My mammy, Cherokee. I know these tribes; they are good people. They don't wish you no harm, either."

Swift Feet placed one hand near his pistol and his other hand near his knife. His eyes were narrowed as he continued to watch the young men circling the boats.

"We have gifts for you," Donelson said suddenly, signaling to the other men.

Noquali's eyes roamed from one man to the next. He estimated about thirty people milling around on deck, mostly black and white men, although there were a handful of women. Two black men were on the bridge, one staring straight ahead while the other worked the tiller. He could hear the sound of children, but they were not within sight; he supposed they had been herded into the confines of the cabin, either because of the foul weather or their unanticipated guests. Their clothes were all stained and many of them wore layers of clothes; they all appeared thin and tired and their faces indicated a prolonged lack of sleep.

Johnny brought forward a small porcelain bowl, which he held in both hands as if it were sacred. He placed it on the table in front of Noquali. "Our gift to you," he said, meeting Noquali's eyes.

Noquali picked up the bowl and examined it. It was painted in shades of blue and depicted sailing ships with birds soaring over the masts; even the inside bottom of the bowl was painted and ringed with an intricate blue border. He nodded his appreciation but he did not speak. Let them think he did not understand their language, he thought.

Another young man appeared with his arms laden with goods. As Donelson directed them, they presented each item individually, allowing the Indians to savor each gift. There was beautiful pottery, leather bracelets, carved wooden figurines, and even tobacco. The latter was most appreciated, and Noquali found himself looking more closely at their other possessions. He wondered if they had liquor in the cabin, how much more china they carried with them, and whether they had furniture for their new home. Jo-leigh would appreciate the china, he decided. It would look nice on her table. He narrowed his eyes so his stares would be less obvious as he looked at the women gathered a few yards away. One of them had a comb in her hair which appeared to be made of bone. It would be beautiful in Jo-leigh's long black hair.

A shot rang out and he jumped to his feet, his hand moving automatically to his rifle. Archie, Night Owl and Swift Feet had also risen quickly. Donelson was already on his feet and hastily crossing to the starboard side where the two young men in the canoe were whooping and pointing at the shore. Donelson yelled out to them, "Rueben! Return to your boat forthwith!"

The Indians on the far shore were rushing for their own canoes and dugouts and hitting the water at breakneck speed.

Donelson turned back to them, frantic. "They were shooting at an animal—not at your people." His words were tumbling over one another. "We do not want trouble."

Noquali grabbed Night Owl's arm. In the Cherokee language, he said, "Stop them. This is not the place."

Without delay, Night Owl and Swift Feet rushed to untie their canoe as *The Adventure* quickened its pace. The woods were alive now with warriors, their red and black painted faces appearing almost magically from the wintry underbrush, their bodies leaping over fallen stumps and limbs, rushing to the water's edge, where a growing number of canoes awaited them. They were streaming out now as far back as Noquali could see.

"Stay close to the northern shore," Archie was directing Donelson. "Direct your men to move quickly, and stay as close to the northern shore as possible."

As the two Cherokee disembarked and raced to the others, he peered at the flatboats and canoes stretched out for a mile behind *The Adventure*. Even with orders to stop, he knew the single shot may have caused him to lose control over the warriors. There would be some who would not be content now until they had scalps and fresh tales to share.

# 27

**M**ary was standing at the bow just below Ike, who was on the bridge when the shot rang out. They had fallen in line with the other boats when the four men had climbed aboard *The Adventure*, but they'd had difficulty getting around one of the shoals and were now third to the last in line; only the Jennings and the Stuart boats were behind them now.

Try as she might, she hadn't been able to get a good look at the visitors on board *The Adventure*; they were too far ahead of them. They had had more than their share of things to look at and contemplate, however, as they watched the Indians running along the shoreline, keeping pace with the boats.

The river was wide here, and Ike had directed them to remain closer to the north shore to provide for a wide berth around the Indians. Some of the Indians had taken to canoes but were remaining closer to the southern shore. One canoe moved alongside *The Adventure*.

When Rueben had won the argument on board the Harrison boat and took to the waters in a canoe with his friend Jim, Ike had announced to no one in particular, "No good can come 'o that boy."

Mary had silently agreed as she'd watched them move dangerously close to the Indians on shore; close enough to call out to them. She saw a small herd of deer higher on the mountainside, standing motionless as though the animals had been engrossed in the action below. And when Rueben had fired off his rifle at them, Mary knew he was too far away to have any chance at hitting his mark.

What she hadn't considered was the Indians' reaction.

It was swift and ferocious, as though Rueben had been firing directly at them. The mountainside came alive with Indians, as if all the trees at which Mary had been idling staring had been painted bodies; they rushed down the steep incline to the shore faster than the boats could react. Somewhere in the back of her mind, she registered the deer fleeing, disappearing with their white tails held high; and turning back to the bow, she caught a glimpse of two Indians hastily leaving *The Adventure.*

For the first time in her life, she heard an animalistic cry more terrifying than anything she had ever witnessed. It pierced the air and grew with intensity, the sound reverberating through the valley with such force that it seemed to be everywhere at once.

"Get the muskets!" Ike yelled as he leaned into the tiller, pushing and turning the long pole. "Push forward!" he yelled to those with poles. "Gather speed!"

Mary dashed to the cabin, her legs spread wide to keep her balance on the swiftly moving boat. As she raced toward the back, she caught a glimpse of the Jennings boat, the people moving about frantically, trying to navigate further to the northwest to outrun the Indians.

She reached the door and slung it open, grabbing the muskets that stood just inside.

"Mary!"

She hesitated only momentarily as Meg cried out in anguish. She was holding onto Johnny with all her strength as he tried valiantly to take his wooden musket and join his older brother Sam on deck.

"Stay here!" Mary ordered as she slammed the door in his face. From the darkened corner, she heard Jane screaming in terror.

She leaped and lunged back across the boat. Ma was racing toward her and as they nearly collided, she grabbed two of the muskets. "Hurry, Mary, hurry!" Ma screamed as she flew past her, tossing one of the muskets up to the bridge.

Mary could see Ike still frenetically moving the pole through the water, his body leaning forward as if he could will the boat to move faster. He anxiously glanced over his shoulder as Mary passed below him.

"Put down the guns and grab a pole!" he shouted over the din.

Mary quickly laid the muskets on a pile of sack cloth, grabbed a pole and paddled like she'd never paddled before.

"Put your back into it!" Ike was shouting. In tandem, the Neelys sliced their poles through the waters.

Mary no longer felt the hunger pangs that had plagued her for days; she no longer experienced the constant ache of muscles unaccustomed to rigorous labor. She was enveloped in sheer panic as the Indians closed in on the fleet like a pack of wolves descending upon sheep. Terrified, she glanced around her, catching a glimpse of Ma, Jean, Beth, Martha, Billy and Sam rowing like the devil himself was after them.

The Jennings boat was dropping back as only Mr. and Mrs. Jennings appeared to be paddling the small, overstuffed boat.

Ike turned to look in the same direction and then his eyes swiftly searched the boat. Seeing Sam at the stern, he called out, "Sam, keep rowin', no matter what! Stay in the center, away from the north shore shoals, so's we don't get hung up. If any Injuns try to board, shoot to kill. *Do not* try to help nobody in the other boats. You hear me?"

Mary watched Sam as he nodded grimly and kept slicing his pole through the waters.

Then Ike called out to Mary, "Mary, take a musket and get to the children!"

She grabbed one of the muskets from the sack cloth and with a final glance at Ike, raced through the boat toward the cabin hatch. As she passed each of the Neelys, they looked at her with the same terror-stricken panic—all but Sam, who had a look of anticipation on his face that was more harrowing to Mary than the others' fear.

"The children—" Ma managed to holler as she worked the pole.

"I'll take care of 'em," Mary shouted as she raced to the cabin.

The cabin hatch faced the back of the boat. When she threw the door open, Meg screamed as though a murderer was bearing down on her.

"It's me!" Mary shouted, rushing inside. In a split second, she'd taken in the image of Meg in the corner of the cabin, her thin arms pulling six-year-old Johnny and four-year-old Jane as close to her chest as she could. Jane was screaming and crying.

"Are the Injuns attacking?" she screamed.

"No!" Mary shouted. "Pipe down! Ain't nothin' gonna happen to you."

She turned back to the hatch and started to push it closed. When the gap was only a few inches wide, she stopped. The boat was gaining speed. "We're outrunnin' 'em!" she shouted to the children. "We're safe!" She hoped God would forgive the lie, and she wondered at her own method in trying to calm the children. But she couldn't think with their screams reverberating through the tiny cabin. And she had to think.

The Indians were stopping the chase, she realized as she watched. Dozens of canoes were simply stopping. As if the world had taken on a surreal, slow-motion quality, she saw their heads turning to look behind them.

As the Neely boat continued to put distance between them, she realized the Jennings boat had continued to drop back. They were too near the northern shore, she thought, too close to the shoals in their effort to escape the Indians attacking from the south. The beaches would jut far into the water, the shallows trapping any boat that came too close to shore. Especially a boat overloaded with furniture and heavy boxes.

And around a curve a mile behind them, the Stuart boat limped into view.

# 28

Noquali and Archie Coody remained on board *The Adventure* even as it gained speed and cut through the waters, spiriting them away from their tribe. They remained calm, waiting until they had rounded the last bend before Tuskegee Island Town before Noquali nodded and rose from the table with Archie by his side.

"You've passed the last of the Indian villages," Archie said, his voice smooth and calm. "You'll be safe now."

"I am so sorry—please tell them we meant no harm," Donelson said, shaking Archie's hand. Noquali couldn't help but notice how his hand trembled as he shook his hand. "He was shooting at an animal, not at the Indians."

"Oh, I'll be sure to tell 'em," Archie said. "We'll be off now."

Donelson motioned to his son. "Help them load the gifts into their canoe, Johnny."

As Johnny hurried to assist with the loading, Noquali climbed into the canoe and accepted the goods as they were handed down. He could see the faces of Archie and Donelson as they shook hands again like old friends.

"You're out o' Chickamauga Territory now," Archie was saying. "You can let down your guard. Any Indians you see now are Cherokee. They're real friendly." He climbed down into the canoe and turned back. "But if you're lookin' to avoid 'em, just stay close to the north shore. They ain't no Indians on that side o' the river."

With that, he pulled his bear pelt over his head to shield him from the harsh winds.

As *The Adventure* swept past and the canoe floated in the swell caused by the larger boat, Noquali watched the inhabitants on board. There were some truly beautiful women aboard, he thought. And they took directions well.

Then he paddled out of the way as the other boats swept past them, slowing now that *The Adventure* had assumed a more unhurried pace.

Then along with Archie, they turned toward shore. They had to hurry if they were to be part of the upcoming wave of attacks.

# 29

Mary remained at the door, her musket still clenched in her hand. Somewhere in the back of her mind, she registered the sweat rolling off her palm, greasing the barrel of the musket, even though the air was frosty.

"They're not behind us anymore," she said to the children.

Meg began whimpering. Her soft sobs did more to Mary's heart than Jane's earsplitting cries. It wasn't fair, she thought miserably. Poor, sweet Meg, who could never even bear to step on an insect, was curled into the darkest corner of the cabin, her body heaving as she cried.

Now that she had declared their safety, Johnny's bravery was renewed and he fought against Meg's embrace to leave the cabin and fight alongside his brothers. Meg relinquished her hold on him, and he flew to Mary's side.

A rising conflict was raging within her. She felt obligated to go to Meg's side, to comfort her and Baby Jane, to dry their tears and reassure them, but she was unable to drag herself away from the partially open doorway. With Johnny pummeling her legs, she remained wedged between the door frame and the door itself in order to block the children's view.

"Ma's gonna wear your hide out," Mary admonished. "You're supposed to protect your sisters, and here you are, trying to run away from the cabin!"

The pummeling stopped and Johnny grew quiet behind her. Thank God, Mary thought as she turned her attention back to the scene unfolding behind them.

The Jennings boat was outdistancing the Indians, but only barely. They were still too close to the shoreline, Mary thought with rising panic, and there was too great a distance between them and the remaining fleet.

The Stuart boat was even worse. The Indians had continued gathering along the shoreline. And now with the boats pulling further away from them, it left them to look back to the east— where the Stuart's lone boat was hobbling into view.

It was like a gauntlet, Mary thought, her throat so constricted she could barely breathe. The boatload of sick and suffering men, women and children would have to outrun the Indians who were now amassing on the shore, departing in canoes that were advancing upon the ostracized boat. Hannah, she mouthed as she watched them. God help her!

"Mary, the children!"

Ma's frantic words came rushing at her and she tore her eyes away to look into Ma's worried face.

"They're fine. They're scared, is all." She let the hatch swing open as her mother brushed past her. She could hear her consoling them and urging them to be brave but her voice sounded distant, almost distracted.

A moment later, Ma was back at the door. She motioned for Mary to step just outside, but she kept the door partially open so the children could still see her. Little Jane was trying to escape Meg's clutches and run after her mother, but Meg was holding onto her despite her own sobs.

"The scouts have been by," she said. "We're past the Indian villages, but they told us to stay to the north shore. There are no Indians on that side. We're moving downriver a few more miles and then stopping."

Mary nodded.

"Keep the children in the cabin until we've put some distance behind us."

"Yes, ma'am."

Ma squeezed Mary's shoulder. "You done good, child. The worst is behind us."

Mary nodded. Ma patted her on the shoulder before walking away. Mary watched her as she moved from one to the other, making sure everyone was okay, and everyone knew what to do.

The river was narrowing now and as Mary stepped out of the cabin and peered around its side toward the bow, she could see a bend in the river up ahead. Soon, the Indians would be out of sight—and so would the Jennings and the Stuarts.

She returned to the cabin door. "Meg, there are some biscuits in the basket over there," she said. "Can you fix a snack for you, Johnny and Jane? Put some strawberry preserves on them."

As Meg dried her eyes and dutifully trudged to the basket, Mary turned back toward the stern. With her body wedged once again between the door frame and the door, she peered at the two boats behind her.

The Stuart boat was more than a mile behind them, but their screams and cries were carried across the water as they fought their way through the gauntlet. The Indians were converging on their boat like a disturbed beehive, surrounding them and boarding them even as they desperately tried to outmaneuver or outrun them. One shot after another rang out; it was impossible to tell the difference between the Stuarts' rifles and muskets and those of the Indians. There were too many shots, Mary thought, as she realized the Stuarts would have to stop and reload. That many shots meant the hordes of Indians were firing upon them.

Out of the corner of her eye, she saw the Neelys converging on the deck, watching the Stuarts fight for their lives. It was silent on board the Neely boat, eerily silent, Mary thought. Deadly silent. Even Sam knew they could not come to their aid.

Mary prayed for God to help them. She pleaded with Him silently as she watched the Indians boarding the boat and swarming over the deck. The boat was foundering now; it had stopped its forward progression and was spinning slowly in the water as all hands fought for their lives. The air was filled with their screams, horrific screams that pierced Mary's soul. There were more shots fired amid the Indians' spine-chilling war cries and gleeful whoops of victory as more of the savages joined in the wild rampage.

Then the Neely boat was around the bend and the horrific scene behind them was replaced with the craggy trees that bent from the north shore over the river's edge, their trunks seeming to bend toward the water in a final act of sorrow.

# 30

Noquali heard the fighting before he caught sight of the flatboat. He'd paddled first to the south shore as the fleet passed by, watching each boat and making a mental note of the number of passengers. The dogs often barked and he noted them as well; but they'd dealt with dogs before and no doubt would make quick work of these when the time came.

He allowed the boats to cruise past him as he remained close to the shore where the reverse current swept him eastward. He would have to hurry to the rear to get in on the initial action before returning to shore and traveling overland to reach The Whirl before the Donelson boat approached it.

The boats at the front were clustered together but as the long column swept past, they became more disjointed, the spread between them widening. The last of the boats were barely in sight of one another.

Now he paddled the canoe quickly toward the rear, listening to the sound of gunfire as he approached the bend in the river. Once past, he was sheltered from the view of the boats to the west.

The last boat had been effectively cut off from the others and now as he approached it, he could smell the gunpowder as it wafted across the water. He made out the distinct sound of the women aboard screaming in terror and confusion while the men shouted back and forth to each other with panicked instructions.

As he neared, a black man reared up from the stern, raising his rifle to his shoulder and aiming at a warrior about to overtake them. Noquali instantly stopped paddling and grabbed his own rifle. Almost before the rifle butt had reached his shoulder, the shot was fired. The man slumped over the side of the vessel, his body hitting the water as canoes churned over it.

The air was filled with smoke, the Indians' war cries blending now with horrified screams. A white man at the bow was grappling hand-to-hand with a warrior and as they fought, another came from behind and scalped the settler. Shrieking in pain, the man lost his grip on the first Indian, leaving himself vulnerable to the quick onslaught that followed. The first warrior slit his throat in one swift movement and his body was tossed into the river like a rag doll.

The water was thick now with bodies: women whose wide skirts ballooned as their bodies drifted; men face down, their heads bloodied and scalps laid bare. There were others scrambling in the water to keep from drowning, even as their wounds prevented the full use of their arms and legs. Noquali watched as a small, blond-haired girl was tossed overboard to be knifed by an approaching warrior.

The flatboat was spinning now and Noquali once again leveled his rifle. It was easy to pick off the settlers as the boat spun about and much more difficult for those on board to aim at their attackers with the dizzying movement of their vessel underfoot. Too easy, Noquali thought as he sensed the adrenaline pulsing through his veins.

Then he was moving his canoe rapidly toward the boat and climbing aboard with the rest of the braves, knifing and shooting anything that moved. It might have appeared like mayhem to an observer with the air thick with smoke, the screams and shrieks of victims, and the river turning red with their blood. But to Noquali, it was well orchestrated; the Indians moved in a fluid, graceful movement, knowing instinctively which brothers were at their sides as they silenced one settler after another. The ones who were not killed instantly were thrown overboard to join the others drowning in the fast-moving current.

Then the sounds of screaming began to die down, the rifle fire silenced. They were all engaged in hand-to-hand fighting now, too close together to raise a rifle or even a pistol.

Noquali sprang across the boat to crack a man's jaw with the butt of his rifle. As the man fell, he leaned over him and with one abrupt movement, slit his throat from ear to ear. He jumped onto his stomach, ignoring the gurgle from his victim as he propelled himself forward to grapple with another man, easily overcoming him as he shoved his knife into his throat. Then he was on to a strapping white man fighting two braves; coming from behind, he reached around his head and slit his throat. The settler turned and faced him with wide, surprised eyes, his mouth open. He was young, Noquali thought, perhaps no more than fourteen. Then he was off to the other side to fight the remaining settlers as the boy fell to the deck.

The screams were now replaced with shouts and as the minutes passed rapidly by, the sounds began to dissipate.

Then the Indians were standing amid the bodies, surveying them, watching for any sign of movement.

Noquali found himself beside the cabin hatch. The deck was soaked with blood that ran like the river itself as the boat continued to lurch and toss against the shoals. Some of the warriors were moving through the boat, taking scalps and tucking the tuffs of hair away for cleaning and the inevitable bragging. Rings were wrenched off dead hands, the braids of young women cut away as special tokens of their accomplishment. Some of the Indians, flush with victory, began rifling through the possessions aboard.

Noquali turned and opened the hatch, his rifle at the ready. But there was no gunfire. As his eyes grew accustomed to the darkness, the stench enveloped him and he took in the mattresses laid end to end, the wooden boxes piled against the walls, and the furniture roped and secured.

Others joined him as he began ripping into the boxes. He felt a wave of disappointment as the first ones revealed old, moldy food. Even in the dim light, he knew the fruits and vegetables and even the meats were no match for what the Indian villages could offer, and he tossed them aside as he looked for better items.

He pulled his knife from his buckskin belt and cut through the ropes that held a dresser secure. He opened the first drawer and rummaged through it, his bloodied hands finding lacy cotton undergarments. At the bottom of the second drawer, he found necklaces; grabbing them in his fist, he ventured toward the door to view them in the light.

He was pleased. And Jo-leigh would be pleased.

A movement caught his eye and his hand rapidly moved to his rifle. His eyes scoured the darkness as he searched for the source.

He stood perfectly still. His own breathing was so slow and measured it was almost as if he had stopped breathing at all. And in the murky light, he could feel the breath of another, could sense it there among the boxes, as he became increasingly aware that he was being watched.

He slowly, methodically moved toward the boxes, his eyes narrowing as he focused. They were stacked from floor to ceiling and so tight from one side to the other that he doubted a mouse could get through—all except for this one spot.

In one location, the boxes were only two high and as he approached, he realized two other boxes had been hastily strewn aside. He turned toward the side, allowing the taller stacks to shield his body as he silently maneuvered closer to the opening. His rifle was ready, and the shouts of the warriors gleefully ripping through items on deck sounded faint and far away. He was focused on the breathing now, the shallow, uneven breathing of one who was trying not to breathe at all.

He knew there were two there before he could see them; and when he was close enough to the opening to spin around and aim downward on the other side of the short stack, no eyes peered upward to meet his. Instead, he found two women huddled together, their arms around each other as if they could protect one another, their heads downward as they shielded their faces.

With one swift movement, he tossed the uppermost box away, revealing more of the women, who trembled with a nervousness he had seen so many times before.

He reached down and grabbed the first one by her hair, pulling her upward. A yelp burst from her lips as she was heaved to her feet and spun around to face him.

She was younger than he'd expected; perhaps all of seventeen or eighteen years old. Her hair was long, spilling outward from a disheveled braid and even in the waning light, it looked like precious copper. She stared at him with eyes wide and filled with horror, her lips parted but unspeaking.

He kept his grip on her hair while he set down his rifle. Then he reached in with his free hand and pulled the second trembling girl to her feet. She was younger looking, her golden hair not quite as long, and as he half-dragged, half-pulled them toward the light at the doorway, he thought they looked like sisters with their high cheekbones and arching brows.

He paused momentarily in the light and yanked their heads backward so he could see their faces more clearly. Two sets of the greenest eyes he'd ever seen stared back at him.

He could feel the warriors closest to the cabin watching as he held each girl at arm's length and took in their slight bodies, their chests heaving now with their laborious efforts to control their frenzied breathing.

"S-de-yi-dv," he used the Cherokee word for *rope* as he spoke to the nearest brave, motioning with his head toward the cabin.

The brave crammed a handful of trinkets into his buckskin pouch and rushed into the cabin, returning with rope.

Wordlessly, Noquali bound the hands and feet of the two girls, first by binding the older one's hands together and then to the other one. Then he repeated the process with their ankles. If they attempted to escape, they would be forced to move as one and they would drown as one.

The other warrior returned to ransacking as Noquali pushed the girls toward the starboard side. He tied them to the flatboat as he clambered over the side and swam to his canoe. Pulling it back to the flatboat with him, he secured it against the larger vessel and called out to one of the braves to assist him. The larger, bloodied brave stopped in deference to Noquali, untied the girls and tossed the younger one over the side to the canoe. The older one, securely fastened to the first, had no choice but to be pulled violently overboard, where she rammed her head against the sharp bow of the canoe. Noquali unceremoniously pitched her flailing limbs into the boat atop the other captive.

Then he was paddling away from the flatboat. He glanced back to see the warriors scattering the goods about the boat, plundering the cargo as if someone had thrown open the doors to a fully stocked trading post. He wouldn't need to return to gather any more possessions. He had the necklaces and the captives as well as the gifts from Colonel Donelson, and he would have plenty of additional opportunity as they seized the remaining boats. For now, he had to move quickly to shore and take the young women overland to the nearest village. Under tribal law, the women he found now belonged to him.

# 31

How does one calm a child who has just witnessed an attack by savages? Mary wondered as she helped Ma, Jean and Sam comfort the smallest Neely children.

"Thank the Good Lord the cabin door was closed," Ma breathed over Jane's head. She was sitting on the mattress with Jane pulled onto her lap, the small child wailing as if she were being spanked.

"Yes," Mary agreed. But as she spoke, she realized it hadn't been the sight of the Indians swarming the Stuart deck that had been so disturbing; they had been far enough way to have been spared witnessing the visual details. No; it was the screams, the terrifying, horrific screams of the Stuart family—the shrieks and shouts amid the gun blasts and the whoops and cries of the savages that caused her blood to run cold. They could not escape those sounds, even when the hatch had been shut. And each time Mary closed her eyes, she heard those sounds again and again.

As Meg sobbed in Jean's lap, Mary knew there was nothing they could say or do that could ever erase those memories. She bent down and stroked Meg's knee.

"I wish we'd never left home!" Meg cried, her small body wracked with her sobs.

"I know, honey," Mary said. "If I had magical powers, I would cast a spell and we would all be back home again!" She glanced up and met Jean's eyes; they were an emerald green, wide and round. Funny, Mary thought, even though Jean was the eldest, she had always thought of her eyes as innocent. Now they were dark and haunted. She wondered if her own eyes appeared the same.

On the other mattress, Sam was trying a different tactic with Johnny, counseling him to remain brave like King Arthur and the Knights of the Round Table. As Mary listened, he told him a story that she suspected he was concocting on the spot about a great battle in which King Arthur, his knights and even their young sons—some Johnny's tender age of six—had fought off attackers. Mary smiled inwardly as Sam told him to take care of Meg and Jane, as he was intrusting in him the role of Protector and Defender. As Sam spoke, Johnny's eyes were dry and his jaw was firm, jutting out as he raised his chin solemnly, his small hands grasping his wooden musket.

With Ma, Jean and Sam comforting the smallest children, Mary made her way out of the cabin and to the bow. She spotted Ike above her on the bridge, his eyes dark and narrowed as he watched the riverbed. Billy was behind him with the tiller. They both glanced down at her as she approached.

"Not scared, are ya?" Billy called out with a forced smile.

Mary shook her head.

"I almost had to take a break to change my pants."

Mary chuckled nervously and glanced at Ike. His face was grave and his brows furrowed, his lips pursed.

The boats were no longer moving at the furious pace they'd set while they were under attack, but they were still moving quickly through the fast-moving current of the Tennessee River. Rather than remain in the center of the river as they had earlier, they were hugging the north shore as the scouts had directed them. The Neely flatboat was larger than some of the others, and Ike directed Billy to steer further from shore because of its deeper hull. In front of them, Captain Blackmore's boat moved closer to the shoreline, although it was the same size. Mary could see Mr. Payne on board the boat, using his pole on the starboard side to try and remain clear of the sandbars and rock that jutted out from shore, where a boat could easily run aground. He was a young man, perhaps in his early twenties; a handsome man, Mary thought as she looked at his sandy hair and ruddy skin.

"They're too close to shore," Mary said to no one in particular.

"Hhmm," Ike murmured.

She suddenly felt presumptuous; only a few weeks earlier, she would not have known the starboard side from the port, would not have understood currents and crosscurrents; and was now struck by the transformation of the Neely family into sailors.

"Mary, take this musket to the stern," Ike said, pulling her away from her thoughts. She glanced up as he handed a musket down to her. "Tell Sam to take up the stern and keep his eyes peeled. Billy, you think you can handle a musket as well as the tiller?"

"I got two hands, don't I?" she heard him say as she made her way across the deck toward the rear. The musket was heavy and cumbersome and now Mary marveled at her ability to carry several of them at once when the Indians attacked. I suppose, she thought, one rises to the occasion—whatever that occasion might be.

As she made her way to the stern, she caught sight of the Jennings boat rounding the last bend. Her heart soared with the sight; the last she'd seen of them, the Indians had been dangerously close. But as she watched, she realized their smaller boat was hugging the north shore even more closely than the Blackmore boat, almost as though they intended to beach it.

The shallows along the Tennessee River, like the Holston, often went much further into the river than one might think; and at high water, it was possible for the river to appear much wider than it actually was. Just beneath the surface was a combination of sandbars, underwater plants, tangled deadwood, and even rocks. While they'd been directed to remain on the north side, the Neely boat had stayed between the center of the river and the north shore, but now as she peered from front to back, she realized the boats on either side of them—the Blackmore boat and the Jennings boat—were much nearer the north banks.

She reached the stern and paused to watch the Jennings boat. They appeared to be gaining speed, as now she could see the shapes of Mr. and Mrs. Jennings at the bow, their teenage son and another young man on the port side, and a black man and woman on the starboard side, all working with their great long poles to catch up to the rest of the fleet.

"Brothers! Brothers!"

Mary turned toward the sound. In the back of her mind, she felt every person on every boat had turned simultaneously and now they were all looking toward the south shore.

A handful of Indians were running along the bank, calling out to them. "Come ashore!" they called. "We are brothers!"

Mary caught a glimpse of Sam standing in the cabin doorway, his jaw firm and his musket firmly in his grasp. A second later, Ma appeared beside him. She was conscious of Billy on the bridge facing the port side, the side nearest the Indians, but the river was wide here and Mary knew any rifle fire could not reach them. As if in response to Mary's thoughts, she saw the tiller shift in Billy's hand and felt the boat turning toward the starboard side, closer to the north shore, and she could feel the pace quickening. Best they remain as far from the savages as possible, she thought, and hurry past this Indian village.

But as she watched, the handful grew to a band and the band to a mob and they were running along the shore and taking to the waters as they had before. With fresh fear rising in her throat, she started to run toward the cabin door. She had already taken several steps when she realized she hadn't left the musket at the stern as Ike had directed, but she was too focused on reaching Sam to turn back.

Out of the corner of her eye, it registered they were moving closer to the north shore. Here the woods were thick with evergreens and jutted closer to the water's edge. As she hurried toward the cabin in the direction of the bow, she caught a glimpse of Mr. Payne still struggling to keep the Blackmore boat from running aground.

She was halfway to the cabin when a shot rang out. Mr. Payne slumped, his long pole slipping from his hands and sliding into the water, where the boat churned over it. The sound of the wood cracking was drowned out by the cries of Indians who were rising from the ground along the north shore and rushing toward them, their guns and rifles filling the air with smoke.

Captain Blackmore was turning around, his mouth open as though he were shouting at the others on deck, his hands moving simultaneously to his side to retrieve his pistol.

The Neely boat surged toward the center, away from the north shore, but the Indians were so close Mary could see the whites of their eyes. Their faces were emblazoned on her mind, the red and black stripes covering every inch except the eyes themselves, which seared from the stripes like hawks eyeing their prey.

"Ambush!" Billy was yelling as he struggled with the tiller to push away from the north shore. "Ambush!"

The deck came alive. Ma rushed to the port side and grabbed a pole. Somehow, Billy managed to grab onto his musket while he wrestled with the tiller. Sam stepped from the cabin, raising his own musket. Jean rushed past him, running for another pole in a frantic effort to outrun the Indians. Beth raced past Mary, heading for the stern and the pole there.

Sam was yelling but Mary could not make out his words above the dreadful cries of the Indians as they swooped down upon the boats. There were dozens of them, and they appeared to be everywhere at once—in canoes attacking from the south side and even more racing through the waters from the north, where they'd lain in wait for the settlers.

A red and black hand grasped the side of the boat only feet from Mary. She saw the top tail of long black hair before she saw the face of the warrior coming over the side. She raised the musket to her shoulder and leveled the weapon at his chest as he came into view. He was still whooping in an animalistic cry that filled her ears when she fired. The blood splattered over the deck like the red paint on his body was convulsing in midair; he slumped over the side, one eye fixing Mary with his gaze. Then his hands released a pistol and a knife onto the deck before his body slid backward into the water.

She raced to the boat's edge and grabbed the pistol from the deck, ducking down to retrieve it just as a round whizzed past her head. The smell of gun powder filled the air. The boat was moving faster now, further from the shoreline and toward the center of the water, and Sam's musket was fired and then Billy's and somewhere Mary heard a voice yelling for her to reload.

Somehow she made it to the hatch and yanked the shot bag and powder horn off the nails where they hung. The sounds of Indians echoed through the valley, their war whoops surrounding her. She glanced up to see Sam standing nearby, his back to her, shouting something over his shoulder to her, but she couldn't make out the words. Somehow, her trembling fingers managed to load and charge the musket. Then as Sam turned back toward her, she passed the loaded musket to him and he tossed her his, and she repeated the process.

Beth raced to the doorway, nearly tearing the shot bag from Mary's grasp, screaming that Billy needed reloading, and they grappled with it momentarily before both realized everyone needed ammunition. Beth raced off with the shot bag and powder horn to help Billy and Ike, while Mary grabbed an ammunition box and ripped it open. She no sooner had gotten the musket loaded than Sam was tossing back the first one. It was hot and burned Mary's hands as she wrestled with it, but fear—pure, unadulterated terror—propelled her onward.

They were moving toward the center of the river now and the muskets were not fired as quickly. Sam was taking his time now, the musket at his shoulder while he pivoted in a semi-circle, looking for targets.

Slowly, Mary ventured a couple of feet from the cabin. She held the last loaded musket in her hand, ready to swap it for Sam's spent one. But they had outdistanced the Indians once again.

Before a wave of relief could sweep over her once more, her eyes caught the Jennings boat in the rear of the fleet. They had run aground.

As Mary watched, the Indians appeared to move in one giant wave, their bodies turning as one as they focused their full attention on the Jennings boat. Half the people on board were trying desperately to push the boat from shore while the others were firing at the Indians, their shots coming fast and furious.

As the Indians doubled back toward them, she could hear Mr. Jennings' shouts. Though she couldn't make out his words, he had no sooner stopped shouting than the entire family was throwing furniture overboard. It was then that Mary realized their only chance for survival was to lighten the boat enough to break from the bank and head toward open water. Even Elizabeth, who had given birth less than twelve hours earlier, was rushing across the deck, dumping boxes, tables, chairs, and other sundries overboard. Everything was being discarded.

As the Neely boat continued westward, she could only watch helplessly as the furniture and boxes floated away from the boat and downriver, while the entire Jennings boat rocked with the efforts of the small crew.

As Mr. Jennings alternately fired and reloaded his rifles and kept up a constant onslaught toward the Indians that drew ever closer, Jonathan, Obediah, and the slave Ezekiel jumped overboard. Grabbing a canoe and taking to the water, they abandoned the Jennings boat.

Mary was speechless as they watched the three men paddle away, leaving only Mr. and Mrs. Jennings, the slave Esther, and Elizabeth to fight the Indians. The last she saw of them, Mrs. Jennings had jumped onto the shore and was trying desperately to push the boat from the banks with her bare hands. Then the river between the Neely boat and the Jennings was filled with canoes, the air full of blood-curdling war whoops and rifle fire.

# 32

Ike wiped his forehead with the back of his sleeve. Although the air was frigid, he was sweating profusely. He had been working a long pole from the bridge in an attempt to outrun the Indians. Now as he climbed down to the deck, Mary reached forward to take the pole from him. She almost recoiled when she realized it was covered in blood.

"Are you—?" she began.

"No," he answered curtly. "I'm not shot." He removed an old handkerchief and bound it around the palm of his hand. He winced but quickly tried to cover his pain as he tied it.

Ma grabbed his wrist. "Son, your hands are blistered!"

"Weren't nothin'."

"I need to tend to that," Ma said. "It'll get infected."

"I'll do it later." He glanced past them toward the stern.

Mary followed his gaze, as did the others. There was nothing but open, rushing water behind them, propelling them further westward.

"Billy," Ike called.

Billy peeked down at them from the bridge. "Yeah?"

"You remember when we'd go huntin' geese?" Ike said.

Billy's eyes widened in surprise. "I reckon I do."

"You remember how I told you to shoot 'em?"

"This ain't really the time—"

"You remember?" Ike's tone was insistent.

A hush fell on the Neely clan as they watched the interaction between the two brothers.

"Yeah, I remember," he answered.

Ike continued looking eastward. "A gaggle of geese flies in a pattern—"

"—like the letter 'v'," Billy interjected.

"And which goose do you shoot first?"

"Why, the last one, of course."

Ike turned his face upward to look him in the eye. "Do you remember why?"

Billy's eyes became even wider as Ike's words began to sink in. He looked from his brother to his mother and then toward the stern, at the open water behind them. "Because," he said, his voice coming fast and strained, "if you shoot the ones in the front, the rest of the gaggle will scatter. They'll know one of 'em's died and they'll break up and fly ever' which way."

"That's right," Ike said.

Mary searched the faces of the others. They appeared just as baffled as she.

"But if you shoot 'em from the rear," Billy continued, "the ones up front won't know the rest of 'em ain't behind 'em. And they'll keep on goin'," his voice becoming rushed, "and you can keep on pickin' 'em off."

Ma sucked in her breath.

"That's right," Ike said. "And that's what them Injuns are doin' to us. They're coming at us from the rear, pickin' us off one boat at a time."

Beth spoke up. "But surely that's just coincidence—"

"Think about it," Ike said. "They came after the Stuarts first. They were already separated from the rest of us; they surrounded 'em and overtook 'em."

"Maybe the Stuarts got away," Ma said. "We don't know that they didn't."

"We don't know that they did."

"Then they attacked the Jennings," Billy said. "Did the same thing; ran 'em aground and overtook 'em."

"And look who's last in line now." Sam's voice was loud and angry. Mary could tell he was ready to circle back and shoot a few more of those Indians.

The women all looked westward at the same time. Mary knew they were calculating the distance between their boat and the others. There were twenty-eight boats left now; so many that Mary was sure they were stretched out for two or three miles. She wondered if Colonel Donelson even knew the rear boats had been attacked.

As if reading her mind, Ma said quietly, "But if we were attacked right here, right now, those boats ahead of us would hear it. They'd know we were in trouble."

"And what do you think they'd do, Ma?" Sam demanded. "Come back to help us? Like we helped the Stuarts and the Jennings?" He shot an accusatory glance at Ike.

"Sam, we couldn't help 'em," Ike said. "They'd have just killed or captured us, too. They outnumber us." He glanced toward the north shore. "And who knows how many more are out there now, just waiting for their chance to attack again?"

Mary shivered. Suddenly, it seemed as though the temperature had dipped below freezing again, and she felt the wind whipping at her face as she stared ahead.

"What can we do?" Billy asked.

"We can do what the geese do," Ike said. "They move up in the column."

"But that would put Captain Blackmore at the rear," Beth said.

"That's Captain Blackmore's problem."

The family fell silent. Mary knew Ike was right. As heartless as it sounded, she'd seen firsthand that each boat had to form its own army. They couldn't depend on the others, just like the others hadn't been able to depend on them.

Ike looked upward at Billy once again. "Billy, steer the tiller toward the center of the river. Y'all listen to me and listen up good: no matter what you're told, stay in the center. That way, if there's another ambush, we can quickly move to the north or south.

"Ma, I need you on the starboard side and Jean, get to the port. I need all three of you to row like the Injuns are firin' at us right now."

"What about the boats ahead of us?"

"They're still stayin' toward the north shore. Go around 'em like we was in a race."

Mary thought that would be easier said than done, but she grabbed a pole as Ma and Jean took up their positions. With the three of them moving their poles rhythmically through the water, they would soon catch up with Captain Blackmore's boat.

"Sam, come with me. We're gonna load every weapon we've got here and make sure they're ready to fire. I want the shot bags and powder horns distributed, too …" His voice faded as they left the bow and marched toward the cabin.

"That leaves me," Beth said.

"Martha's with the children. I'm sure they all need you," Mary said. "Poor Meg, she's been through so much. Johnny and Jane, they're so young, they don't know all that's happening, but Meg…"

"Yes," Beth said. "She's been like a pint-size version of Ma, hasn't she? Strong and brave."

Mary nodded, but she wondered how Beth could have slept through those nights when Meg was crying, her little body wracked with her sobs. She felt helpless to rescue her from this terrible journey, and she suddenly felt a surge of anger at her father for bringing them west. What was wrong with their lives back east? She wondered. They had a nice home, plenty of land and livestock, friends and church and family. What was the point of traveling all this way in this God-forsaken country?

As Beth left her side and made her way toward the cabin, Mary glanced at the cliffs rising on either side of the river. Sure, it was beautiful, she thought. Even if the leaves were off the trees this time of year, even with the snow still on the ground, it was beautiful. But what was the point of beauty when wild savages were firing at them, trying to kill them?

Her thoughts turned to Hannah. How sick had they all been? She wondered. Had most of them been in their beds with fever and chills? Had they even been able to stand and fight? How many were left on deck to try and fend off the attack?

She couldn't help but wonder and worry about their fate. If they had not been able to escape, she thought, a quick death would be merciful. God have mercy on their souls, she mouthed.

She could still hear their screams reverberating in her mind, could still close her eyes and see the vision of the Indians swarming over their boat. She had heard so many stories of scalpings and captures—surely Hannah had not been captured, she thought. That would be a fate worse than death. Oh, far better for her to have been killed with a single shot than to live and be carried into an Indian village like prey into a viper's pit. Surely God would not have done that to her!

What am I thinking? She thought suddenly. She tried to focus on Captain Blackmore's boat ahead of them. She couldn't keep thinking about Hannah—or poor Elizabeth! Elizabeth's baby! She thought as her throat tightened. Oh, God, this is too barbaric to even think about. Help me! Help me!

She quickened the pace of her pole, shouting, "To port!" as she struggled to move closer to the center of the river. She could sense Ma and Jean watching her as she struggled to steer the boat, their own frantic movements coinciding with her own.

The faster they poled, the more terrified Mary became, as if the movement itself intensified their vulnerable position. She could see Captain Blackmore on board his boat now, standing alongside the body of Mr. Payne, who was stretched across the deck with a quilt across him.

"Is he dead?" Mary found her voice rising, though she was speaking to no one in particular.

"They don't do that to live folks," Billy said from the bridge.

The captain was speaking to the men on board, pointing toward the south and then to the north. As they came alongside them, he stopped speaking to watch them move past. He stepped to the side and shouted something, but Mary couldn't make out his words.

Ike emerged from the cabin and shouted to Captain Blackmore, "We're movin' closer to the fleet! Closin' ranks!" as they sped past.

Then they were upon the next boat, passing that one as well as the women stood with mouths agape while the Neely women poled for all they were worth. Mary's arms felt leaden from the effort and with each movement, she told herself the next one would be the last. But it wasn't and she knew it wouldn't be until they had more boats behind them.

Then, exhausted, they fell in behind Robert Cartwright's boat. Ike and Sam, now armed and ready, took over as the women returned to the cabin to rest. Mary rubbed her shoulders and marveled at their ability to reposition themselves in the fleet. They had to be safe now. They just had to be.

# 33

This had to be the longest day they'd had yet. Had they really awakened this very morning at the abandoned Indian village? It seemed like ages ago when she'd stayed up all night helping to deliver little Ephraim Peyton, Jr. The image of the cabin where they'd slept with its fire pit in the center and the beds arranged in a circle around it, seemed now like a sketch out of a book and not a place she'd actually visited only hours before.

But as she looked at the sky, she realized it was perhaps only mid-afternoon and Ephraim, Jr. was at best only twelve hours old. The sky was almost white and there wasn't a cloud to be seen; she knew that would make the coming night frigid. She wondered what they would do when nighttime fell; thus far, they had halted their journey rather than travel in the dark waters, where shoals and floating debris could cause them to run aground or damage the vessels. But as she looked at the craggy mountains on either side of the river, she knew it would be too dangerous for them to remain in this region; they had to put miles behind them and they had to do it as quickly as possible.

Ma was at the bow now with Ike. Mary stood near the front on the port side with Sam a few yards away. Jean was on the starboard side, and Beth and Martha were at the stern. Ike and Billy had traded places and now Billy was watching the waters from the front of the bridge and Ike was working the tiller. Their labor with the poles had slowed from their earlier frenzied efforts to pass other vessels, but the fact that eight of the Neely clan were working in concert did little to reduce the strain on her body.

A great mountain loomed ahead. The river seemed to cut a swath right through the center of it. As Mary studied it, it appeared as though the mountain's ridgeline ran straight down into the water, reducing the river's width to half what it had been just moments ago. She watched as the boats ahead of them navigated toward the center of the river to avoid the rocky, treacherous shores.

Directly in front of them, the Cartwright boat swung toward the center. Tied to the large flatboat was a canoe that belonged to John Cotton.

John and his family were not as well off as some of the others. Instead of purchasing a flatboat and filling it with a lifetime of possessions, he had secured a large canoe instead. It was filled almost to overflowing with all their worldly possessions, but now as Mary watched the boat bobbing with the current she realized their belongings were meager. It occurred to her that most of the bundles wrapped in gunny sacks consisted of food or clothing, items that would be vital for their survival. There was little room for other things, such as the furniture and keepsakes each Neely child packed. Unlike some of the other families, the Cottons had no room for livestock, dogs, or non-essentials and the few keepsakes they did manage to pack must have had enormous sentimental value.

The small family had managed to remain in their boat amid their bundles until the attack. At some point during the attack, the Cotton family boarded the Cartwright boat, where they would be more secure and more protected from further assaults. The canoe was tied to the larger flatboat and now it swayed and dipped in the river as the wakes from the larger vessels caught it.

The mountain was beginning to block out the light from the pale winter sun, casting the river into a blackness akin to a bottomless pit. As they hurried eastward, Mary began to spot whitecaps and the sound of rushing, burbling water reached her ears with increasing turbulence as the river continued to narrow. The boat quickened its pace and now the Neelys were no longer trying to propel the boat forward; they were, instead, caught in a downstream current that was propelling them onward at a breakneck speed.

Billy yelled from the bridge, "Rapids ahead! Secure everything!"

The women sprang into action as the men took over the perilous task of keeping the boat from capsizing in the dangerous waters. Rocks began to appear in every direction as they approached the rapids, and Mary found herself struggling to remain upright as she lurched and tumbled across the deck, gathering items that had not been tied down.

"Secure the weapons!" Sam called to her. "We can't afford to lose 'em!"

Mary quickly grabbed the shot bags and powder horns and carried them in her skirt, somehow managing to lug two muskets to the cabin as well. The river was roaring now, the spray pummeling the boat as vigorously as if they were caught in a violent thunderstorm.

The hatch was open. Ma was telling Meg to watch over the smallest ones, her voice sounding shrill and urgent as she struggled to be heard over the sound of the river. Jane was crying again and Meg was doing all she could to prevent her from running onto the deck to be with the others while little Johnny was ready to fight more Indians, his lower lip quivering despite his bravado.

Mary barely had time to put the shot bags and powder horns down before the boat took a sudden lurch and the items careened across the floor. A giant wave swept over the deck, drenching everything and everyone in its path. Everything that wasn't tied down was flung from one side of the cabin to the other.

"Close the door!" Mary yelled. "Close the door!"

But as she struggled to reach the doorway, she realized all of the women had jammed the entryway at once and the hatch was swinging helplessly in the wind.

She yanked Martha through the door, yelling, "Stay with the children!"

Martha didn't waste time arguing; she dived onto the mattress and huddled with the others, her wet clothes drenching the bedding.

The rest of the women were back through the door in an instant. It took Ma's and Mary's combined strength to get the hatch closed again, but it popped back open as soon as they let go. Mary caught a glimpse of Martha rushing to the doorway and as they struggled to close it again, she was ready to latch it as soon as it shut.

They were soaked now, the river spray pelting their bodies as the boat pitched and listed in the treacherous waters. The women rushed to the four sides of the boat, each grabbing onto the poles held by the men, who were frantically trying to keep the boat from capsizing.

Ahead of them, Mary could see the river bending around the mountain, its width so narrow that it appeared as though each boat's inhabitants could almost reach out and touch the side of the cliffs. The rocks had become boulders now, their massive bodies jutting out of the water like an obstacle course.

Ike was shouting over his shoulder but Mary could not make out his words over the roar of the river. She could only watch helplessly as each boat was caught in the dangerous waters and pummeled mercilessly downstream. Somewhere in the back of her mind, she realized she had to watch the course the others used before them, memorizing where to remain to prevent their own boat from capsizing, but the thought was fleeting and worthless as the vessels were battered within seconds.

The Cartwright boat hit the rapids with a force so great that Mary could hear the women's screams over the sound of the rushing water. The little canoe seemed to be lifted by an unseen hand, removed completely from the water, and then tossed back down again on the rocks with a force so great that the attached flatboat listed dangerously in the water.

As Mary watched, her eyes caught the movement of the boats in front of them. Just past the rapids they were entering, it seemed as if the river was doubling back upon itself. She watched in horror as the first boats turned completely around in the water so the passengers were facing those behind them.

Every boat was alive. Every available occupant raced to their poles, their oars, or their paddles and desperately tried to maneuver past the danger. The tillers were useless against the river's onslaught. The water was churning now in a circular motion, the center of the circle seeming to disappear in a downward spiral. It was as if the entrance to Hell itself was opening up before them.

As the Cartwright boat was caught in the circling current, Mary struggled to keep the pole from crashing into their boat. She could hear the sound of wood cracking and moaning, but she couldn't tell whether it was the Neely boat, the Cartwright boat, or one of the others that was now moving in a precarious circle.

"Stay away from the center!" Ike called out as he leaned his full weight against the tiller, but his words were futile. Everyone on board knew if they reached the center of the circle, the river would swallow the entire boat and everyone on board. But as they all battled the current with every aching muscle, it felt as if they were grappling with Nature itself. If they won, they would simply make it to the other side—and if they lost, the river would swallow them whole.

As their boat spun around, she caught sight of others on the remaining boats, their faces mirroring her own terror, as they too struggled to keep from crashing into each other or sliding into the watery abyss.

She caught sight of John Cotton and Robert Cartwright, and then of Captain Blackmore. She hadn't thought they were together on one boat. Then she suddenly realized they were all swirling in the waters; she was seeing men on different boats so quickly that they blurred together.

The boat crashed into the side of the great mountain with a loud crack that sounded like the vessel had been ripped in two.

Then Ike was shouting, struggling to be heard above the din. Mary realized, as if coming out of a trance, that they were at the edge of the Whirl. One more massive effort could spit them out on the other side. It was then she became aware that she had been struggling so hard to keep the boat from capsizing that her hands were bleeding, the blood mixing with the river water as it streamed down the pole.

Everyone on board rushed to the starboard side in a desperate attempt to cause the boat to rise on the port side in order to thrust them to the extreme edge of the Whirl. As the boat listed, they held onto the railing and watched the immense cliffs loom above them. The side of the boat scraped the rocks with a thunderous rage as Mary held her breath.

Then the mountain was gone and in its place was the open sky. The sound of the rapids halted unexpectedly. As suddenly as they were caught up in the maelstrom, they were ejected, more or less intact, on the other side.

The waters were calm here and the river opened back up, as though the towering cliffs were parting to allow them access.

*The Adventure* was stopped a quarter mile from the Whirl, its inhabitants watching the others as they were propelled out, one by one.

As the Neely boat limped toward them, Mary caught sight of a package swirling in the gentle current, moving eastward. She leaned over the boat in an attempt to snare it, but couldn't. Sam joined her, thrusting a long pole into the water. He managed to snag it beneath a rope wrapped around the bundle, and together they hauled it onto the deck. Mary knew before they had it on board that it had been aboard John Cotton's canoe.

Now as she looked back, she could clearly see the rest of the cargo swirling toward the larger boats like stray cattle rejoining the herd. And somewhere in the distance that was growing wider by the moment, she could see the Cartwright boat still swinging wildly, its passengers still fighting the watery monster as the canoe, now tiny in comparison, was flung above the water like a loose kite in the wind.

# 34

The odor of gunpowder clung to Noquali's skin and clothes and crept into his nostrils as he paddled northwestward toward the waning sun. It served to strengthen him, causing his spine to straighten and his chin to jut forward. To some, the smell of gunpowder and death would frighten and horrify; but to Noquali and his fellow warriors, it was a heady perfume, an enticing aroma that caused their minds to become clearer and their blood to pump more keenly.

He noticed the weakening sun's rays lying gently across his arms as he paddled and he took in the quieting waves as they lapped against the side of his canoe. It was a good day, and it was not yet over.

In front of him sat the two captives. The one he placed in front was older, perhaps eighteen years old. Blood continued to stream down the side of her face from where she'd fallen against the canoe, but she seemed oblivious to it. As she turned to look behind her at the warriors teeming over the flatboat and dividing the goods with fervor, he saw in her vivid green eyes a vacancy, as though her brain was barely registering the carnage around her. He had seen it before; had seen that look of shock in almost every captive he took. Sometimes it remained for hours and sometimes it never quite went away, even after years of captivity.

The one who sat between them was younger, perhaps thirteen or fourteen years old. Like the older girl, she had long hair the color of the rich earth. She glanced back only momentarily, her eyes unblinking, wide and empty.

Their skin was wet with heavy perspiration although the air was cold, and as he paddled, he noticed their clothes were also damp. It wasn't out of the ordinary for captives to become feverish when they were first seized, but he had to admit their fever was beginning sooner than most. Most were attacked by their own bodies and emotions soon after entering one of the Indian villages, when their fates hung in the balance. It was then that they would prove either their cowardice or their dignity.

According to tribal custom, the girls were now his property as he was the one who had seized them. There were times when the local or presiding chieftain would claim the captives as his own and rank would take precedence, but Noquali knew this would not be the case. Not today and not with these captives. They were his to do with as he chose.

He noticed they held hands tightly, their knuckles red and raw in the winter air. The younger one pressed against the older one. No doubt they are sisters, he thought.

Their fate was his decision and his alone. Captives generally fell into four categories: those who were killed outright, those who were enslaved, those who were adopted into the tribe, or those who were tortured. With the last group, their final fate depended on how they responded to the torture; if they were brave and noble, they might live; and if they cried out or screamed or begged for mercy, they would die a slow and painful death.

But torture was almost always reserved for men. If women and children were to be killed, it was more often than not done quickly. It didn't enhance a warrior's image to torture an enemy captive that was so obviously weaker.

As he neared shore, he took note of others who were returning with the spoils of their brief battle: there were fine china plates and pewter mugs, cooking utensils and clothing of every description; there were rifles and pistols and ammunition, which were perhaps some of the most prized trophies. There was also furniture. One canoe overturned as the inhabitants attempted to unload an unwieldy wood cabinet as tall and wide as their own height.

When all was done, the boat would be stripped bare and dismantled; the only evidence that it had ever existed would be a few pieces of wood that would eventually be reclaimed by the river.

As he came ashore, he hopped out of the canoe and dragged it away from the crosscurrent. The two girls remained inside, their eyes so wide they almost appeared to engulf their entire faces.

Two braves approached him as he prepared to unload his captives.

"You are Noquali?" one asked.

He stopped and turned toward them. The one who spoke was taller than most, his body taut and muscular as only those braves in the prime of youth could be. But his long, straight hair was brown, not black. And as Noquali looked into his eyes, he saw not the black eyes of an Indian but the hazel eyes of a white man. And yet he had spoken the Shawnee language perfectly.

"Yes," Noquali answered.

"I am White Messenger," the man answered. "And this is my brother Msipessi."

Noquali greeted them with respect. His brother was a full-blooded Indian; he was sure of it. He had the raven hair and ebony eyes typical of the Shawnee. He was shorter and stockier and powerfully built. "I have been expecting you."

White Messenger reached for the older girl, easily pulling her to her feet. He spoke to her in English. Her face was glazed in shock, but a glimmer seemed to ignite in her eyes as she recognized her own language. Her lips moved silently, almost as if the words were tumbling through her head too quickly for her lips, previously frozen in fear, to catch up. When the words began to escape from her, they were fast and tumbled and almost incoherent.

White Messenger turned to Noquali. "We have come too late to fight alongside you?"

Noquali reached his arm around the girl's waist and hauled her from the boat onto the sandy bottom of the shoreline. The younger girl, still bound to the first, let out a yelp that sounded like a wounded dog as her sister was torn from her. The yelp then turned to surprise as she was yanked overboard by the rope that joined them, but Noquali caught her with his free arm and set her upright in the frigid water.

Then he led them onto the shore as White Messenger and Msipessi followed.

"No," Noquali said, "you have not come too late. Our work is only beginning."

"Then tell us what you would have us do," Msipessi said. His words were in contrast to his brother's; where White Messenger's voice was measured and calm, Msipessi's was boiling with an inner rage.

"You have horses?"

"Yes." White Messenger pointed.

"That stallion over there is mine," he said. "We will take the trails along the cliffs westward." He began walking toward the horses, leading the girls with the rope. Their feet were unsteady on the unfamiliar terrain and they appeared to be very weak. White Messenger and Msipessi followed. "We have counted more than twenty vessels. They are headed for the Whirl, where the spirit of the river will spit them back to us. Our brothers await us there. We attack them there, and bring the spoils to Tuskegee Island Town."

"Bloody Fellow's village."

"Yes." He reached his horse and turned to untie the girls from each other.

"And the captives?" White Messenger asked. His words were not spoken with compassion but as a soldier awaiting orders for the disposition of cargo.

"There is no time to waste," Noquali answered. "We must bring them with us. Afterward, they will go with us to Tuskagee Island Town."

"I can take one on my horse," he said.

Noquali tossed him the rope. "Take the older one. Tie her to a tree when we reach the Whirl, well out of range of the battle. I do not want one of our brothers to mistake her for a fresh captive."

"Understood." White Messenger spoke to the girl and she climbed onto the horse. Noquali thought she appeared relieved to be riding with him, but her expression changed suddenly when her sister was directed to climb onto Noquali's stallion.

White Messenger spoke to her calmly and she settled uneasily onto the horse.

"I told her they will not be separated," White Messenger said to Noquali's inquiring glance. "She need not know more."

Noquali nodded. "We must make haste," he said as he mounted his horse. "The sun will soon be gone, and we must strike them before sunset, as soon as they reach the Whirl."

With that, he spurred the horse forward. The stallion located the familiar trail easily. Urged forward by its master, it moved quickly through the woods, climbing steadily upward toward the peak. Behind them, White Messenger followed closely, the older girl clutching him to keep from falling onto the steep, jagged rocks below. And Msipessi hurried only a few paces behind.

Below them, the sounds of the other braves grew faint, the cries of battle now replaced with the enthusiasm of victors dividing their spoils. With everyone else who'd traveled on board the flatboat now dead and scalped, the goods that remained were theirs for the taking.

# 35

I f Mary had been physically beaten by one opponent after another, she didn't think she could have felt any more spent and battered. It seemed as if every time she thought her body could take no more punishment, she was called upon to rise to even greater challenges—and now she truly did not know how she could continue.

To everyone's relief, Colonel Donelson had ordered them to stop at a level spot along the northern shore just west of the Whirl. As each boat limped to shore, it was inspected for damage. Some had sustained minor damage but miraculously, only one had been destroyed—John Cotton's large canoe.

"We got to go back," Sam argued. "Every last thing the Cottons own is in that water. It wouldn't be Christian for us to leave it here. Why, that family would face ruination."

"You're right," Donelson said. His shoulders seemed more rounded than usual, and Mary could only imagine the strain he must have been under. "Take several canoes and round up what you can—Sam, Captain Hutchings, John Caffrey—and Russell Gower. Take others with you as you need."

"I'll be going, too," John Cotton said. "The supplies were my responsibility, after all."

Donelson nodded and the men began untying the canoes from the larger boats. When they launched a few short minutes later, there were three men in each boat, all setting their direction for the east, back toward the Whirl.

"Children," Ma said as she watched Ike and Sam paddle away, "we have a lot of tidying up to do. All that tossing has dislodged a lot of boxes and furniture in the cabin. We'll need to pull a few things out and repack."

Mary fought to keep her jaw from dropping. If anything, the ones remaining on shore should have been given an opportunity to rest. But as she looked at Ma's increasingly haggard face, she realized there wasn't a one among them who hadn't endured more than they'd ever dreamed was possible. They were all hurting, hungry and cold.

As Mary returned to the Neely boat, she passed Jed Cobb as he beached his canoe. He walked past her without a sign of recognition, his eyes focused intently on Colonel Donelson. Mary turned and watched him catch up with him as he was preparing to board *The Adventure.*

"Colonel," his voice wafted over the shore so softly that Mary strained to hear him.

Donelson turned to face him. "Yes? Have you news?"

"I've counted all the boats, sir," Jed said, "and two are missing."

"Two?"

"The Stuart boat—"

"God help them," Donelson breathed.

"Yes, sir. Being in the rear like they were, it's likely they were overtaken by the savages."

"And the other?"

"The Jennings. They didn't make it to the Whirl, sir."

Donelson nodded silently, his eyes drifting toward the east as if he could spot them somewhere behind them. They appeared sad—no, Mary thought, beyond sad. He looked devastated.

"I can go back, sir," Jed was saying. "I can carry my canoe on land past the Whirl and then row upriver aways."

Donelson peered at the mountains that bore down on the river where it narrowed to the Whirl.

As if in answer to his silent musings, Jed said, "The mountains will stop the Indians; they'll keep them to the east. They won't come through the Whirl, and these cliffs are steep.

You'll be safe here. Perhaps put up for the night, give the folks a chance to rest—"

"Yes," Donelson said. "That's an excellent idea." He turned back toward *The Adventure*. "Take another man with you, and see what you can find out about the Jennings—and perhaps the Stuarts, too."

As Jed hurried back to his canoe and Donelson disappeared into his boat's cabin, Mary turned, almost bumping into her mother. She had been so absorbed in the men's conversation that she hadn't even noticed her standing directly behind her. As their eyes met, Mary noticed her eyes, always so full of spirit, were dimmed now. It startled her; she'd never thought of a woman's eye color changing but there it was, her own mother, whose emerald eyes had been replaced with someone else's— now sunken and the color of a stagnant lagoon.

She had always been a large woman, buxom and formidable. But now her skin hung loosely about her frame.

"Are you getting enough to eat, Ma?"

"What?" She looked at her as if seeing her for the first time. "Oh, yes, of course. Now run along, Mary, you're needed at the cabin. We mustn't waste time."

03809

The Gower boat was put ashore next to the Neelys and as Mary toiled alongside Jean, Beth, Ma and Billy, she noticed the Gowers were sweeping the water from their deck. The Gower's daughter, Nancy, was younger than Mary; she had long black hair and a ready smile. Thin as a rail, she didn't appear to eat enough to keep a bird alive but was always willing to share whatever food they had for a pot of stew. She was brushing the water over the side of the deck as if she wasn't the least bit tired, but Mary knew otherwise. She thought perhaps the hard work kept them all from considering their dire circumstances and the tragic end the Stuarts and Jennings must have met.

As Mary helped to move boxes that had shifted during their tumble through the rapids, she took the opportunity to survey the other boats. They had moved up in the line and were now within five or six boats of *The Adventure*, which was heartening to her if the Indians were indeed intent on attacking from the rear to the front.

Then as quickly as Mary and her siblings had carried the boxes outside, they were directed to restack them in the cabin and secure them tightly with rope.

Mary longed for nightfall. If only the sun would drop below the horizon, Colonel Donelson would certainly order them to make camp for the night. Then the women could go about the chore of finding sufficient food to add to a pot of water and make not a stew, but a watery soup.

Mary's eyes scoured the mountains around her. A sheer cliff stood between the shore and the woods far above. It was too steep an incline for the men to reach the woods and hunt for game, she reasoned. If only they had another deer or even rabbit—any meat would do. They would cook it over an open spit and afterward, throw the bones into various pots and cook off every bit of meat. Even the water used to boil the bones would be used for soups and stews for days to come.

"Are we almost there?" Meg's voice was small and weak and as Mary turned to face her, she forced herself to smile reassuringly.

"We've been through the worst," Mary said, wrapping her arm around her. "We're more than halfway and we're out of Indian Territory now." She hoped God would forgive her if she hadn't spoken the truth, but she wanted with all her heart to believe her own words.

"Mary, I'm hungry," Meg said. She didn't whine and when Mary looked into her eyes, she knew she had waited to say something until she felt as if she couldn't delay it a moment longer.

"Why don't you get some biscuits and put a spoonful of preserves on them? You eat one and give one each to Johnny and Jane."

"There aren't any more biscuits, Mary." Her eyes filled with tears.

"Mary!"

At the sound of her voice, Mary looked up to find Nancy watching them from the next boat over. She hadn't realized how close the boats were and wondered whether she had overheard their conversation. Nancy's next words removed all doubt.

"We have extra biscuits," she said, "and we'll be happy to share them with you."

Mary knew there wasn't a family among them with extra food, and whatever was given to them would be taken out of the Gower family's own mouths.

"Just three of them," Mary said, almost apologetically. "Just for the younger ones. We'll repay you. Somehow."

"I know you will, Mary. You would do the same for us."

Nancy disappeared into their cabin and reemerged a moment later, carrying three biscuits that were no more than two bites apiece. They stood on the decks as Nancy passed them from the Gower boat to the Neely boat.

"God bless you, Nancy," Mary said as she took them. She handed them to Mary and walked with her to the cabin, where Jane and Johnny were playing on the mattress. Jane was cranky and Mary leaned down and scooped her into her arms.

"Let's get some food in that belly," she said with a broad smile, though her own stomach was growling fiercely. "Meg is going to put some sweet fig preserves on these biscuits, and they're going to taste delightful. They're a gift from the Gowers!"

"A gift!" Jane exclaimed, putting her hands together.

"Yes, a gift, and you'll have to eat it real slow, so you can savor every single bit. These are special biscuits!"

Mary watched as Meg pulled a jar of preserves from one of the crates. She scraped the sides of the jar with a long-handled spoon, barely pulling out enough to moisten each biscuit. Back home, Mary thought, they might have tossed that jar into boiling water to ready it for another batch of homemade preserves. But now, they would be more likely to pour a bit of boiling water inside the jar to loosen any bits still stuck to the sides, so they could savor every morsel.

Her own stomach growled. Unable to watch the children eat, she left the cabin. Her legs felt heavier with each step she took and she wondered what they could possibly cook for supper.

All of the fresh fruits were long gone; the vegetables that hadn't been canned were moldy or spoiled; and those that had been canned were precious few. And they had no idea how much longer they would be on this river or when they would ever reach Fort Nashborough.

As she walked across the deck, she could see some of the canoes returning with the Cotton's possessions—at least those they could recover. They would be soaked, no doubt, but one of the other flatboats would take them in and they'd be laid out tomorrow on the deck, where the winter sun would have to dry them. They were fortunate, Mary thought, to have climbed aboard the Cartwright's boat before reaching the Whirl or they might have lost more than their cargo.

Some of the settlers had disembarked from their boats and were beginning to make preparations for supper. Others were still inspecting their boats or conferring with Colonel Donelson about the trip ahead.

Jed Cobb had paddled a good distance from the others when he suddenly changed course and began returning to the fleet. He was shouting but his words were drowned out by the distance between them.

Ike half-stood in his canoe and turned toward him, shouting something in return.

Jed waved wildly at him before returning to his paddling, heading almost straight for shore, though he was still some distance from the fleet.

Mary watched as Ike turned away from Jed and looked toward the cliffs that loomed above them. She heard the shot ring out at the same time as Ike stumbled in the canoe, teetering so fiercely that he almost capsized the boat.

Mary opened her mouth to scream, but her voice was lost in the sound of gunfire. The women were running for their children, desperate to protect them and retreat to the safety of the cabins. Men were shouting and running to their guns and rifles.

"Cast off! Cast off!"

The frantic command was shouted from boat to boat. With Ike and Sam in the canoe some distance away, there was only Billy and the Neely women aboard.

"He's been hit!" Ma shouted.

The Neelys raced to the side of the boat nearest the canoe. A shot grazed the side of the vessel and Ma pushed them back. "Cast off!" she shouted.

"But Ike—"

"There's no time!"

The boat was already beginning to lurch as men on shore were untying the boats and pushing them back into the water, anxiously ordering them to move quickly. Every second counted now as Billy took the bridge. Amid the gunfire that fell all around them, he maneuvered the tiller as the others used their poles to push away from the shore and toward the center of the river, out of range of the gunfire.

The Neely women were spread out along the sides, each desperately moving the poles through the water. It seemed an eternity before they were able to push the boats off and move into the river.

A thud hit the side of the boat and a moment later, Sam's head popped over the side. Ma and Mary raced to help him aboard as he scrambled over the side. Then all three reached down and seized Ike by his coat and arms and hauled him onto the deck. Sam grabbed the rope and as the flatboat began to struggle toward the open water, he secured the canoe to the flatboat. John Cotton's possessions bobbed behind them as gunfire ripped through the crates.

"You're shot!" Ma shouted.

"Not now!" Ike bellowed. "Aim for the south! Aim for the south!"

As Ike climbed onto the bridge to help Billy with the tiller, the others grabbed the remaining poles and pushed and rowed as if the devil himself were upon them.

Ma stumbled and Mary screamed. But as the others turned in her direction, Ma shakily raised herself to her feet and continued to push her pole through the water.

Somewhere in the confusion, Mary's mind registered Ma's ripped skirt and screams coming from the Neely cabin, where the children were terrorized by the fresh Indian attack. And somehow her eyes took in Ike frantically working the tiller with both arms as if one entire sleeve wasn't covered in blood and dripping onto the bridge above her.

And somewhere in the back of her mind, she saw the other boats scrambling beside them, racing for the southern shore, Nancy Gower at the helm of her family's flatboat, her tiny body steering the huge vessel even as a hail of gunfire rained down upon them.

And somehow she managed to look upward at the cliffs, where the savages had gathered along the ridgeline and were shooting at them as if they were ducks in a pond.

# 36

Mary felt dead on her feet. She held the pole in an icy grip, her fingers so numb from the cold that she could no longer feel them. Though they were covered in two pair of mittens, one atop the other, they seemed fused to the frigid pole. She watched the dark water roll past the flatboat in the pitch blackness of the night, but although her eyes followed the wake and the current, her mind barely registered that they were moving.

It had been two nights since the attack and the boats had not stopped once in all that time. During the daylight hours, they moved with precision and purpose, hastily attempting to put miles between themselves and the Chickamauga tribes. And when darkness descended, they continued floating along the Tennessee River in the numbing cold, mindlessly keeping the boats from drifting too close to shore.

Four people had been wounded in the last assault. Nancy Gower had bravely held onto the helm of her boat, steering it to safety as the Indians attacked. It wasn't until they had placed enough distance between the boats and the Whirl that Nancy's mother noticed blood on her daughter's dress. A shot had gone clear through her thigh, entering from the back as she steered the boat away from the cliffs, and exiting through the front. Mrs. Gower thought it was a miracle the round hadn't hit bone. Nancy said she never felt a thing; her adrenaline was pumping too fiercely in an attempt to outrun the Indians to pay attention to much of anything else. Mrs. Gower had cleansed the wound the best she could and wrapped her thigh in a makeshift bandage but now Nancy was back on deck in the dark of night, steering again.

Mrs. Jones, a lady Mary hadn't previously had occasion to meet, had also been wounded but it was said the round only grazed her.

A man had been hit but his boat was far behind the Neelys, and Mary hadn't received word yet on who he was or the injuries he'd sustained.

And the fourth had been Ike, who had been hit in the upper arm while he was returning with some of John Cotton's possessions.

Once they were out of range of the rounds and the fleet had slowed to take an assessment of their damages, Ma had descended on Ike like a mother hen. Despite his objections and his assertion that he remain at the bow, Ma had insisted on taking him to the cabin, where he'd stripped off layer after layer of clothing to reveal the extent of his injury.

The shot had gone through his coat, a sweater, a shirt and an undershirt and lodged just below the skin. Ma dug it out while the boat continued to pitch with the current. They used river water to clean it and Ma pulled out her sewing kit, sewed it up and wrapped a bandage around his upper arm with rags made from worn clothing. Mary heard some of the others had cleansed the wounds more effectively with whiskey, but since Pa and Ma were opposed to liquor, they had none on board.

Ike never winced though his brow was heavy with sweat and Mary thought she detected his chin trembling under the beard he'd grown on their river journey. But his only complaint was the Injuns had ruined his favorite coat. Jean had promised to wash the blood out of his clothes once they could set ashore, and Beth promised to mend them.

Now he was back on the bridge above Mary, looking for floating debris that might slow their progress and issuing instructions to Billy, who worked the rear tiller.

When Ma had gone to relieve herself, she'd returned with an expression of wonderment as she held up a round. While she'd toiled at the height of the attack, it had gone through her dress and lodged in her petticoats. She had laughed ironically about it, as she wouldn't have been wearing petticoats while working the job of a sailor, had it not been so bitterly cold. She'd simply donned them for the extra warmth. Her dress had a neat hole at the back but one that could be easily mended. They all had stared in astonishment and shook their heads in amazement.

It was snowing lightly now and as Mary gazed at the moon, she remembered all the nights she'd lain in bed and watched through the window at the falling snow. She'd been snug then, comfortable under a down quilt; there'd been a fireplace in every bedroom that kept them all comfortably warm.

Now she shivered in the night air, the shawl that covered her head soaked through, her hands frigid and raw, and her face so cold the snowflakes didn't even melt when they struck her skin.

It had to be close to midnight, she reasoned, when the inky sky was reaching its darkest and the air was piercingly cold. Thickening black clouds obscured most of the moon as they moved swiftly from the northwest. Gradually the clouds began to drift apart until a ray of moonlight was able to peek through to lead the way.

Ma, Sam and Beth had navigated the boat through the frosty waters after sundown until Mary, Jean and Ike had taken over. At midnight, Martha, Billy and Ma would take their places while they grabbed a few hours of much-needed rest.

And so it had been for two nights and Mary wondered how much longer they could possibly continue in this manner.

She saw the scouts ahead of her, moving past each boat as they had for two days. They generally inquired as to their welfare, but unless there was an attack or a grave illness to report, they called back in turn that "all was well" even though each of them knew they were far from well. They were hungry and the children were crying themselves to sleep, only to awaken a few hours later to begin anew. They needed meat and the only way to get it was to go ashore, where another attack might be imminent. The fruits and preserves were all gone and what flour and grain remained had to be watered down so much to make it go further, that it was like eating poorly cooked flour soup.

They ate the last of the raw vegetables; limp carrots, potatoes filled with eyes and peas that had shriveled to half their size.

Meg had stopped crying throughout the night but her silence was even more alarming. She had stopped speaking and stared ahead with large, unblinking eyes. Ma had tried talking to her, as they all had, but it was as if she had gone completely deaf. Even when Jane crawled atop of her and begged to be held or fed, Meg seemed blind to her attentions.

Jane's coughing continued and her little face was beginning to look skeletal. The bouts of coughing came from deep inside her tiny chest and seemed most persistent during the nighttime hours.

Mary had held Meg in one arm and Jane in the other as they tried to sleep last evening, and while Jane coughed and squirmed and kicked in her sleep, Meg was as still as death. The last Mary had seen of them was when she closed the door of the cabin around eight o'clock; Ma was lying down beside them, stroking Meg's hair and talking to her quietly and reassuringly, though Meg was unresponsive.

Now the scout approached their boat and Ike prepared to call out the familiar refrain that all was well. But before he could speak, Jed shouted, "A mile ahead, we're making encampment on the northern shore."

And then he was gone in the murky darkness, moving to the rear of the fleet in his small canoe.

# 37

**M**ary had just drifted off to sleep when the shouting began.

They had made camp along an open stretch of the northern shore, far enough from the thick woods to minimize the chance of a surprise attack. Each boat was instructed to appoint at least one person to guard the fleet during the hours before dawn. Ike and Ma agreed to remain awake until Sam and Billy relieved them two hours later.

Some of the settlers started campfires to keep warm while others boiled water for a brackish drink that might have been coffee if they'd had ample supply. But many were too exhausted to do more than tie up their boats and climb into bed.

Mary lay with her arms wrapped around Meg. When the shouts began, they were so faint she thought she was dreaming. She tried to convince herself that the men were effectively guarding them in a vain attempt to succumb to sleep. But as she continued lying there with one eye partially open, the shouts grew louder and more insistent.

"Help poor Jennings! Help!"

Mary bolted upright as Beth and Jean came to their feet. Ma remained in bed on the other side of Meg, but raised to one elbow.

"It's a trick," Jean whispered hoarsely.

In the darkness, Mary could barely make out her sister's silhouette as she made her way to the door. She glanced at the boys' mattress but only Johnny was upon it, sound asleep as if nothing were amiss. She started to rise but she felt herself pulled downward with startling force. She gasped and peered through the darkness. Meg was holding onto her clothing with both fists.

"It's all right," she whispered to her little sister. "I'm not leaving you."

Meg didn't relinquish her hold on her and Mary gently but firmly opened her tightly clenched hands. As soon as she extricated herself from one hand, Meg grabbed her clothing in a different place so that it was impossible to get away.

"Meg, you have to let me go," Mary whispered.

By the time Jean slid the door open a few inches, Ma was also up. Mary caught a glimpse of her retrieving the musket they kept at the ready.

"Help poor Jennings!" the call came again.

Jean opened the door wider and stepped to the threshold.

"What are you doing?" Beth called hoarsely.

"Ike and Sam are running along the shore," Jean said over her shoulder. "And others are getting into canoes!"

"Are we under attack?"

"No—no," she answered hesitantly. Then her voice grew breathless. "It's a boat! A flatboat!"

Mary jumped almost straight up on the mattress with Meg still clinging to her. Gathering the girl into her arms, she crossed the cabin and stood beside Ma and her older sisters. As the clouds parted, the moonlight filtered down to the river below, casting the current into glistening waves that rolled toward shore. And there, not a quarter mile away, was the Jennings boat limping toward them.

The canoes met them, the men sending up shouts of cheer. John Caffrey climbed aboard the Jennings boat and took control of the poles while Mr. Jennings sank to his knees.

Mary flew past her sisters and clambered off the boat with Meg still clinging to her, her face pressed against Mary's chest. By the time they reached the ground, Meg had slid from Mary's body but as she raced toward the others, Meg grabbed onto her skirt and hurried along. The air was so frigid that all of them had long ago begun sleeping in their clothes, a habit of which they were grateful as they journeyed through Indian Territories. Now Mary ran with dozens of others as the Jennings boat came ashore.

But as they neared, Mary's enthusiasm turned to sorrow as she saw Mr. Jennings' face. He looks nearly dead, she thought. The memory of their own boats running swiftly through the waters came rushing back to her, as they'd tried to outdistance the Indians while the Jennings were left behind to fend for themselves—

She stopped at the bow as the men secured it on shore. Mr. Jennings was half-carried from his boat. Mary searched for any other signs of life, but saw none. The hulking boat began to take on the shape of an apparition, eerily silent and tragic, the shadowy cabin blocking the moon.

"Get him some food and water!" Captain Blackmore ordered. Someone brought blankets forward and they tried to lay him upon them, but he insisted on standing. But too weak to argue, he sank again to his knees, his eyes filling with tears of relief.

"I despaired of ever seeing you again," he said, taking the cup of water that was offered to him.

"What happened?" Colonel Donelson said. "Where are the others?"

He gulped the liquid as if he hadn't touched water in days. He tried several times to speak before he gathered enough strength to let his words escape from his lips.

"We ran upon some rocks," he said, "and grounded the boat. We were trying to cast off, to catch up with the rest of the boats— but the Indians, they saw our distress and they descended on us like—like the savages they are."

Though the crowd had grown thick, they were completely silent. Mary grew aware of Meg, her face buried in the folds of her billowing skirt, and realized her child's ears shouldn't hear Mr. Jennings' story. But she was too riveted to move, too determined to hear him out. She placed her hand on one ear and pressed Meg's head deeper against her as if she could muffle his words.

"Where are the others?" someone asked in a hushed tone.

When he looked upward at the crowd, at his friends and his former neighbors, his eyes appeared to be those of a man twenty years older. Mary thought she had never seen such pain and agony in all her life.

"My son Jon and his friend Obediah," Mr. Jennings said, choking on his words, "and the young negro servant, Ezekiel—"

"Yes?" Donelson asked, kneeling beside him.

"They—they fled."

There was a collective gasp.

"You mean, they escaped?"

"They ran. They took the canoe tied up to our boat and they left us there on the rocks."

"Oh, my God," a lady toward the back exhaled. It was the thought that every one of them had; Mary was sure of it. As if it were happening again right before her eyes, she recalled the Indians swarming over the Jennings' boat and the three men leaving three women, a baby and an aging man behind to fend for themselves.

"Cowardice!" one man shouted from the rear. "If they'd been in Washington's Army, they'd have been hung for desertion!"

"Now, men," Donelson said, straightening. "There'll be plenty of time later to deal with them—if the Indians haven't captured them already." He turned back to Mr. Jennings. His face was pale and drawn and he appeared to choose his next words carefully. "Your wife, Mr. Jennings? And Elizabeth and the baby? What happened to them?"

Mr. Jennings' face was wracked with indescribable anguish. "My wife and Elizabeth—" he motioned toward the cabin.

Mary was pushed aside as Ma bolted for the boat. Before anyone could stop her, she had climbed aboard with Mrs. Gower and Mrs. Donelson fast on her heels. Mary felt a surge within her blood and she raced to join them.

When Ma opened the cabin door, they were met with total disarray. It appeared as if half their possessions were gone and those that remained were tossed about the small cabin. Furniture teetered atop wooden crates, some of them half-crushed; and clothing, dishes and cooking utensils were scattered across the floor. The walls were peppered with holes; so many that Mary could see the river on the other side.

Mrs. Jennings and her maid servant were kneeling on a mattress and as the door flew open, they scrambled for the rifles before realizing they were not being attacked yet again. Then Mrs. Jennings pulled herself away from Elizabeth, who lay on her side on the mattress. She motioned for the women to step outside the cabin.

As they met on deck, Mary's heart hammered at the sight of her. Her dress was in tatters; riddled with so many holes that it was a miracle she hadn't been shot in two.

"Jonathan told us what happened," Ma said, wrapping her arm around her shoulders. "Dear God."

Mrs. Jennings rested her head against her. "They deserted us," she said, her voice filled with disbelief. "They left us there to be slaughtered."

"How—how did you manage to get away?" Mrs. Donelson tentatively asked.

"We were stuck on the rocks," she said, her voice sounding almost disembodied. "I had no choice but to jump off the boat and push us back into the water."

"You pushed the boat by yourself?"

She shook her head as if not believing it herself. "God knows where I got the strength." She spread her skirt for the others to see. "The angels were with us… Jonathan was shooting at the Indians—he was the only one left to protect us—and Elizabeth and the servant girl, Esther, were trying to lighten the load to get us off the rocks." Her voice choked. "They were throwing our furniture, food, crates—whatever they could grab onto—and tossing them overboard."

Ma squeezed her shoulder. "I know it's tough, but all those things can be replaced. You'll start life anew in the Cumberlands, and you'll soon have a new home filled with new things. The important thing is, you and Jonathan, Elizabeth and Baby Ephraim are all right."

Mrs. Jennings drew away from her and stared at her with wide, unblinking eyes. The blood seemed to drain from her face and when she spoke her words seemed to hang in the air. "We'd made a crib out of one of the crates. Baby Ephraim was in it."

# 38

Noquali awakened to the comforting warmth of a fire and the bitter aroma of kanohena brewing. He drew himself onto one elbow and peered from the loft in Jo-leigh's tiny cabin to the floor below.

She was moving from the table to the fireplace, her tall, slender frame graceful and lithe against the candlelight. She reached toward a kettle, adding bits of meat to a morning stew, her lean forearms extending beyond her buckskin sleeves.

He watched the light from the flames as it danced against her gleaming black hair and he pictured his fingers sweeping through the silky strands.

He glanced toward his feet at White Messenger and Msipessi sleeping on the opposite side of the loft. Quietly, he rose to his feet, gathered his clothing and slipped on a few garments before heading down the ladder. He carried his beaver leggings and moccasins with him, placing them silently beside the table.

Jo-leigh was busy stirring the pot when he reached his hand around her neck, gathering her hair in his palm and waving it briefly beneath his nostrils, where he took in the full, sweet aroma.

She turned to him, glancing apprehensively toward the loft. "The others—"

"Do not worry. They are not yet awake."

She placed a finger across his lips. "But they will be shortly," she whispered.

He reluctantly dropped his hold on her hair and watched it cascade down her back.

"Where are the girls?" he asked, drawing up a chair. "Why are you cooking, and not the girls I brought you?"

She glanced at him out of the corner of her eye but continued to work silently.

Frowning, he perused the cabin. Across the room on Jo-leigh's small bed lay the two girls, entwined in each other's arms in slumber. He quickly pulled on the beaver leggings and the boots before rising.

"No," he said. His voice was low but firm.

She turned and placed her hand upon his arm. The gentle gesture was enough to keep him from striding across the room and jerking the girls awake, but he felt his face growing hot.

"I brought you two slaves," he said, "to do with them as you will. But I did not imagine you would become a slave to them, cooking the morning meal while they sleep like chiefs in a warm bed."

Her hand tightened on his wrist. "They are ill."

His chin jutted forward proudly. He knew as he narrowed his eyes and looked down upon her that his expression was immobile, but his emotions were surging. The gift of one slave was a major achievement, one that bespoke his love for her and his commitment to caring for her. The gift of two slaves enhanced her status in the village. Only Bloody Fellow's wife owned more than one slave and most owned none at all.

His eyes roamed from Jo-leigh to the two girls. To have given her sick slaves was an insult. He would be laughed at behind his back; looked down upon by other warriors. This was totally unacceptable.

"They are faking," he said firmly. "They are playing you for a fool. They will lie in your bed and have you wait upon them, bringing them their food and doing their bidding." He shrugged her hand off his arm and marched to the other side of the room, where he threw the covers off the two girls.

At the sudden act, one of the girls groggily opened her eyes. She tried to raise her head but it fell back upon the straw mattress with a slight moan. The other remained asleep, curled within her sister's arms.

Jo-leigh was beside them instantly. "Look at their faces," she urged him. "The fever is upon them. It is cold on this side of the cabin; can't you feel the chill? But their skin is hot." She grabbed his hand and placed it upon the smaller one's forehead. "They have a fire within them."

He pulled his hand away. It was wet with their heavy perspiration and he wiped it on his leggings.

"I have been tending to them," she said gently. "I have been giving them kanohena. The hot liquid will cause the fever to break and escape them. See," she said, pointing to their skin, "it is already working."

The light was dim here but as he looked at their bodies, he could see beads of perspiration so large they almost appeared to be boils.

"Give me a few days to tend to them. I will make them well. And then *they* will serve *me*."

Noquali scowled. "Get them out of bed," he directed. "They can toil over the fire. While they make the morning meal, they can sweat out their fever."

"Noquali," she urged, placing both her hands upon his forearms and looking him squarely in the eyes, "one of them can barely move. The other is not much better. If I work them now, they will surely become worse and then what good would they be to me then? Let me make them well so they can serve me well in return. Do we not also tend to a sick horse so that it may heal and return to work?"

He opened his mouth to argue her point, but he was interrupted by a quick rap on the door. As he made his way across the cabin to the door, he was aware of White Messenger and Msipessi stirring in the loft above.

"Two approaching the Whirl," the young warrior said as soon as he opened the door. "Bloody Fellow is on his way; he wishes for you to join him."

⊂⊃

Dawn was barely breaking across the wintry sky as Noquali, White Messenger and Msipessi made their way from Tuskagee Island Town toward the Whirl. It had been more than a day since they had stood upon these cliffs and fired down upon the flotilla as they stopped along the northern shore. It had been a disappointing attack; there had been nearly 250 white men, women and children directly below them and 70 warriors amply supplied. Yet they had failed to kill or capture any of them. Their rounds had fallen short or missed their mark and the boats had moved out more hastily than they had anticipated. They had followed them for some distance but the flatboats had outrun them.

Still, just east of the Whirl, they had managed to kill 26 in the last boat and Noquali had snared the two survivors. And as soon as he returned to Jo-leigh's cabin, he would take up the issue again and insist that her new slaves work as they should.

There had been another boat as well that the warriors had converged upon but in the end, it too had escaped. They had spotted only seven aboard, but it had been a much smaller boat. And when it ran aground, to the Indians' delight they had begun throwing their goods overboard, leaving behind a treasure trove. Though they had failed to capture the boat itself, the warriors had eagerly carried what spoils they were able to recover from the river back to their families—jewelry, linens, blankets, cooking utensils and kettles, and ornately carved furniture.

Three young men had jumped off the boat as the warriors approached: two white men and a black man. They had managed to untie a canoe and they'd set off toward the east, back upstream toward the last boat.

Noquali had managed to shoot the black man. He'd watched him fall out of the boat, his arms flailing as he tried to grasp the side of the canoe to haul himself back on board, but his companions had sped away, leaving him in the middle of the river. They had watched him drown, his head bobbing above the water as it turned red with his blood.

They hadn't pursued the two others, as their help was needed at the Whirl with the greater prize of the remaining flatboats, and Noquali was still irritated that they had managed to allow their escape.

Now he joined Bloody Fellow and a few of his men on the cliffs above the river. They watched in silence as the canoe came into view; it was the same one he'd seen two days before and the same two young men who had escaped.

"They must have been biding their time," Bloody Fellow said, "thinking we would move on after the attack."

"Yes," White Messenger said. "And now they must think they can rejoin their party."

Noquali smiled. "Then it is time, my brothers, for us to teach them the ways of our fathers."

CBEO

They remained amid trees with great branches extending over the water like a mother's arms. Their canoes were still except for the occasional current that lapped against their sides, causing them to roll gently. Noquali kept his paddle extended over the side, steadying the canoe and preventing it from emerging from the tree line until the time was right.

Those birds who had braved the harsh winter were awakening now, their songs insistent in the morning sun. The dew was still on the shoreline. Just behind them, the forest floor was still covered in snow and thin sheets of ice.

The canoe made its way downriver. It remained close to the opposite shore, hugging the shoreline as if the shadows cast by the trees could conceal them. But as they moved ever closer to Noquali and the others, the river grew narrower. Soon it would change to rapids before converging onto the Whirl.

As they grew closer, Noquali made out the tow-haired man in the back of the canoe, nervously casting his eyes along the shoreline and jumping at every sound. The one in front had light brown hair and he seemed to keep his attention focused on the water, as if trying to avoid sandbars. They were both unkempt, their hair thick and disheveled above rail-thin bodies.

Noquali, White Messenger and Msipessi remained perfectly silent and as rigid as the trees as the canoe swept past them. Neither white man turned in their direction. They continued on as the southern shore grew closer to the northern one; the only sound was that made by their paddles as they swept through the water.

He heard the war cries of Bloody Fellow and his warriors before their canoe emerged from their hiding place fifty yards downriver. They appeared so quickly that the two young men froze for several seconds as if unsure of what was happening. When they realized they were under attack, they appeared uncertain whether to go for their rifles or try to outrun them. One grabbed a rifle, his fingers clumsy and thick, while the other attempted to turn the canoe around and head back toward the east.

But as the canoe was turned, Noquali emerged from his hiding place and swiftly overtook them from behind, squeezing them between the two groups of warriors.

Realizing they were no match for seven warriors converging upon them, they paddled in a frenetic circle for a few confusing moments before laying down their paddles and rifles and raising their hands in defeat.

They had captured the two young men without a single shot.

# 39

Mary stirred the contents of the kettle as she kept one eye on the activities surrounding her. There wasn't the faintest aroma of food emanating from the pot and as she peered inside, it looked like nothing more than a pot of water with a few aged and shriveling vegetables floating about. It was the sorriest soup she'd ever seen and her heart sank as she thought of an entire day on the river with only this hot liquid to sustain her.

Meg sat a few feet away with Jane in her lap. Johnny had erected a miniature fort with sticks and was using twigs for men as he played a solitary game of settlers and Indians. Billy had given him the feathers he'd found that day that seemed so distant in time and place; and Johnny was wearing them as he played. At one time, it might have brought a smile to Mary's lips but as she watched him on this dreadful morning, she winced with the thought.

Ike, Billy and Sam were helping the Jennings move their furniture to various boats as could accommodate the extra weight. The Jennings boat was riddled with rounds and was taking on water. As it sank ever deeper into the Tennessee River, Mary could only imagine Mrs. Jennings bailing the water as her husband hastened to catch up with the rest of the boats. It was a miracle they'd escaped the Indians, and another miracle they'd been able to keep going with nothing more than hope and faith that they'd be reunited with the rest of the families.

The women spoke of the horror of poor Baby Ephraim in hushed tones, becoming quiet when Elizabeth or Mrs. Jennings came into view. The amount of speculation sickened Mary as some debated whether he survived the water in his makeshift crib, was jostled so harshly that he was killed on impact, or drowned as he floated helplessly away from his mother. Still others held out the hope that he had survived and some Indian woman was caring for him and might raise him as if he were her own. With each fresh set of conjectures, Mary wanted nothing more than to cover her ears and hear no more.

She had seen Elizabeth only once. Mrs. Donelson and Ma had spent a great deal of time in the Jennings cabin. Eventually, they had emerged and had walked straight away to *The Adventure* with Elizabeth between them. Her skin appeared pasty, her eyes sunken deep within her skull as if she had been crying without respite. She did not look at anyone but kept her head downcast, using her hair and her clothing in an ineffective attempt to shield her face from the others.

Mrs. Harrison had moved forward as if to say something but Ma shook her head and fixed her with an uncompromising stare and they had continued on without missing a step. Once at the Donelson cabin, they had all disappeared within and had yet to emerge.

"I can't imagine what she must be going through," Jean said as if in answer to Mary's thoughts.

"She must have relived those moments a hundred times over," Mary said as she stirred.

"With just the four of them aboard—her parents, the servant girl and herself—who's to know who tossed the crate overboard?"

Mary focused on Sam approaching them, as if to rid her mind of thoughts of the Jennings. "It doesn't matter. What's done is done."

"Still, the guilt—"

"I hope she doesn't feel guilty. They all did what they had to do. And by throwing the furniture overboard, they probably saved their own lives."

"I suppose you're right," Jean said. "And we can only hope and pray that Baby Ephraim died a quick death, or was taken in by some kindly—"

Her words were cut off by the sound of men arguing. They watched as Colonel Donelson strode quickly from his own boat toward Captain Blackmore's, a dozen men following him. His son-in-law, Captain Hutchings, bellowed in anger. "This is a fool's journey!" he shouted as he passed by Mary, his eyes spitting fire at the back of Colonel Donelson's head. "You have taken us into this God-forsaken land and you appear totally incapable of bringing us out of it!"

Colonel Donelson stopped and glared at him for a long moment before answering. "We are moving as quickly as practical."

"Quickly? You call this quickly? We were scheduled to arrive at Fort Nashborough months ago. Four weeks, you told us! Four weeks down the river with barely a moment spent in Chickamauga Territory. And they wouldn't pay us a nevermind, as we were moving straight through!"

"Tom, you know as well as I," he said, his jaw tightening, "there have been factors beyond our control."

"I'd say so!" he thundered.

By this time, others were joining them.

"Another family airin' dirty laundry?" Sam whispered near Mary's ear.

They watched curiously as Donelson argued with his daughter's husband. As the crowd around them grew, others began to join in.

"Our families are starving," Mr. Harrison said. "We'll begin dying off if we don't get decent food."

"How far westward will we encounter the Chickamauga?" another said. "How great are their numbers?"

"How much longer will this insufferable trip take?" still another demanded.

"We're not going all the way to Fort Nashborough," Captain Hutchings said. "At the first river crossing, we're taking it to other points."

"Now, why on God's green earth would you do such a thing?" Donelson demanded, his normally cool exterior showing obvious signs of exasperation.

"With all due respect, you don't know where we're going. You've never been this way before. All you have is a simple drawn map that shows a river that should have been navigable in a month. How do we know if we're even halfway to the Cumberlands?"

"Yeah!" another shouted.

The crowd was growing larger and more unruly. Mary whisked Meg off her feet. "Take Jane and Johnny back to the boat," she said, "and I'll be behind directly."

As the smallest children were herded away, Mary searched the crowd for Ma. She finally sighted her departing the Donelson's cabin. As she made her way through the crowd, Ike spoke up.

"We're gonna survive this trip only if we stick together," he said. "If any one of us goes off on their own, it'll be the kiss o' death for 'em."

"Ike's right," Colonel Donelson said. "And we're closer to Fort Nashborough than many of you might think." He grabbed a stick and crossed to a patch of smooth sand. He made a crooked mark, followed by three small x's. "This is where the Tennessee begins," he said, "and this is the distance we've come thus far."

As the rumblings continued, he raised his voice to be heard above the crowd. "We're within two days' time of reaching Muscle Shoals. Robertson's men are to meet us there with ample food and supplies."

"How do we know we're that close?" Mr. Harrison demanded.

"We're here," Donelson said, pointing to the second mark. "And we're still moving with the current. We're not that far, men." As they continued mumbling and debating among themselves, he added, "And just where do you think you'd be going, should you desert the others? The river runs that way—" he pointed to the west "—and that way." Pointing now to the east, he continued, "And we know what dangers lay to the east. We're out of Chickamauga Territory now, and as we continue to the west, we'll put even more distance between us. We'll soon be reunited with Colonel Robertson and his men, if you'll only listen to me!"

"If we're out of danger here," Mr. Harrison said, "then allow us to hunt, even if it's only for a few hours. Our families are starving, Colonel, you have to see that with your own eyes!"

"Yeah!" another man shouted. "We need some decent grub!"

Donelson turned away from the others and searched the surrounding terrain with his eyes. Mary was close enough to see the doubt and she wondered if they were truly out of danger or if the savages still lurked on the other side of those trees.

"When we reach Muscle Shoals," he said, "we'll rest and hunt."

"But you said that was two days' time!" Captain Hutchings was becoming more infuriated. "We need food *now*!"

"I got me a hankerin' for some *real* vittles!" another exploded.

Donelson strode to the Neely kettle and slipped the dipper inside. As he pulled up the liquid, his eyes widened at the water, still fresh and clear. Mary was suddenly ashamed. They hadn't enough food to even turn the water into a broth.

But as he released the water back into the kettle, his face softened.

"What about fish?" Sam asked.

Donelson looked at him for a moment and then stroked his chin.

"Which one of us has netting aboard?" one of the men said sarcastically.

"We can make netting easy enough," Ike said, coming to his younger brother's defense. "Each of us has some sort of rope on board, haven't we?"

"It's too cold," one of the men argued. "The fish are all in deep waters to keep from freezing."

"Mary, bring me some rope," Ike said.

Without hesitation, Mary rushed back to the boat. She found Meg, Jane and Johnny settling uneasily into the cabin, the younger children complaining because they were unable to remain outside. She found some rope and hurried back to the men.

Ike was waiting for her. As she approached, he pulled out his knife. "Tie that end up to that tree over yonder," he ordered.

As Mary complied, he ran the rope to a nearby tree and cut it, leaving just enough to tie it securely. Then as the others watched, he began tying pieces vertically so they hung down to the ground, and then crisscrossed them with other pieces of the rope.

"This is crude," he admitted, "but if those women who are more adept at weaving could help, we could create nets that are sure to catch some fish."

One of the men laughed. "Then what are we to do? Spend all day sittin' out in the river, waitin' for the fish to jump in 'em?"

When Ike answered, his voice was frosty. "We get two boats within a few yards of each other and stretch the nets out between 'em. As we travel downriver, we're sure to catch somethin'. How many of you haven't seen a fish or two jumpin' out of the water as our boats went past?"

"They're the stupid ones," one man mumbled. "The smart ones are in deep."

"I ain't aimin' to check their schoolin'," Billy said, stepping forward. "Dumb or smart, they're food."

Donelson strode to the center of the gathering. "It's worth a try," he said, "and it won't slow us down. Are there any women here who can fasten some nets?"

"No disrespect," Mrs. Gower said, "but I can make a much better one than that one, Mr. Neely."

The crowd laughed uneasily.

"And me, too," Ma said, stepping forward. "Each of us can make the nets as we travel, and when we've got them ready, we'll call to the nearest boat. We might snare enough fish for a meal— but one thing's for certain: if we don't try, we'll be having more water and pretending it's a meal."

"As soon as the Jennings are situated," Donelson said, "and we can pack up and move out, we'll be closer to arriving at Muscle Shoals. And give me just two days, men. Robertson and his men will be there waiting for us, just as we arranged. And if they've cleared a trail overland, we'll be leaving these boats behind in two days time and all of this will be just a distant memory."

A memory, Mary thought as she helped Ike untie the rope from the trees. A memory was something that didn't destroy you from the inside out, something that didn't make a mark on your soul so deep you know you'll never shake it, as long as you live. No, she thought as her jaw jutted forward and her teeth clenched, this was no memory. This was a nightmare.

# 40

When a woman was captured, it often occurred without fanfare by the Indians. They took no more notice of her than a dog, for she was worth little more. But when a man was captured, it was cause for a celebration that would herald the start of an important custom.

So as Noquali and Bloody Fellow marched the two young men into Tuskagee Island Town, the villagers rallied around them. The men's hands were tied behind their backs and their ankles were bound together to prevent their strides from reaching more than a half-step. Women rushed them with clubs and beat them upon their heads and backs, until blood streamed down their faces and bled through their clothing. They stumbled and the tow-haired man fell upon his knees, where he was kicked by the village children.

Though the warriors came out of their homes and observed their passing, they did not strike them as they made their way toward the center of the village; their work would come later and Noquali knew it would be observed by all.

They reached Bloody Fellow's home and he stepped around the men and addressed his village.

"These animals have been captured as they attempted to escape," he said. "They are cowards. When the warriors attacked their women and their children, they left them to die. They did not fight but ran like mice from the eagles.

"Let us prepare a great feast for today we shall rid the land of our fathers of these cowardly rabbits!"

A whoop began in the throats of the Indians and increased to a fever pitch.

Noquali held his head high as he grasped the tow-haired man's forearm and led him toward the communal building. Women were already busy preparing huge kettles over fires; others raced forward with fresh venison and buffalo, hominy and corn. There was much laughter and gaiety as they kicked and beat the men while they passed and when one cried out, it only intensified their efforts.

"Please, please let us go," the tow-haired man pleaded with Noquali as they reached a set of poles that rose about seven feet high in the center of the compound.

He said nothing in return but continued staring straight ahead as if he did not understand his language.

While the tribe watched, he marched the man through several inches of charred wood as they approached one of the poles. The man's eyes grew wide as the cinders reached above his ankles. They were cold now, but as the day progressed and the celebrations began, Noquali knew they would soon begin to smoke again with the burning of fresh wood—and flesh.

He kept the man's hands bound behind his back but cinched his elbows so close together on the other side of the pole that he cried out in agony. The pole was too wide for them to meet but Noquali pulled on them almost to the point of dislocating his shoulders. Finally, he tied them together as the man begged for mercy.

As the darker haired man was tied to another pole so they faced one another, Noquali wrapped a buckskin strap around his neck to keep his head upright. Then he lifted his feet from the ground and bound his ankles around the pole. His body tried to pitch forward but the ropes and strap held him in place, as Noquali knew they would.

Soon women and children were piling brush at their feet, some of which were piled high enough to tickle their knees.

A short distance away, the fires grew hot as the women cooked the meals. And Noquali, Msipessi and White Messenger retired to Jo-Leigh's cabin to rest and prepare for the afternoon's events.

ଔଷୋ

The sun was high overhead when the meals were laid out before them on great tables. It was a feast: there were sweet corn cakes piled high on wood platters; a wild boar roasting over a giant spit; slabs of venison so tender, the meat could be torn off with bare hands. Enormous chunks of buffalo were laid so high on the tables that one could barely see over them. And there were bowls filled with tender hominy, crisp corn, wild onions and Noquali's favorite, kanuchi soup. There were bowls of dried plums and figs and drinks made from the sweet syrups of fruits preserved since they were harvested the previous summer.

He watched Jo-Leigh as she helped to carry the food from the pots to the table, chatting with several other women as she worked. Her slaves were not with her, a fact that did not escape Noquali.

White Messenger and Msipessi spoke quietly in the Shawnee language. Noquali did not know their language fluently but picked up enough to understand they would soon be leaving. Their Shawnee family awaited them to the west, and they would shortly begin a pre-arranged trek northward with what they hoped would be several captives. The Shawnee were gathering in the land called the Kain-Tuck, and under the leadership of Chief Blackfish, the Indians were mounting raids against the settlers, killing the men and capturing the women and children.

As Noquali listened, he knew the white men did not stand a chance against the Cherokee, the Shawnee, Delaware, Creeks, and other tribes. The tribes knew these lands as well as they knew the palms of their own hands. They understood the ways of the animals here, the various purposes provided by the rich, dark soil. They practiced their ancient rituals in these lands, and used the abundant herbs to cure every ailment. They were adept at living in the starkest winter months and the most humid of summer days. In contrast, the white men were weak, unable to run for miles as the warriors often did. They did not understand the plants here, their medicinal purposes, or the ways in which the Great Spirit provided for those who were worthy in every season.

As he stared at the two young men who called out for water and mercy, his anger rose within him. They came with the intention of pushing them from their own lands, the lands of their fathers; they signed agreements to which his people were expected to abide but the white men did not; and many seemed intent on annihilating the red man.

He rose from his table and wiped his mouth as he approached the tow-haired man. With the eyes of the villagers upon him, he removed a long knife from his belt and sliced open the head of the young man, stripping away part of his scalp. He held it by a tuft of hair above his head as blood dripped down his forearm. He shook the scalp as he marched around the campfires, showing it to all. He could feel Jo-Leigh's eyes upon him and his chest expanded as he approached her.

As the man screamed in terror and anguish, his cries only served to excite the villagers. Soon the darker haired man's scalp was also sliced away, exposing bone at the top of his skull.

The minutes ticked by slowly. They would not hurry this celebration but they would savor every moment.

He eventually returned to his table and placed the scalp beside his food. He ate eagerly, hungrily.

"Noquali." The voice was thin and higher pitched than most of the Cherokee males. He turned and faced John Rogers, the white trader.

Rogers flowed easily between the white men to the east and the Indian tribes. He brought them ammunition, weapons, and clothing. The women enjoyed his visits, for he frequently brought china and bowls from far-off places, the likes of which the Indians had never seen before.

Noquali stood and greeted him.

"That man," Rogers said, pointing at the tow-haired man he had scalped, "what do you plan to do with him?"

"Burn him," he answered.

Rogers nodded. He seemed to be studying the two men and when he spoke his words were slow and studied. "Can I buy him from you?"

He looked at him briefly before turning his attention to his captive. Had it not been for the strap around his neck, his head no doubt would have lolled forward. His entire body seemed slumped against the pole and blood poured from his head, soaking him from his face to his chest. Occasionally, children would poke at him with sticks to try and rouse him from his stupor. When they did, the screaming would commence again.

"Why would you want him?" Noquali asked. "He is useless."

"Perhaps."

He tilted his head. "You were captured once, were you not?"

Rogers avoided his eyes. "Yes. I was."

"By the white men."

"Yes. John Sevier." He turned to look at him. "But he let me go. And because he allowed me to be released, I am here with you now and I am able to continue supplying you with all manner of goods. Please allow me to repay that act of goodwill. Allow me to purchase that boy from you."

Noquali watched the boy. His skull was exposed and he doubted he would live much longer, even if he were cut down from the pole. "What is he worth to you?"

"Come to my trading post," Rogers said. "Pick out what you want, what you think the boy is worth."

Noquali walked resolutely toward the two poles. He removed the strap from the boy's neck. As his head dropped forward against his chest with a long moan, he cut his ankles from the pole and then his arms.

The villagers began an outcry as it became obvious that he was freeing the young man. As he led the stumbling boy, now blinded by his own blood, to Rogers, he spoke to the others.

"The other captive is Bloody Fellow's," he said. "Ask him what he wishes to do with him!"

Bloody Fellow rose from his table. "Burn him!" he ordered.

Noquali handed over the young man to Rogers. As they meandered through the village to the trader's post, he could smell the wood beginning to burn as the screams of the other young man filled the air.

# 41

March 12 was the most beautiful day Mary could remember. The clouds parted, revealing a blue sky that was unlike the cold gray they had become so accustomed to seeing. They were traveling south now, and it was if the temperatures were warming with every hour of their journey.

Their bellies were closer to being full than at any time in the past three months. The women and children had sprung into action, making nets out of any appropriate materials they had on hand. It was tricky stretching the nets from one boat to another, as the boats had to stay a constant distance from each other and travel at the same speed, so in the end many fixed their nets to poles and cast them off the sides of their vessels. As they'd traveled downriver, they encountered dozens upon dozens of fish. Many of them were too small and slipped right through the squares they'd so carefully tied, but occasionally a good-sized fish would become entangled in the ropes. When that occurred, a cry went up from boat to boat, as if they were in a tournament.

Pots were set to boiling on each deck and the smell of fresh fish permeated the air as they cooked. Some of the luckier families had enough cornmeal to thinly coat the fish and enough grease to fry them. The Neelys boiled theirs for the briefest of time, and they all admitted it was the best fish they'd ever tasted.

It didn't seem to matter anymore that their fruit and preserves were gone or their vegetables consisted only of what was left in their canning jars, which was pitifully few. They had rowed downriver with a new vigor for almost two days now, and they knew that before this day was out, they would be reunited with James Robertson and his men, and ample, fresh supplies would be waiting for them.

"Do you think Pa will be there?" Mary asked Ma as they cleaned the plates and utensils after their meal.

Ma stopped and looked westward. Though she had lost a lot of weight, her eyes were brighter than Mary had seen them of late, and her skin had a certain glow about it.

"I hope so," she said finally. "They have to have been worried about us, as far behind schedule as we've fallen."

"Yes," Mary said thoughtfully. "But when you look at each of us, we weathered this trip fairly well, all considered. Ike's arm is healing and no one else has been injured."

Ma glanced at Meg, who was quietly talking to Jane and reading her a picture book. "And Meg seems to have conquered her fear," she said quietly. "I have worried about her so."

"Why did we leave our home back east?" Mary asked.

Ma dried a plate as she tilted her head, deep in thought. "Why does anybody move to a new place?" she said at last. "Isn't it always the notion that what's ahead is better than what we had before?"

"But we were happy. We had a big house with plenty of room for each of us. We had a working farm; we'd always been able to provide for ourselves and always had enough left to sell at the market. We had livestock, barns and fresh water—what could possibly be on the other side of the mountains that we didn't have back home?"

"It isn't just what you have at that particular point in time," Ma said. "It's what promise the future holds for each of you." She glanced about the boat at Ike and Billy on the bridge with the tiller and Sam on the deck sweeping the water with a long pole; Jean and Beth hanging clothes to dry on makeshift lines; Martha sitting quietly, writing poetry as she so often did; and Meg, Jane and Johnny playing a game of jacks. "There's more land for the taking out west. For each of you, that means the promise of a farm or a ranch, or whatever you want. It's fertile land, land that will sustain your children and your children's children for generations to come. They have needs out there, for doctors and lawyers and land surveyors, all manner of educated men. The opportunities for each of you are limitless."

Ma finished drying and carried the plates back to the cabin. Mary sat on a bench built onto the deck and surveyed the hills and woods that rose from the shoreline. Their speed had increased as the terrain dropped in elevation. They were through the mountain range now, she thought. They had made it.

Her thoughts turned to Hannah and her heart wanted to cry in pain. She longed for her friend and she knew as long as she lived, she would never forget her. There was still a chance, she told herself, that the Stuarts would appear just as the Jennings had, and all would be well once more.

She found herself searching for the sight of the Donelson boat, *The Adventure*, but it was too far ahead of them. She tried not to think of poor Baby Ephraim, but his tiny, trusting face as she'd held him at the abandoned Indian village kept popping up in her mind's eye. She wondered what Elizabeth must be going through at this very moment, knowing when they reached Muscle Shoals, her husband might be there waiting for her, anxiously awaiting his first glimpse of their baby.

She caught sight of Catherine Hutchings and her son, and her heart sank at the thought of Simon suffering with frostbite, his body buried somewhere behind them at a place none of them would ever see again. And young Mr. Payne, shot through with an Indian's round, stricken down in the prime of his life.

She thought of the Cotton family, what possessions they could save spread out among the other families, their boat gone.

And the Jennings wondering what fate had awaited their only son, Jonathan, his friend and their servant, and living with the thought that they had been abandoned in the moment of their greatest need.

Ma was right, she thought. Men always moved because they were looking for something more. They believed their futures would be brighter somewhere else; that fortunes were to be made on the other side of the mountains. But at what price were these fortunes won?

The vessels were slowing up ahead and a shout came back from boat to boat to pull ashore within the next mile. The river had begun to drop at a rate that even the scouts had difficulty navigating, and they'd taken to shouting from one vessel to another.

As they prepared to stop, the Neely children lined up along the side of the boat, eager to get a glimpse of the men who had come to meet them. Even Meg's face was lit up like the candles on a Christmas tree.

The oldest children joined Ma and Ike in using the poles to slow the flatboat. It was easier said than done, as the current was strong. They finally navigated to the northern shore and beached the boat alongside Captain Blackmore's.

There were no men ashore.

As the clamor and din of the boats coming ashore ceased, they were met with an eerie silence. The families stood motionless on their boats, staring into the woods and along the shoreline, searching for signs of the loved ones who had journeyed to Fort Nashborough by land and were to have met them here. But there were so signs and no sounds. Even the birds were quiet.

"I don't see 'em," Billy said. "But I don't see no Injuns neither."

"It's when you *don't* see 'em that you ought to be worried," Sam said, keeping his musket close.

At last, Captain Blackmore and Colonel Donelson climbed down from their boats. Captain Hutchings joined them, and slowly the men from other boats began to disembark. When Ma climbed off the boat, Mary took it as a cue to follow her. They joined the men as they gathered along the shore.

"Where are they?" Mr. Harrison was asking, his eyes wide.

"Don't panic," Colonel Donelson said calmly, though Mary thought his skin had grown paler. "We are weeks behind in our journey. They most likely returned to Fort Nashborough when we didn't arrive as expected.

"Fan out, men, and look for the provisions they promised to leave us. There will also be a map with directions for the overland trip, if it is practical for us to finish our journey by land."

As Captain Blackmore and Colonel Donelson divided the men into groups and pointed them in various directions, the women set about planning the next meal and caring for their broods. The dogs, now not much more than skeletons, joined the men, racing through the woods and barking, gleeful at finally leaving the confines of the boats.

With the prospect of an overland journey, those who were left behind began emptying the cabins as if engaged in spring cleaning. All manner of crates were unpacked and tallied and unscientifically weighed to determine how they would be moved overland. Furniture was dusted and checked for damage and mattresses, long kept in the confines of stifling cabins, were brought out and aired.

Clothes were washed along the shore and hung over bushes and the sides of the vessels, anywhere space could be found.

Having found nothing near the river, the men ventured deeper into the woods until they could no longer be seen. Only a few remained behind, guarding the families and boats.

As the minutes turned into hours, the women set about cooking a fish soup from their catch. But as Mary ventured to one boat after another to compare ingredients that could be combined to feed more families, she realized that a pall was settling over them. Instead of a victorious and happy reunion with those who had gone overland with Robertson, they were left only with empty hearts. And as the men hiked further inland, those left behind wondered whether the food they still possessed would have to be rationed for the unknown journey ahead.

In the end, the soups were nothing more than fish and water with a pitiful sampling of an occasional onion.

"What I wouldn't do right now," Mary said to Ma, "for just a bit of sassafras bark to flavor this water with!"

As the men began to return, their long, solemn faces spoke of their failure to find any sign that Robertson had ever been there. One after another shook their heads in silence, too stunned and weary to say more as they gathered in a circle along the shoreline.

"What are we to do now?" Captain Hutchings said. His voice was thin and strained.

As Colonel Donelson eyed the families about him, Mary thought he looked positively mortified. "It is too risky to journey overland," he said at last. "We must continue by way of the river."

A cry of protests grew, the voices becoming one.

Mr. Gower's voice rose above the rest. "How do we know Robertson even made it to Fort Nashborough?" he demanded. "How do we know they were not attacked by Indians and killed or captured?"

At his words, the clamor increased and the crowd pressed closer to Captain Blackmore and Colonel Donelson.

"We have nothing but faith," Donelson said. "If we give up now, what do we do? Settle here, while the Indians are still too close for us to live peaceably? Or continue our own journey westward to a place we know is habitable?"

"Colonel Donelson is right," Captain Blackmore said. "We have been to Fort Nashborough and we know what awaits us there. We have no choice but to continue our river journey."

"We will rest here," Donelson said, "and eat. Then we shall trim our boats and prepare ourselves for the next part of our journey. We have come so far—and we have only a short distance yet to go."

Mary listened to the protests and debates but in the end, it was settled. It was, as Captain Blackmore had said: they had no choice but to follow the river. And as she set to work scooping out the fish chowder, depositing a ladle full in each person's bowl, she hoped and prayed that Donelson was correct and their journey would soon be over.

# 42

It was early afternoon by the time every boat had been carefully inspected. Mary found it rather curious, as up to this point each family had been responsible for their own vessel in determining its seaworthiness. But today was different. Today, Captain Hutchings, Colonel Donelson and Captain Blackmore personally inspected each boat. They were tight-lipped and solemn, and Mary could only assume they were still mystified about James Robertson's absence.

But as they met along the shore for some final instructions, there was something different about this day that she just couldn't quite put her finger on.

The sun was still shining and the sky was bluer than she'd seen it since late last summer. Though there were clouds in the sky, they were the beautiful, fluffy ones that never heralded the approach of rain.

Most had shed layers of clothing, as it was a particularly warm day, unusual considering the freezing temperatures they'd endured thus far. It was as if spring was in the air, and as she peered toward the woods, she almost expected the trees to begin budding.

"We'll be continuing our journey in a short while," Donelson was saying. "And we're going to need each and every one of you to be fully prepared."

"Do you anticipate more Injun attacks?" a man in the rear asked.

"No. We have passed through Chickamauga Territory, and we don't anticipate any more Indian attacks… We're going to be heading into a treacherous part of the river."

Billy chuckled. "Seems like we just done that."

Donelson cleared his throat. "This is going to be a bit different. When we were briefed about the journey before leaving Fort Patrick Henry—by those who had journeyed here before—we were told that Muscle Shoals stretches for twenty-five or thirty miles."

The crowd remained silent, waiting for him to continue. His eyes scanned the men, women and children gathered around him. "These are rapids and we'll be experiencing a steep drop."

Several people moaned.

"Is that all?" Mr. Harrison asked. "With all we've been through, we can handle some rapids."

Captain Blackmore spoke up. "We've asked several of you to place your families on larger boats. Those with canoes, however large, have been asked to tie them up to larger vessels.

"We need all of you to check and double-check your cabins and secure everything, no matter how large or small. Remove everything from your decks that isn't necessary for navigation."

"I strongly suggest," Donelson added, "that you consider lashing yourselves to your boats in some fashion. There's a likelihood that the vessels will be pitched and tossed as we descend the rapids. We don't want anyone tossed overboard."

"And to that end," Captain Blackmore said, "if you find yourselves in trouble, we cannot go back for you. It won't be a matter of choice. We will be physically prevented from taking the river toward the east."

"Children and dogs should remain inside the cabins."

"Any questions?"

There were a few brief murmurings through the crowd. Mary looked at Ike, who motioned for the Neely clan to follow him back to their boat.

Once they had gathered at the Neely boat, Ike said, "I talked with Captain Hutchings a short while ago, and we're going to have to take the whole twenty-five or thirty miles at one time, without a break. There is no place to stop; no place to even slow down."

"Ike, Billy and Sam," Ma said, "check the cabin to make sure everything is tightly secured. Meg, Johnny and Jane will remain in the cabin. Martha, you stay with them and keep them safe."

Martha nodded but Mary could see from the look in her eyes that she wondered how she would manage that feat if anything were to go awry.

"Ike and Billy, I assume you two are planning to work from the bridge?" Ma continued.

They nodded.

"Then I will be at the bow," Ma continued. "Mary, you'll be at starboard, close to the front. Sam, you take the starboard close to the rear. Beth, port side. Since you'll be the only one on that side, stay toward the middle. Jean, you'll be at the stern."

As the family dispersed, Mary set about with her sisters fastening down or removing everything on deck. Each tied a rope around their waists and prepared to secure it to the flatboat before they launched.

"This seems about as necessary as slaughterin' a dead hog," Sam grumbled.

With the children and Patches secure in the cabin, they were ready to embark.

They watched *The Adventure* push away from shore, but the second one in line was holding. Mary could sense everyone's impatience; they were all ready to get this over with.

She spotted Jed Cobb walking along the shore, calling out to each boat in turn. When he reached the Neely boat, Mary strained to hear him as he shouted toward the bridge at Ike.

"Wait 'til the boat ahead o' you rounds that bend," he said.

Mary glanced downriver. The bend was a quarter of a mile away, leaving more space between each boat than they'd ever had before.

"Keep that distance between you and the next boat 'til we're through Muscle Shoals."

With that, he was off to the next boat.

Mary, Ma and Ike looked at each other in silence. Ma's eyes were taking on a hunted look, and Mary felt her stomach begin to tie in knots. She wished she hadn't eaten as much of the fish as she had. She was unaccustomed to the richness and already her stomach was churning.

Ike turned back to the bow, his brows furrowed and his face dark.

The minutes crept by as each boat cast off. It seemed as if the entire fleet was watching each individual boat as it gathered speed and moved downriver.

Finally, Captain Blackmore's launched. Mary found herself holding her breath, a tingling sensation starting up her arms toward her chest as she watched it approach the bend.

"Our turn," Ike shouted from the bridge.

All hands used the poles to push away from the shore before assuming their designated positions. As instructed, they tied their individual ropes to a secure point on the boat nearest them. Mary checked the knot once more before picking up the pole again.

They navigated toward the center of the river and moved toward the west, where the sun was shining brightly.

CR&D

They heard the noise before they spotted its source.

It sounded like a roar; at first, it was faint and distant but as they continued westward, it grew with frightening intensity. The river was moving swiftly, carrying their boat effortlessly. Mary was relieved; she'd had little to do except an occasional poke at the water to keep the boat from moving too far to the northern or southern shore.

Sam was complaining about the necessity of tying himself to the boat, as if it somehow infringed on his manhood, but Mary noticed he kept his grumblings just low enough so they were not heard by Ike or Ma.

"With this speed," Sam was saying, "we'll be through Muscle Shoals in short order."

"I'm glad!" Mary called back to him. "It puts us that much closer to Fort Nashborough and Pa!"

She realized she was shouting to be heard above the roar of

the rapids and as she turned to look westward, she spotted whitecaps along the river. She had only seen the ocean once in her life; she thought whitecaps only appeared in oceans and never in rivers.

She watched Captain Blackmore's boat gain momentum. It pitched as it hit the whitecaps and the hands on board struggled to keep it from turning sideways.

"Brace yourselves!" Ike shouted.

Though Mary thought they were prepared for the onslaught, when they hit the first set of waves it nearly knocked her off her feet and she scrambled to keep the pole securely in her hands.

The river was moving more swiftly now and the boat was picking up speed.

Somewhere in the distance, she heard a woman scream and then another, but their voices were quickly drowned out by the constant roar. It was deafening now, and the river was beginning to spray over the sides of the boat, coating the deck with slick, cold water. Mary's feet slid on the smooth deck and she struggled to remain upright.

Her pole was worthless now; the river was shallow but it pitched and tumbled so strenuously that she was unable to push off the river bottom to keep the boat leveled toward the west. The waves splashed over the sides with growing ferocity.

She glanced toward the west to get a sense of the width of the river and as she did, her hands froze around the pole. She felt her mouth drop open and despite the water lashing at her, it was as dry as a cotton boll.

Though they had been traveling downstream, it was as if they suddenly found themselves at the top of a great mountain. And as she looked below, she saw the river charging down the mountainside at an incline so steep that she felt despair welling up inside her.

"My God!" Ma exclaimed.

Mary wanted to look toward her or to look upwards at Ike for instructions, but she couldn't drag her eyes away from the horror that faced them.

The current no longer coursed westward but swirled in every direction as it wound down the mountainside. The whitecaps were as high as the tops of the boat cabins, soaking every person as they struggled to remain aboard their boats. They pitched from side to side, their boats swirling in the waters like leaves. She lost sight of the smaller boats entirely, only to see them pop up again further downstream.

"Hand me some soap!" Billy called out. "It'll be the best bath I've had in months!"

As Mary stared downward, she saw islands jutting out of the water directly in their path. They were littered with debris of every description—driftwood heaped as high as a house, tops of evergreens struggling to remain afloat, and against one island a battered canoe was raised high atop driftwood as if to warn others to stay away.

Ike shouted but his words were lost in the bellow of the river.

Mary wanted to stop, to go back, even if it meant returning through the hostile territory of the Chickamauga. They would never make it through this alive, she thought desperately. It was impossible.

She felt thunderstruck as her eyes scoured the surrounding terrain. There was no place to stop, no way to maneuver out of the river, no safe haven.

The boat pitched forward and then slammed downward as it took the first of the rapids. She caught a fleeting glimpse of Ike, his face contorted as he desperately tried to keep the boat pointed westward. The wind was sucked right out of her body as the boat dragged along the shallow river bottom, its speed increasingly as it swept through the water.

She swung her pole outward, though she wasn't sure if she was trying to row or trying to right the boat. Her movements were as ineffective as if she'd been slapping the waves with a kerchief.

She heard a scream and then another before realizing it was her own voice she heard as they careened downward. A mountain of floating debris soared in front of them and then it was beside them, so close she could have reached out her hand and grabbed it; but in the next instant it was gone.

The sound of wood splintering rose above the roar of the rapids and as she looked toward Ma, she caught the horror in her eyes. The blood was drained from her face and her skin appeared glazed with shock. She wondered briefly if her own face appeared the same, but then the boat was bouncing again and dragging the river bottom again and she was fighting to remain upright.

They looked like leaves in a rainstorm, unable to prevent the onslaught and powerless to stop it but fighting until they had no more breath in their bodies. Mary pitched against the side of the boat as it began to spin sideways, and she felt the desperate struggle of the entire family trying to right it before the next rapid dashed them against the islands of rocks and debris.

Above her, she was vaguely aware of Ike at one tiller and Billy at the other and as the boat spun, one tiller would lift while the other tried to right the boat, only to repeat the process with the opposite tiller a moment later.

The river no longer appeared like water but like the foamy hands of a giant mauling them unmercifully. The boat became airborne; Mary could feel the sensation of her stomach dropping, as if her head was floating and her body was not. Then it pounded downward against jagged rocks and the whole boat seemed to cave inward from the port side. Billy was suddenly swinging in the air, grappling to hold onto the tiller, appearing as if he would fall upon Mary and Sam at any second. Then between Ike's frantic efforts and the ropes tied about Billy's waist, he was snapped backward. From somewhere behind her, Mary caught a glimpse of a pole sailing through the air before it hit the deck and rolled toward the stern.

Then the starboard side was rolling upward, the pitch so steep that it knocked her to her knees. No sooner had she come to her feet than they were slammed again. Driftwood appeared in mid-air and then it was crashing down upon them.

Through the chaos, she saw blood streaming down her forearm and across her hands, but she felt nothing. It was as if she had already died and she was now looking downward at herself and her family, struggling onward against a foe they couldn't defeat. The water sprayed over the sides of the boat like an aggressive conqueror, rolling into her open mouth and causing her to choke.

This must be what drowning feels like, she thought.

She *was* drowning, Mary thought as the world around her became a watery swirl of faces and flying debris and the deafening roar of the river. They were all drowning.

# 43

Noquali tore off a piece of fresh, warm bean bread and chewed it thoughtfully as he listened to White Messenger.

"Our brothers, the Shawnee, have been forced to move farther and farther to the north and the west, away from the homes their fathers knew and their fathers before them," he was saying.

As he spoke, Noquali thought how unlike a white man he sounded and how much like a true Shawnee. He glanced across Jo-Leigh's cabin at his dead brother's wife and wondered what she thought of her newfound half-brother. They didn't physically resemble each other in the least, he thought as he watched her. But in their mannerisms, they were both calm and reserved, given to thoughtful dialogue in lieu of fiery speeches.

"Stay here with us and fight," Noquali urged. "We will push back the white men. Our vantage point here is excellent; we are almost inaccessible by the white men by land and we have the river defended well. We can drive them back to the other side of the mountains."

"What of those who escaped?" he asked quietly. "Boats filled with white men who move further west, even as we sit here speaking of their destruction."

His eyes narrowed. "They have not escaped. Not yet. Our brothers, the Creek, wait for them even now."

"And what of the others who come behind them?"

"We will kill them all. And the word will pass to those on the other side of the mountains that this land is defended by those who have a rightful claim to it. And they will learn to live to the east of the mountains and we shall remain to the west."

White Messenger ate of a mixture of corn and walnut before speaking. "My father, Eagle Feathers, had a dream in which he was visited by wise elders who have gone to the spirit world. In this dream, the elders told him our people would not be successful in keeping the white men from our lands. They will come with bigger guns and armies and drive us westward."

Noquali sneered. "So do you surrender like a dog to its master?"

White Messenger fixed his gaze upon Noquali. When he answered, his voice was calm. "We do not surrender. But our family is small and it grows even smaller. Eagle Feathers wishes to move to the north and west, where we might be greeted with peace and friendship."

Noquali nodded and broke off another piece of bread. He watched Jo-Leigh as she labored in front of the fireplace, occasionally stopping to mop sweat from her brow. He felt his skin grow hot as his eyes roamed from the beautiful woman to her bed on the other side of the room, where the two girls he had captured still remained.

"You are a fool," he said to Jo-Leigh. She turned to him, her brow arching as her eyes narrowed. "I bring you slaves and you treat them like chieftains." He motioned toward the bed.

"They are ill," she said.

White Messenger peered through the darkened cabin. The girls did not move but remained in each other's arms. "What is wrong with them?" he asked.

"They suffer from a great fever," she said.

He sipped a sweet fruit drink and gazed across the room. "How are you treating them?"

"With mullein. Their fingers and hands are swollen; it will reduce the swelling and the fever." She poured a tea-like substance into a cup and began walking toward the girls.

"I will take my leave," White Messenger said.

She stopped at the edge of the table and turned back to him. "I am glad we met."

He rose and placed his hand on her shoulder. "Though we will be far from each other in body, our spirits will remain as one."

Noquali rose and joined them. "Where do you go now?"

"It will soon be spring. We will journey to the lands toward the setting sun, where the hunting is said to be plentiful. We shall remain there through the summer before moving northward."

"These men we have fought, they also are moving to those lands."

"But they will not reach them," he said smoothly. "Our Creek brothers will stop them."

"Yes," Noquali said. "Our brothers." It was not lost on him that during another day and another time, the Cherokee fought against the Creek. The river had become the dividing point, keeping the Cherokee to the north and the Creek and the Chickasaw to the south. Now they were joined together in a common fight, the fight for the survival of their peoples.

"What became of the man you scalped yesterday?" White Messenger asked.

Noquali shrugged. "The white trader, Rogers, has enslaved him. They left Tuskagee Island Town early this morning."

"So he is yet alive?"

"Barely." Noquali smiled and pointed to the woven belt around his waist, where a dozen scalps hung. "This one is his," he said, staring at one in adoration. "I took a good portion of his scalp. If he lives, he will be worthless, as I sheered it to the bone."

"Rogers paid well for the boy."

"Yes." He puffed out his chest.

"Why?"

"Perhaps he thinks he can sew a new scalp on him," he laughed. "Perhaps one of those furs he is always trading."

Jo-Leigh started to move toward the girls, but White Messenger gently stopped her. As she turned to look back at him, he said, "If you are in need, you are always welcome within our lodge."

Noquali felt his cheeks grow hot. "She will be well cared for," he said abruptly. His eyes landed on the cup she still held in her hand. "Why do you give in to these slaves, feeding them in your own bed, giving them drink? They play you for a fool."

He took the cup from her hand and set it on the table, where it sloshed onto the warm wood. "It is time they work."

With White Messenger and Jo-Leigh on his heels, he strode to the other side of the cabin and flung the furs off the girls. He expected them to appear startled or frightened, but neither moved. Scowling, he wrapped his large, bronzed hand around the younger girl's neck, but as he did so, his eyes widened.

"What is it?" Jo-Leigh asked.

"She is cold," he said. His voice was low and disbelieving.

Jo-Leigh rushed to her side. She sat on the bed and as Noquali withdrew his hand, she felt of her forehead. "She had been hot with the fever," she said.

Noquali watched as Jo-Leigh's hands moved from her forehead to her cheeks and chest. Her hands were clammy-looking. He wondered if she had become too warm herself while preparing their meal.

When she looked up at him, her hazel eyes were wide. She began blinking rapidly. "She is dead," she managed to say.

Noquali reached for the other girl. She moaned slightly, her voice barely audible. "When did you give them mullein last?"

"Before I fell asleep last night," she said softly. "I held each one in my arms and fed them the drink." She mopped perspiration from her brow and gathered the other girl in her arms. Her head lolled backward and Jo-Leigh gently cradled her.

"One girl is dead and the other is dying," Noquali said.

Jo-Leigh looked up at him. Her eyes were moist and sad, but there was something else there. As Noquali stared into them, he wondered if she had come to like these girls. No; it was impossible. They had been weak when he captured them and they had only remained in her home for a few short days. Besides, they were white women and slaves.

But as his eyes locked on hers, he noticed a pain that had not been there before. The perspiration grew on her brow and her cheeks were flushed. Abruptly, he took the girl from her, returning her to the bed. Then he took her thin clothing in his fist and ripped it away from her body, revealing her naked skin.

Her chest was covered in dome-shaped lesions filled with pus. He spread her clothing away from her, revealing the lesions amid ugly scabs and pitted scars across her entire body. The girl moaned again but her eyes did not open.

He turned to the dead girl, ripping her clothes away from her body. Her skin was even more ravaged by the sores.

"How long have you known they were like this?" he demanded.

Jo-Leigh moved to cover the surviving girl with her ripped clothing and the bedding.

"How long have you known?"

"I bathed them the first night they were here," she said. "And I discovered their fever then. It was so intense that it broke through their skin. I thought if I reduced their fever, the sores would stop…"

As Noquali stared at her in disbelief, he realized the perspiration had grown so heavy that it was beginning to drip off her onto the bedding. With one rapid movement, he reached for the nape of the buckskin dress and pulled it from her.

She gasped in astonishment and moved to cover her neck. White Messenger grasped his hand, and he reluctantly let go. The skin had been too thick and tough to tear, but he had seen enough. Moving upwards from her chest and covering her neck were tiny red spots, so flat and small that in the semi-darkness, he could barely see them.

"Come to the light," he ordered. "Let me see your skin."

"No." She held her dress against her neck, her arms now covering her body as if protecting herself.

White Messenger covered the cabin in a few short steps, grabbing a candle from the table and returning to their sides. As he held the candle close to her, the flawless skin Noquali loved began to take on an uneven look. The red spots had covered her face, but unlike those on her neck, they were beginning to bulge outward.

He stared at her in stunned silence. Somewhere out of the corner of his eye, he once more became aware of the two girls on the bed, one dead and the other dying. He felt White Messenger's breath close to him as he continued holding the candle near Jo-Leigh's face, perhaps too confounded to move it away. And he became intensely aware of Jo-Leigh's beautiful face now marked with these mysterious red bumps, her hair drenched with perspiration and her eyes revealing a feverish pain.

"I brought them into your home," he said at last, "and they have placed a curse upon us."

# 44

Mary's legs were so unsteady she thought she would surely fall before she had walked the short distance from the boat to the others gathering along the shore.

They had made it through the rapids. For three grueling hours, they had battled the waves that pounded their boat unmercifully. Each of them had been whipped off their feet more than once and saved only by the ropes they'd tied around them. She'd thought many times of Meg, Johnny and Jane in the cabin, but she was helpless to go to their aid and had prayed that God would take care of them.

When they were through the last of the rapids, Ma had quickly untied herself to check on her youngest before making the rounds past the others to make sure everyone was alright. They all had bumps and bruises and several had rope burns around their waists despite their heavy clothing, but they were alive.

"That was the most incredible experience I've had in my whole dang life!" Sam was exclaiming.

Mary sank to the ground beside Elizabeth Peyton and Catherine Hutchings before looking at Sam's face. It was lit up like a candle. He wasn't sitting but standing among the other young men, comparing their experiences.

"Did you see that one waterfall? It dropped fifty feet, I swear it did! Straight down!" Reuben Harrison said.

"Our boat turned all the way around so's I was lookin' at Captain Blackmore!" another one added.

"If I live to be a hun'ered an' ten, I will never, ever forget this," Billy said. "I wish I could go back and ride it again!"

Ma dropped to the ground beside Mary, pulling Meg and Jane into her lap. Little Johnny raced to Billy's side, jumping in with his own experiences as though he was already a teenager rather than barely six years old.

"The furniture was a-teeterin'," he was saying, "and we thought it was gonna collapse right on our heads!"

Mary shook her head. "I can't believe they were on the same boat I was on," she said.

"Isn't that just the way Life is?" Ma said quietly.

"What do you mean?" Elizabeth asked. It was the first time she'd ventured off *The Adventure* since the Jennings had been reunited with the rest of the group, and Mary thought she looked utterly spent.

"We can all go through the very same experience," Ma said. "But each one of us handles it differently. Take those boys there; they're acting like they just had the time of their lives." She pointed toward the far end of the shore nearest the woods. Mrs. Harrison was bent almost double with dry heaves and a short distance away, several others were following suit. "But look what the same experience did to them."

Mary glanced around the camp, taking in the line of boats along the shore and the people milling around on deck and disembarking. "And those folks over there," she said, waving her hand, "look like they've just seen a ghost. I don't think they looked that terrified when the Indians attacked."

"Maybe," Ma said thoughtfully, stroking Meg's hair, "it's not what happens to us in Life, but how we handle it. We're goin' into a dangerous world, and we're gonna need to be strong in mind and spirit to survive it."

Their musings ceased as Colonel Donelson approached the group. "Gather 'round, folks," he called out.

He stopped a short distance from Mary. The women remained on the ground as he spoke.

"We're stopping here for the night. A few men have agreed to do a bit of hunting; anybody who wants to join in, see Captain

Blackmore. Game should be plentiful around here, from what I've been told.

"I'll need for each family to check their boat thoroughly. Report any damage to me, especially if there's any question of how sound it is. We leave here early tomorrow morning."

"How close are we to the end of our journey?" Mr. Harrison asked.

Donelson rubbed his chin before answering. "According to my calculations, we should be within a week to ten days from the Ohio River. We travel north on the Ohio until we reach the Cumberland River, which should only be a few days' travel. Then it's smooth sailing right into Fort Nashborough, which sits on the banks of the Cumberland."

"Fort Nashborough is just about due north from where we sit this minute," Captain Blackmore said. "That's why it was so important for Captain Robertson to send an envoy to Muscle Shoals. Had we been able to travel overland, it would have cut our time just about in half. But without a message waiting for us there, we had no way of knowing whether any Indians were nearby. We're safer staying on the river."

"The good news is, we've passed Chickamauga Territory," Donelson added. "We're safe now. They won't follow us this far."

A series of whoops and hollers went up from the crowd. People patted each other on the back and congratulated each other on surviving not only the rapids but the constant Indian attacks.

For Mary, it was bittersweet. She paused to look at her family—Jean and Martha already pulling out cooking utensils and planning the night's supper; Ma with Meg and Jane hanging onto her as though they'd never let her go; Beth writing a note to a beau she'd left behind—though only God knew how it would ever make its way back to him; Ike, dutifully inspecting the boat's hull; and Billy, Sam and Johnny amid their friends with the silliest grins Mary had seen in a long time.

Her heart yearned for George and she wondered how he could ever follow her out west through this perilous river and past Chickamauga Territory; she wondered if she'd ever see him again. She longed for her old home and her comfortable bed and warm fires, the familiar trails, the flower gardens and the hounds. She thought of that night that seemed so long ago, when she and Hannah had peered to the floor below, excited to be embarking on their first real adventure.

How she missed Hannah! She feared she might never see her again. The hours that had turned into days and then weeks, when she'd thought of reuniting with her on the river had turned to distress when she'd learned she had small pox. And only the Good Lord knew where she was now… and whether she was dead or alive. She said a silent prayer for her, but it did not ease the ache in her heart.

"Mary, did you hear me?"

Ma's voice interrupted her thoughts and she realized the other women had already come to their feet.

"Ma'am?"

"Get some pots of water boiling so we'll be ready for the meat when the men bring it back."

"Yes, ma'am." She rose shakily to her feet and made her way back to the Neely boat.

CB&D

That night they dined on buffalo. It was the first time most of them had ever tasted it, and Mary had to admit it was rather good, though Billy was quick to point out that it didn't taste like chicken. The men had come upon a herd not far from camp and had brought back enough meat to sustain them for several days. Some had found a cache of hickory nuts and though they'd no doubt been lying on the forest floor for several months, they were a nice addition to the meal. One enterprising man located some mulberry trees and while it was too early in the season for the fruits to emerge, he uprooted one and brought it back to his boat, where it now sat in a kettle of soil, hopefully to bear fruit in the coming weeks.

Some of the men spotted coyotes in the distance and were debating whether their meat was edible.

"It'd be like eatin' a dog," one of them was saying, "I just couldn't force myself to do that."

"We just 'et buffalo and that's one ugly critter," Sam said, "but the meat's mighty good. And as hungry as I've been, I'd eat just about anythin' I could shoot. 'specially since there ain't no more vegetables—or fruits—or nothin'."

As Mary looked upward at the sky filling with stars, she wondered how soon spring would arrive and how quickly Mother Nature would begin her cycle of replenishment.

It wouldn't be soon enough, she thought as she leaned against a tree. It wouldn't be soon enough.

# 45

Noquali stood at the entrance to the communal building beside Bloody Fellow. In a few weeks, winter would be gone and the trees would begin to sprout their leaves and flowers; their heavy clothing and furs would be put away for another year; and another season of planting and harvesting would begin. During any other year, this would have invoked in him a lighter, more carefree spirit as the end of yet another wicked winter drew to a close.

But as he stared across the village at the log cabins with their roofs providing steady drips of melting snow, his heart was heavy. His eyes fell upon the path to Jo-Leigh's home, and he fought the impulse to tear his clothing from his body in a gesture of frustration and guilt.

"You could not have known," Bloody Fellow said quietly.

"I have brought a curse to your village," Noquali said. "And a curse upon my brother's wife."

Bloody Fellow stepped onto the path and turned toward the edge of the village. Noquali followed him as he walked. As they passed other villagers, he avoided eye contact, keeping his focus on the ground in front of him. The word would have spread like wildfire and now everyone would know it was he who brought sickness into their midst.

"Both girls are dead?" Bloody Fellow asked.

"Yes. The second died during the night."

"And Jo-Leigh?"

"She is afflicted with their disease."

He stopped for a brief moment, deep in thought. After a moment, he continued on without speaking.

"White Messenger has gone to find his Shawnee mother, Medicine Woman. It is said she can cure the diseases the white men bring," Noquali said.

"That is good. But we have no time to waste. I have sent for the shamans, who will prepare the ceremony to drive the curse from our village. They will be here today and they will bring the strength of the Great Spirit with them."

They reached a fork in the path and Bloody Fellow stopped again. He stood for a long moment, his eyes tracing the path toward Jo-Leigh's cabin before turning in the other direction.

"Go to her," he said. "And bring her tonight wrapped in blankets for the shamans to cure."

"Yes," Noquali said. He started down the path before stopping abruptly. He turned to apologize again for bringing the curse to Tuskagee Island Town, but Bloody Fellow was already well down the other path, and he turned back with a heavy heart.

He felt a wave of sadness sweep over him as he continued toward Jo-Leigh's home. By the time he reached her doorway, his stomach had contracted into a tight knot.

He eased the door open. An oppressive heat swept over him, making it difficult to breathe. He stood in the semi-gloom, waiting for his eyes to adjust to the darkness.

"Close the door!" a woman's voice begged in the darkness. "Close the door!"

He stepped inside and complied. Stepping toward Jo-Leigh's bed, he came face to face with Adsila, a crippled Cherokee woman.

"She is resting," she said, taking his hand in her gnarly fingers and leading him to her bed.

The cabin was thick with the stench of wood fire and sickness, and he immediately began to shed his heavy outer garments. As he neared her bed, he could barely make out her form as she was covered from neck to toes in layer upon layer of furs and blankets.

"The sickness can be driven from her by sweating it out through the skin," Adsila said. "We must keep the fire strong and many blankets atop her. She must not have fresh air or cold air or the sickness will grip her."

Noquali walked to the side of her bed and gazed into her face. She opened her eyes slowly and at first, she did not appear to recognize them. Then a tired smile crawled across her face.

He sat on a stool beside her. He wanted to take her hand into his own, but her limbs were beneath the heavy blankets; and he would not have impeded her recovery for his yearning to uncover and hold her hand.

Her face was swollen now with growing sores that seemed to emerge even faster and larger in the oppressive heat. Her skin had been so smooth, so radiant, he thought miserably. The Cherokee prized beautiful skin and Jo-Leigh was the most beautiful one of them all—

He placed a fist against his forehead and leaned against her coverings. How could he have done this to her?

"Do not worry."

The voice surprised him; it barely sounded like his beloved Jo-Leigh. He raised his head and looked into her eyes. They were filled with pain and sweat poured from her, drenching her head and her lovely raven hair.

"Do not worry," she repeated. Her lips were cracked and dry and when she spoke, her voice was barely more than a parched whisper.

"Water," Noquali said, motioning for Adsila.

"She cannot drink of cool water," Adsila said, hobbling toward them. "She must remain in the heat, inside and out."

Jo-Leigh closed her eyes and a single tear escaped and ran down the side of her face.

"She must have water," Noquali urged.

Adsila limped toward the opposite side of the cabin, where she scooped a cup into a kettle that hung over the raging fire. She was back in a moment and handed the cup to him. "It is a special mixture," she said, "that will help to draw the curse from her."

Gently, he raised her head. Her hair was so wet that it hung in folds and left a trail of perspiration across his arm. He held the cup to her lips. At first, she tried to turn her head as the steam rose from the brew, but he urged her to drink and after several seconds, she tried but could barely swallow more than a couple of small sips.

He handed the cup back to Adsila but he hesitated to return her to the bed. Instead, he gathered the blankets and furs around her and pulled her to him. She opened her eyes again, briefly resting them on him before a chill overtook her and she began to shake.

Adsila handed him more blankets, which he continued to pile on top of her and he sat there with her head and her upper body in his lap, stroking her face and her hair as she returned to sleep. And he remained there, rocking her and cradling her, as the hours crept by and the candles burned to tiny puddles of tallow.

# 46

On March 14, Mary observed the sun rising earlier and she wondered how she had not noticed during the past month. The night before, she'd also taken note of the fact that the sunset occurred later, as much as an hour later than it had only the month before. It seemed to herald the beginning of a new phase in their journey, a more peaceful, tranquil phase as they traveled westward on the Tennessee River.

The last two days had been filled with the monotony of the river. They'd all taken turns with the poles and tillers and keeping the boat in line. The currents remained strong but manageable, propelling their vessels westward with a new urgency. They'd stopped at mid-day and some of the men had gone hunting but returned with pitiful rations—not much more than a few rabbits and squirrels.

The fruit and vegetables were long gone and the cornmeal and flour about finished as well. It would soon be necessary to live off the land entirely and with spring not yet ready to arrive, it meant living off what they could hunt or fish.

They continued using the makeshift fishnets, but had caught only a few meager fish.

The nights were worse. It seemed when the blackness set in, their fears rose to terrifying levels. Though each boat had to provide sentries through the night, there was always a sense that an Indian attack could be imminent and the entire fleet seemed to sleep with one eye open.

Meg was experiencing an alarming number of nightmares, waking them all with her screams and cries. Jean, Ma and Mary took turns cradling her and soothing her, but she slept fitfully, often sleeping upright with her back pressed against the corner wall. She had dark circles under her eyes and often fell asleep during the daylight hours, though never more than a few minutes at a time. Her reflexes were slowing; Mary noticed that Johnny and Jane were becoming too much for her to handle alone, and dutifully, Jean had stepped in to fill the void, often washing dishes with Johnny at her side or working the poles with Jane wedged against her skirts.

Beth spent a lot of time combing her long sandy hair and lamenting over the lack of toiletries. She'd had so many beaus back east and although there were many men of marrying age in the fleet, no one had an interest in courtship. No; it seemed that everyone had only one thing on their minds these days: survival.

That now meant finding enough to eat each day. And on an emotional level, it meant trying to look forward to the end of this hellish journey and to the day when they could leave these boats forever.

"I swear to God," Sam had said more than once, "when we reach Fort Nashborough, I aim to burn this here boat. I don't never intend to look on it again!"

As the afternoon wore on, Mary took a much-needed break from poling and sat on a wooden bench near the center of the open deck. The sun was warm enough for her to peel away some of the outer layers of clothing. She removed her gloves and stretched out her hands in the sunshine. Her nails were dirty and broken and her skin rough, and she wondered with a sinking heart whether they would ever again be as smooth as they once were.

Jean was sitting cross-legged on the deck as she taught Johnny and Jane how to play fivestones. She'd picked up some pebbles during their last stop, and now she was tossing a ball into the air. Mary watched her snatching as many pebbles as she could and then grabbing the ball before it hit the deck on a second bounce. Patiently, she taught Johnny and Jane to pick up a onesie, then a twosie, working their way up to a tensie. They were immersed in the game and Jane's squeal of pleasure was enough to almost make her forget the hardships of the river.

Meg was sitting close by but her head had lolled forward so her chin was resting on her chest. Her eyes were sunken and periodically she jerked and gasped in her sleep. Mary wondered if she would ever recover from her terrors, but she quickly pushed the thought to the back of her mind. She would have to recover; they all would. They had no choice.

Sam and Billy were on the bridge. Sam was cleaning and oiling one of the muskets and bragging about the time he'd shot two deer with one shot. They'd been standing so close to one another that one shot had gone clear through one animal and into the other. Billy was listening intently as he half-heartedly worked the tiller.

"Why it's necessary for me to stand here like this, I'll never know," Mary heard him say. "We ain't goin' nowhere but west on this here river."

Ma was at the bow, occasionally using her pole to help keep the boat in the middle of the river behind Captain Blackmore's boat. Captain Hutchings' boat was closer to the southern shore and would have been almost between the Blackmore and Neely boats, had he been closer. Behind him was Mr. Boyd's boat.

Ike was in the cabin getting some much needed sleep. It seemed to fall upon him as the eldest son to monitor the sentries during the long, black nights. He'd lost a great deal of weight, as they all had, but he never complained. Mary often saw him giving some of his food to Johnny, though she knew even if he'd eaten his full ration, it wouldn't have been enough.

Martha was sitting nearest the railing, writing. She often wrote poems, which she would read to the others and Mary had taken to putting some of the poetry to music.

It was an idyllic afternoon, inasmuch as it could be, considering their circumstances.

Mary stretched her legs and rubbed her aching calves through the thick skirt.

Meg jerked again and raised her head, her eyes flying open as if from a fresh nightmare. As her head fell back against the cabin, Mary caught a glimpse of a small object sailing through the air just under her chin. At the moment she spotted it, she heard a rapid cluster of gunfire cutting through the still air.

"Get down!" she screamed, throwing her body across the deck. She brought Meg to the wood floor with one swoop of her arm as gunfire erupted around them. Out of the corner of her eye, she saw Jean throwing herself similarly on top of Jane and Johnny, trying to shield the youngest children from the onslaught.

Sam had raised his musket and was instantly returning fire. Ma was at the bow, her arms frantically pushing the pole through the water in a desperate attempt to outrun the Indians. She was shouting over her shoulder at Mary and Beth, but Mary couldn't make out her words above the din.

Ike burst through the cabin door as a round splintered the wood beside his head. He tossed a musket, shot bag and powder horn to Mary before he began to return fire.

It was then she realized what her mother was shouting: the weapons needed reloading.

"Stay down!" Mary shouted to Meg as she half-crawled, half-ran toward the cabin, below Billy and Sam. She tossed the musket up to Sam as he passed his own back down to her, and she hurriedly reloaded. No sooner had she finished than he was passing the other back down and she was tossing the first one up and repeating the process. Then Billy was grabbing the musket before Sam was able, and Mary was struggling to keep both of them ready to fire.

As she glanced about her, she realized Beth was doing the same for Ike and Martha had rushed to the bow to help Ma propel the boat forward. As she turned her face upward, she saw a rush of air ripple through Billy's coat as he cried out in pain. He stumbled, almost falling off the bridge before he struggled to regain his footing.

"Keep on a-shootin'!" he shouted to Sam as his brother halted to help him. "Don't worry 'bout me!"

Sam redoubled his efforts as Billy got back to his feet. Mary's eyes were unblinking now, as though in a flash she could miss the very thing that would mean the difference between life and death. She kept the muskets loaded as best she could even while she saw the blood beginning to soak Billy's coat and run down his pants leg.

She heard another cry from an adjoining boat, and she turned quickly to see Captain Hutchings grappling between two rifles as Catherine kept them loaded. His arm was bleeding but he didn't seem to notice as he fired repeatedly toward the southern shore.

A servant on Mr. Boyd's boat was struck, his scream piercing the air as he sank to his knees.

Then as quickly as they'd begun, the shots from land began to diminish.

Mary's heart was pounding so strongly that her chest felt as if it would explode. The world was swimming around her: Ike shooting with Beth by his side, Billy and Sam firing more slowly now with more careful aims, and then Billy's musket sinking to his side before he turned unsteadily on his feet and stared with glassy eyes over the water.

As the fleet raced westward, Jean got the smallest children to their feet and hustled them into the cabin. Then as the last of the shots died away, the Neely clan sprang into renewed action. Sam raced to work the tiller while Ike climbed the ladder and brought Billy down from the bridge.

"Get my sewin' kit!" Ma called to Mary. "Bring me some water!"

They cleared the deck, making a place for Billy to lie down. Then Ike joined Sam on the bridge, keeping one eye on the water and the other on Ma and his sisters as they gathered around Billy.

Billy grimaced and fought back a moan as his coat was pulled from him. His shirt and waistband were in tatters and soaked in blood. But as Ma poured water on the wound to clean it and she began to poke and prod him, she declared the shot had passed cleanly through.

While she bandaged him, Mary glanced at the other boats, where Catherine was tending to Captain Hutchings' arm and Mrs. Boyd was removing a round from their servant. There was a flurry of activity on the other vessels, and Mary wondered how many had been shot.

For the first time, she realized Meg was gone. She rose unsteadily to her feet and made her way to the cabin, where she found her on the mattress with Johnny and Jane pulled close to her. It was an image Mary had seen too many times, an image she had hoped she wouldn't have to see again. Only this time, she wondered if Meg realized how close she had come to being shot. Mary shuddered at the thought of the round coming so close to her little sister's face; and she closed her eyes as if to ward off the image.

She returned to the hatch and looked eastward at the wake their boat made in the river as it sped away from the Indians, who now stood amassed on shore watching them fade away.

# 47

Colonel Donelson declared they had been attacked by the Creek and possibly Chickasaw, though Mary didn't know how anyone could have positively identified them in the heat of the attack. Ike said they were too far west now for the Chickamaugas and the traders and pioneers who had traveled this route before had most likely informed Colonel Donelson of the possibility of Creek Territory.

"You'd think he might'a shared that information," Sam had complained. "We might'a been better prepared."

But as they made camp that evening near the mouth of a creek, Mary didn't care whether they were Chickamauga, Creek or Chickasaw. They were Indians, and as far as she was concerned, all Indians were out to kill them.

The woods here were set back from the shoreline. Colonel Donelson decided it was too dangerous for the men to hunt while in Creek Territory. Mary was grateful they still had some buffalo broth left and a few fish that had been snared during the afternoon. A handful of women ventured along the wood line, searching for kindling.

The air was warmer here, Mary thought as she gathered the small pieces of wood into her apron. She could hear the laughter of small children as she worked and she marveled at their resiliency.

A spot of greenery caught her eye and she instinctively recoiled. Why, it's grass, she thought. It's green grass! Her heart soared at the thought of springtime arriving, and she began to wonder what types of flowers would bloom where they were going, what types of trees they had, and what their new land would look like.

She spotted a plant nearby and meandered deeper into the woods to examine it. It was a fern, she thought in wonderment. A wild fern. She quickly began pulling off the fresh, tightly curled tops. This would be an amazing delicacy, she thought with pride, green salad with their evening meal!

They were everywhere—twisting and snaking their way through the forest floor, their little green hats seeming to beckon to her to follow. Her apron was filled with them now and with bursting pride, she realized she had enough to feed the entire Neely clan.

She hadn't realized how much time had passed until she discovered how difficult it had become to spot the ferns in the waning light. She stood upright and peered around her. The women who had been working alongside her were gone.

She cocked her head and listened but she no longer heard the laughter of the children. There was nothing but the occasional bird calling out in the dusk.

She narrowed her eyes and studied the ground around her. Which way had she come? She wondered with rising panic. She tried to see the ferns but the ground was in shadows now. She took what she thought was the path she had taken, using her feet to feel for the plants whose tops she had so recently cropped. As she scrutinized the trees around her, she realized in her earnest effort to gather the ferns, she had kept her head and eyes downward, taking no notice of her surroundings. As a result, the trees appeared totally unfamiliar.

The forest floor was uneven and she repeatedly stubbed her toes on protruding roots; even with her shoes protecting her feet, she winced with the pain. Twice she stumbled and fought to keep her precious cargo from spilling out of her apron as she regained her footing.

I couldn't have come this way, she thought. The mere notion she could be lost threatened to unnerve her. The trunks were too close together; she would have noticed that as she bent to pick up the ferns. She tilted her head back, trying to peer through the tops of the trees to the disappearing sun. Which way was west?

She stopped in a small clearing, her heart pounding so strongly she could plainly feel it in her head. They had camped on the northern shore, the shore opposite the Indian attack. She stood facing the last of the light that filtered through the trees. That had to be west then, she thought. She turned to her right. Then this is north. She whirled around to the opposite direction. Then this is south, she thought, pursing her lips. This was the way back to the boats and the river.

A movement caught her eye and she jerked her head to her left. She caught a flash of red through the forest. It was a face, watching her, she thought. It has to be. She took two steps toward it. It appeared again as it peeked around a large tree trunk, and then it was gone.

"You're not scaring me this time, Billy," she hollered with more conviction than she felt. With her brother's mischievous eyes following her, she felt a renewed sense of confidence. She couldn't be that far from the boat, and she wouldn't give him the satisfaction of knowing she'd been frightened.

She continued through the woods with her head held high, hoping she was going in the right direction or she'd never hear the end of it. She kept her hands knotted in her apron and tried to concentrate on the joy of showing the fresh vegetables to her family.

When at last she broke through the wood line, the sun was nothing more than a red glimmer quickly fading on the horizon.

As she made her way to the Neely boat, she spotted Ma standing over the kettle, stirring the broth that would be their supper. She stood upright as Mary approached.

"Where have you been, girl?" she demanded.

Mary opened her apron. "I found ferns for a salad!" she said, her cheeks flush with pride.

Ma took one of the curled ferns and bit into it. Her eyes closed and a wide smile crept across her face as if the tiny bit of greenery was a sweet and rare delicacy.

"I had forgotten how good they taste!" she said, opening her eyes. "Where did you find them?"

"In the woods over yonder," Mary said, motioning toward the wood line. As her eyes swept behind her, her blood froze. Billy was painstakingly helping to move a heavy piece of furniture from the cabin of *The Adventure*.

"What's Billy doing?" she asked.

"Oh, it's just some of the Jennings' furniture. They are trying to redistribute it so some of the boats can move faster. I think that piece is going onto the Hutchings' boat."

"How long has Billy been helping them?"

Ma shrugged and went back to the broth. "He started right before you left to get some kindling. Don't you remember?"

"And he's been there the whole time?" Mary felt her throat constricting.

"Between there and the Hutchings' boat," Ma said. "Now Mary, don't dawdle. Get that salad rinsed off and we'll have it with our soup tonight."

૦૩૪૦

The dogs began barking almost as soon as the sun disappeared. Colonel Donelson ordered the fires extinguished after supper, choosing safety over warmth. Mary was actually relieved, as the light from the campfires glowed around her.

Billy had been quiet during their meal and unusually serious. As the dogs continued their incessant barking, the attention of the entire family was focused on the woods. Mary barely tasted the salad she had so carefully harvested and while the buffalo soup warmed her throat it tasted like nothing more than boiled water.

Sam was the first to finish eating. He laid his plate upon the ground and picked up a musket. He stood at the edge of their campfire, staring into the woods. His mouth was tight and his eyes narrowed.

"I swear, somethin's out there," Sam said.

Ike's eyes wandered from his brother to the boats and finally to the other families. As Mary followed his gaze, she noticed the others were also watching the woods and the dogs.

"I'll take the first watch," Ike said.

"I'll stand it with you," Sam immediately responded.

Ma rose to her feet and kicked dirt over the campfire. "Jean and Billy, get some sleep. You'll be relieving them in a few hours." She picked up Sam's plate, her eyes turning toward the darkening forest. "Mary and Beth, wash the dishes. Don't waste any time."

Mary sprang to her feet. "You don't have to tell me twice," she said as she gathered them. "This place is giving me the willies."

She hurriedly carried the plates to the river, where she rinsed them out. The dogs were growling now, their teeth bared as they stared toward the trees. As Mary and Beth hoisted the kettle onto the boat deck, she noticed Patches' fur was standing straight up along her backbone.

She had no sooner returned to the cabin than the word was passed from boat to boat that everyone was to remain aboard during the night, including the sentries.

CR80

Mary was sleeping fitfully when she felt the boat jerk under her. She bolted upright. Through the murky darkness of the cabin, she made out Meg, Jane, Johnny and Martha, but Ma and the others were gone.

She climbed off the mattress.

"Mary?"

Meg's voice was tentative and high-pitched.

"Stay here," Mary said.

She felt her way to the hatch, grabbing the musket they kept next to it. Then opening the hatch a small crack, she peered into the darkness.

Ma and Jean were using the poles to push away from shore. As Mary ventured further out, she spotted Ike and Billy on the bridge, steering the boat toward the center of the river. Sam and Beth were on the port side.

"Go back to bed," Ma said when she spotted her.

"What's happening?"

"We're leaving. The men think Indians are afoot; they may be aiming to attack us in our sleep."

"Then why do I have to go back to bed? Can't I help?"

"You'll be taking the next shift," Ma said, grunting as she struggled to push the boat further from shore, "and you'll be up the rest of the night. Now go back to bed and get some sleep—while you can."

# 48

By the time Mary awakened, the sun was shining brightly through the door crack. She was in no hurry to rise; she'd spent much of the night on deck, helping to move the flatboat westward in the darkness. They'd stopped at dawn on the opposite shore and no sooner had they come ashore than Mary was slipping under the covers on the flattened mattress.

She pulled the quilt over her shoulders and turned on her side. No one else shared the bed; she thought of stretching out luxuriously, but it was too cold and she remained almost in a fetal position. She heard soft snoring across the cabin and peered over the quilt at Sam, who had also remained on deck throughout the night. He was now fast asleep; his long, lean body obscured by the mountain of quilts atop him, his dark brown hair tussled.

She closed her eyes and tried to go back to sleep, but each time she almost drifted off, she thought of Indians lurking in the woods; Indians firing upon them, killing and capturing them. It was daytime, she reassured herself, and so many would be afoot along the shore that the likelihood of an Indian attack was greatly diminished. But the logic did little to calm her fears and finally, she reluctantly sat up in bed and began to stretch.

She heard the murmur of voices just beyond the boat. It wasn't unusual, with so many brothers and sisters. But as her mind began to shift from the comfort of the warm bed to the events of another day, she recognized another voice: that of John Caffrey.

She climbed out of bed and ran her hands through her hair, attempting to straighten it before opening the cabin door. When she emerged, Mr. Caffrey, Colonel Donelson, his son Johnny, and Ike were deep in conversation.

While Mary had been sleeping, Mr. Caffrey and Johnny had returned to the clearing they'd left so hastily the previous evening. They were anxious to determine whether the Indians had intruded into their campsite after their departure.

"It was just as we'd left it," Mr. Caffrey was saying.

"Two pots had been left on account of 'em bein' too hot to move," Johnny added, "and they were still there with soup left in 'em."

"There was even a servant still asleep agin' the tree!" Mr. Caffrey said with a chuckle. "One of Captain Hutchings' men. He was sound asleep and when we roused him, he didn't even know we'd all left and he was there by his lonesome!"

They all got a good laugh out of that, and Mary thought they might have been laughing more out of relief than from the humor. If the Indians had not ventured into the clearing, it meant they might not have been in imminent danger last evening.

"Then what were the dogs barking at?" Ike mused, as if reading her mind.

Johnny shrugged. "Might have been wild animals. We saw a black bear on our trip back there... Or could have been deer... 'coons... anythin'."

Colonel Donelson had been listening quietly as he rubbed his chin. His eyes wandered from the small group, and Mary followed his gaze. He was watching Captain Hutchings in the next boat, and his face began to darken.

"There are rumors that some of the others are not happy with Colonel Donelson," Ma whispered.

Mary had not noticed that her mother had joined her at the cabin door, and now she turned to look at her in surprise. "Why?"

"There are some—including his own son-in-law—who blame him for the delays. They think he doesn't know how to get us to the Cumberlands, or how long it will take."

"Well, it seems like we've already been on this river longer than Moses wandered in the wilderness," Mary said.

Ma let out a laugh so quiet, it was almost imperceptible. "That it does, child," she said. "Somebody—I don't know who—underestimated the time this trip would take, that's for sure. I don't believe they understood the Indian threat, either."

"Are we finished with the Indians now?" Mary mused.

Ma shrugged. "Who knows, Mary? We may reach the Cumberlands and still be in constant danger. We just have to take it one day at a time and see what develops."

Mary's stomach began to growl and the sound was not lost on the two women. When Ma didn't speak, Mary asked, "How are we set for food?"

"We're out of food, Mary," she said. "We are plumb out of food."

"What does that mean?"

"It means we eat what God provides for us along the way, or we starve. It's as simple as that."

Mary turned back as the group of men began to break up. The call went out to break camp and prepare for another day on the river. As Ike called out to her to untie the boat and help to push it from shore, she realized she was starting another day of grueling work on an empty stomach. Already fatigued beyond anything she ever thought she could endure, she crossed the deck to the nearest pole and stood side-by-side with her brothers to push off and begin another day.

# 49

The air was thick in Jo-Leigh's cabin as she lay under thick blankets, shivering from the fever that had taken much of Tuskagee Island Town in its grasp.

The curse had spread rapidly through the village, leaving few families untouched. And as the Chickamauga traveled to surrounding towns, word came back that the curse was beginning to extend to the Creeks and non-warring factions of the Cherokee. It was casting a pall over the Indian nations as their people were afflicted with sores that overtook their bodies, leaving them unable to walk, to speak, or even to move without anguish.

Every cabin sent thick clouds of smoke from their chimneys as they fought to drive the fever from their homes with yet more heat.

The shamans had failed in their attempts to stop its progression. Though they conducted their ceremonies continuously, day and night, their chants, music, drums, and masks did nothing to ease the suffering.

White Messenger had returned with his Shawnee mother, Medicine Woman, and she had worked tirelessly with special herbal remedies, but the Indians were dying now in growing numbers. She spent hours with Jo-Leigh, who became weaker with each hour and was now no longer able to swallow.

Medicine Woman pulled the blankets away from the once-beautiful woman. Noquali looked upon her with an overwhelming sadness as he surveyed her ravaged body. There was scarcely an inch of her skin that had not been affected; those blisters that had burst had left scars that reminded him of Dragging Canoe's pockmarked face, and he let out a long, low wail.

The Cherokee prized their appearance and now the most beautiful woman of all was scarred forever. And it was he who had brought this curse upon her and upon the village. His anguish was almost unbearable.

He took a damp rag from Medicine Woman and began softly, tenderly wiping her body. As soon as the hot liquid touched her, she broke out in a renewed sweat. But unlike the previous days, she no longer groaned with the heat and discomfort. Instead, she lay with eyes that stared blankly at the ceiling; eyes that now lay sunken and emotionless.

In the five days preceding, Medicine Woman had followed the bathing ritual with a fresh poultice made from herbs and plants, held in place with the long leaves of river plants. But today when the bathing was complete, she turned to Noquali and shook her head in silent sadness.

He sat on the edge of Jo-leigh's bed. He took her head into his lap as he had so many times in the last few days. As he rested his hand against the side of her neck, he sensed from her labored breathing that today would be different.

He kissed her forehead, not caring about the raised scars that touched his lips. He kissed her cheeks and her neck and ran his hands through her long, black hair, now wet from the days she'd lain in a bed made hotter from her fevers and the fire that had continuously raged in the fireplace.

He spoke to her and told her he loved her, that he'd always loved her, and would always carry her spirit with him. He cried as he held her and rocked her. And he didn't notice when White Messenger, Medicine Woman and Adsila quietly left the cabin, nor did he notice as the fire died down and a chill crept over every inch of the tiny cabin.

∞

They buried Jo-Leigh as the sun rose. He had dressed her himself in her best buckskins and boots, wrapping her carefully to stave off the last remnants of winter. She was buried on the side of the mountain facing eastward toward her old village with her prettiest jewelry and beads wrapped about her neck and wrists and held within her cold hands.

As Noquali had covered her face with blankets, he hoped he would not remember her as she appeared on this day, but as she had looked that day so long ago when he had reappeared in her cabin and took her in his arms.

Villagers had come to her funeral and had mourned with him, but they were scarcer than he would have wanted for her. Too many of them had already died or were dying yet, and too few had the energy to make the trek to the top of the mountain where she was now laid to rest.

They moved away one by one until only White Messenger, Medicine Woman and Noquali were left. And as Noquali knelt beside her grave, the others quietly faded away, leaving him with only the brisk chill of the mountain air.

He looked toward the east, toward the village where his brother had lived, where Jo-Leigh's family had been slaughtered. This war was not over yet, he thought with a weary gloom.

His eyes wandered to the river below that snaked past the Indian villages. As he watched, a dozen Indians wandered into the frigid waters and allowed themselves to be swept away by the currents to be drowned downstream.

It had been this way for days now, and the sight of the braves killing themselves no longer evoked passion within him. With the shamans no longer able to help them, those afflicted with the sickness were choosing to drown themselves or throw themselves onto raging fires. The bravest slit their own throats or ran sharp spears through their bodies, their faces devoid of expression as if their souls had already expired.

He turned his own hand over and peered at his palm. It was covered in the same sores that had raced over Jo-Leigh. His skin was burning beneath his clothing, and he knew without looking that he, too, was succumbing to the sickness.

He stood shakily, his head light as though it was barely attached to his body. He turned toward the narrow path that led back to the village. But as he took one step away from Jo-Leigh's grave, his knees gave way under him and he sank to the soft, cold earth. The last thing he saw before he fainted was the mound of earth over her grave.

# 50

They reached the Ohio River as the sun was setting. The Tennessee continued to flow swift and strong, eventually spitting them into a river far wider than any Mary had ever seen before.

"It's the ocean," Meg said in awe.

"It ain't the ocean unless we missed our turn," Billy said.

Mary didn't have time to answer, as they quickly learned the Ohio River current was flowing south, and they were heading north. The order went out from boat to boat to aim for the eastern shore, where they would determine their next course of action.

The order was not easily complied with. As strong as the rapids had been on the Tennessee, their boats had moved with the current. Now they were battling a stronger, more powerful current that seemed stubbornly destined to work against them. Though they had been on the water for months now, they found themselves without the expertise to navigate these mighty currents and they fought vigorously to keep the boat from turning circles in the river as other boats were doing.

Two boats slammed into each other with a deafening *crack*, sending the crews scrambling to remain on their feet. Shouts went up from boat to boat as each tried valiantly to reach the shoreline.

"Aim for the crosscurrent!" Ike called out from the bridge.

"There is none!" Billy yelled back desperately.

And indeed, as Mary locked her eyes on a grove of trees and labored toward them, she realized what Billy said was true: the great river was moving so fervently that it was overwhelming the normal crosscurrent near the shore.

It took the better part of an hour for every boat to work its way ashore. When at last they were still, they wandered one by one onto the beach. Some were kneeling forward to grasp their calves, trying to still their aching muscles; others were rubbing their shoulder muscles; still others were simply collapsing onto the safety of solid ground.

Mary stopped near some trees and dropped to the ground, trying to catch her breath. Now that they were out of the water, she could look back at the Ohio River with nothing short of complete awe.

The setting sun drenched the water in its warm, red glow, making it appear as if it were on fire. An island rose nearby and she was amazed that she hadn't noticed it before. She reasoned that she may have mistaken it for the shoreline as they spun about in the current. It rose now, a massive mound of woodland, its white beach stark against the red waters.

Captain Hutchings was marching from his boat at the southern end toward *The Adventure*, which was moored beside the Neely flatboat.

"Oh, Lord," Billy said under his breath. "Here we go again."

The captain and the colonel met just a few feet from where the Neelys had huddled. Mary could see the exhaustion on Colonel Donelson's face; he was pale and thin and his mouth and forehead were deeply lined. He mopped perspiration from his brow with a worn, soiled handkerchief.

The men from the other boats gathered around them in an instant. They all seemed to be talking at once.

Ma pulled Meg, Jane and Johnny toward the tree line. "Keep your eye on them," she directed Jean before she and Ike joined the growing crowd.

Mary stood to get a better look as Captain Blackmore and Jed Cobb pushed their way to the center of the group and stood beside Colonel Donelson.

"How the devil do you expect us to go north on this river?" Captain Hutchings demanded.

Jed Cobb was quick to reply. "It's springtime. All the snow up north is meltin' and it's makin' its way downriver. It's swelled over the river banks."

"That's all well and good, but that doesn't answer my question." Captain Hutchings waved his hand toward the river. The crowd turned in unison to peer at the ferocious current, the whitecaps less visible now that the sun was dropping below the horizon. "You cannot expect us to row against this current. It's not possible."

Everyone began shouting at once. Mary could hear only bits and pieces of conversation as Colonel Donelson raised his hands and attempted to quiet the crowd.

"We haven't eaten—"

"We'll collapse—"

"Maybe we ought to head south with the current—"

Then Captain Hutchings' voice rose above the rest. "My journey is just about at its end," he said in an authoritative, booming voice. "I intend to follow this current south to the Mississippi River. I should reach the Mississippi within a day. And I intend to settle in the Illinois Territory."

"Please, I beg of you," Colonel Donelson implored, "We will only be on the Ohio River a short time – no more than a day or two, at most. The Cumberland River is not far from here, and it will take us straightaway into Fort Nashborough."

"Straightaway, like our journey has been thus far?" John Caffrey bellowed.

Mary watched as the crowd parted to allow Mr. Caffrey close to the center.

"Gentlemen," he announced, "we have reached a crossroad. We can either continue this wild goose chase northward against the current and Mother Nature herself, not knowing when—if ever—we will reach this fairytale that's been touted as God's chosen land. Or you can head south with me, with the current, to warmer lands and plentiful game."

"Men, men, I implore you," Donelson said, attempting once more to quiet the discord, "We have come this far. We are out of the Indian Territories now, and we haven't much further to travel. I beg you to think seriously about the ramifications of leaving the fleet. Stay with us, and I will lead you to Fort Nashborough."

"Or come with me," Mr. Caffrey said, his voice rising above the others. "I intend to take the Ohio to the great Mississippi River, where I will follow it south to Natchez—or perhaps all the way to New Orleans. It is civilized there with many settlers, traders, and commerce. We don't know what we will find at Fort Nashborough other than what you see right here." He waved his hand at the river and trees.

"Or join me," Captain Hutchings said, "and this time tomorrow, you will be able to say your journey is ended. It is time we stop living on food that barely keeps us alive; it is time we stop driving ourselves like we are slaves."

"Yeah!" a man called out from the back of the crowd.

Others joined in, voicing their support for the trip south or ending the journey altogether.

Finally, Captain Blackmore stepped forward. "Men! Men! Listen to me!" He towered over the others and his voice boomed above their heads. As the crowd began to grow silent, he said, "I will not press you to go forward to Fort Nashborough. You have endured much—we all have. You should return to your boats and to your families and spend this night considering your choices. Tomorrow, I intend to travel northward with Colonel Donelson to Fort Nashborough." As the crowd began to grumble, he added, "But others may not. It is each family's decision whether to continue onward. Whether you choose to remain here, turn south toward Natchez and New Orleans, or set your sights for the Illinois Territory or Kain-Tuck, it is up to you to appoint your own leaders. We will part ways tomorrow morning from those choosing not to continue to Fort Nashborough."

The crowd began to slowly disburse. Mary watched and listened as several remained clustered around Colonel Donelson, discussing their strategies for navigating the powerful current of the Ohio River. Others formed groups a distance away, where men were beginning to draw crude maps on the soft earth. Still others quietly returned to their boats.

Ma and Ike rejoined the rest of their family. While Sam, Billy and Ike leaned against the trees and observed the rest of the fleet, Ma joined Mary and her sisters on the open ground. They were silent for a long time before Ma finally spoke.

"Your father is waiting for us at Fort Nashborough," she said.

"It never occurred to me that we'd be headin' anywhere else," Ike quickly added.

They remained silent for several more long minutes. Then Billy, who had been staring at the darkening landscape, said, "Then we'd best come up with a plan for rasslin' this bear."

The entire family turned their eyes to the raging river. Finally, Ike said, "We'll sleep on it tonight. In the light of day…"

Jane sat in Ma's lap and tugged at her. "Ma," she said, "I'm hungry. When're we gonna have supper?"

Ma stroked her hair. "We don't have anything to eat, Sweetheart," she said quietly, pulling her close.

# 51

Noquali opened the door to Jo-Leigh's cabin and stepped outside. The blisters that had formed on his eyelids prevented him from opening his eyes more than a crack, causing his surroundings to appear as if through a mist.

He closed his eyes and took a deep breath. The air was cool and refreshing compared to the thick, pungent atmosphere of the overheated cabin. He was tired of remaining under mounds of blankets and furs; tired of keeping the fire raging until the smell of wood burning permeated everything, including his skin. The fevers had not helped to drive away the curse, just as it had not helped Jo-Leigh.

He took another deep breath. He smelled the sweet odor of fresh grass. He remembered the previous spring; how the green blades managed to shoot up overnight, overtaking the brown, dormant ground from the winter. He detected a slight chill in the air and wondered if the final snows of winter had left puddles that would soon be swallowed by the rich earth.

He thought of Jo-Leigh working in the corn fields, her long, slender fingers turning the soil, and the fresh scent of the ground beneath their feet. This was his favorite time of year, when the trees began to bud, the grass began to sprout, and the wild fruits began to emerge from a winter nap.

He opened his eyes. He tried to look about him but he saw only swaths of blurred color: the gray-brown wood of Jo-Leigh's small home; a trail along the ground the color of leather that wound its way from her home through the village; a mixture of misty blue and puffs of white overhead; and various shades of green that seemed to bend and wave in the soft breeze. There were no edges to any of these objects; they simply appeared to blend into each other like swirling waters.

He took a tentative step onto the path and felt the mixture of pebbles and earth under his moccasin. His other foot followed and he continued one slow step at a time, until he reached a fork. He knew if he turned to the right, the path would wind its way through the village, past Bloody Fellow's home, past the communal building, past the fires of those who were preparing the morning meal.

He turned instead to the left. It was steeper and he caught himself several times as he began to slide along the steep grade. He stopped frequently, marveling at how easily he traversed this terrain just a few short weeks before. But the soles of his feet were covered in blisters that made him wince with every step he took. Though he couldn't see his feet through his filmy vision, he knew they were swollen and his moccasins were unable to adequately support them. Finally, he leaned against a tree and pulled off the moccasins, leaving them beside the path.

The pain radiated through him as he continued; each pebble feeling like a knife with sharp edges all around.

He stopped at the edge of the cliff. His breath was shallower now as he gasped for air. His lungs felt scorched and small and no matter how deeply he attempted to breathe, it was as if the Great Spirit was withholding the air from him.

He felt a drop of rain against his cheek and he lifted his face to the heavens. Another drop followed and then another. He took in the fresh, clean aroma of a gentle spring rain, closing his eyes once more and relying only on his sense of smell.

The sound of rushing water reached his ears and he listened for a long time. It was the sound of The Whirl; he knew that although he could not see it. After a bit, he began the descent to the riverbank, slipping and sliding along a path that was quickly becoming overcome with muck and mud as the gentle drops became a deluge.

He fell and slid unceremoniously on his backside down the path. He tried once to stop his slide, reaching out for a sapling that quickly broke off in his hand. Then, his strength sapped, he allowed the rain and the ground to propel him forward, tumbling once and then twice, bouncing over boulders and rocks, their sharp edges scraping his skin.

Not once did he cry out, though he gritted his teeth from the pain. It was fitting, he thought; fitting that the Great Spirit would punish him so for bringing the curse down upon his beloved Jo-Leigh and the Chickamaugas.

He stopped abruptly at the edge of the woods as his breath escaped with a loud whoosh. The path was gentler here and no longer steep and he lay back upon the ground and tried to breathe once more.

The sound of The Whirl had grown to a roar that filled his ears and his senses. After a bit, he rose painfully to a seated position and tried once more to view his surroundings.

He wiped his hand across his eyes. He drew his knees to his chest and rested his chin upon his buckskin breeches. Then with great effort, he grasped a nearby tree and dragged himself to his feet once more.

He slowly removed his jacket and then his shirt. The rain and the growing wind brushed his bare chest and he shivered involuntarily. Then he removed his breeches along with his belt of scalps and ornaments. He felt for his knife, finally feeling its sharp, pointed blade against his fingers.

He moved rhythmically now as he traversed the last bit of path and felt the sandy shore beneath his bare feet. When his soles touched the water, he almost jerked away from the razor-like iciness. He stood for a moment, willing himself to feel the water, to feel the chill against his feverish skin, to hear the constant roar of The Whirl.

He wanted to stroll into the water but his sores would not allow him to enter it gracefully. He felt himself jerking and shuddering as he rambled into the waters, feeling his body swept downward into its icy depths.

He placed his knife between his teeth and wandered further from shore, allowing the sound of the water to lead him. The waves grew stronger and his body was pelted with a ferocity that swept him off his feet. He almost lost his blade but managed to bite down upon it even as he cringed with the growing pain. And then he was pushed backward as if the waves were fighting against one another. He swallowed a mighty gulp of the water and he realized as it slid over his tongue that it was mixed with his own blood. He struggled to reach the knife that was cutting into the sides of his mouth even as the waves tugged and pulled his arms in every direction.

Finally, his fingers wrapped around the knife handle. As he gulped massive amounts of water, he tried to lean back to peer into the heavens once more. His eyes opened wide and the film that had covered them was swept away with the pelting of the waves. He glimpsed the bright blue sky and the white, tumbling clouds—and the sun peeking through the clouds. Strange, he thought, it was raining and yet the sun was shining. And the sky was blue, not gray and not angry. It was as blue as he'd ever seen it.

Then with a swift movement, he plunged the knife into his heart and allowed The Whirl to draw him into the arms of the river spirits.

# 52

Mary leaned back on the moist earth, too exhausted to enjoy the spring air. It had been three days since they had first laid eyes upon the Ohio River. Three days, and it felt as if they had scarcely moved. It wasn't for lack of trying; they had struggled to remain in the crosscurrent but it was no match for the stronger current moving south. The water frequently washed over the banks and boats were grounded on the shallower riverbed, forcing them to push further from shore and directly toward the opposing current. There were no more shifts assigned but every able-bodied person was forced to labor with the poles and tillers, battling the river to push northward. A hostile wave could push them backwards fifty yards or more and it felt as if it took hours to regain the distance they'd lost.

They desperately wanted rest but the effort required to row ashore was painfully slow and often exhausted them. So they had struggled onward, fighting the current in unison, until their strength was utterly depleted.

They were stopped now on the eastern shore where the water rushed past them in great, hurried whitecaps, heaving their boats as they rested against the banks. Most of the settlers who still had the energy to walk disembarked and gathered near the trees, where they lay down or propped themselves against the trunks and tried to regain their strength.

Mary peered upward into the trees, her eyes widening at the sight of two bluebirds building a nest.

"What day is this?" she asked.

"Thursday—no, Friday," Jean answered, plopping down beside her and closing her eyes.

"What's the date?"

"Haven't the foggiest."

"Late March," Ike said, leaning against a nearby tree, "the twenty-fourth."

Mary watched Ike as he tightened the bandage around his arm. Most of the blood on the bandage was old, but she knew all his exertions only aggravated his wound. "The twenty-fourth," Mary repeated dreamily. It had been three days since they had eaten. She tried to remember their last meal but the only image that surfaced was that of water that was supposed to have been soup.

She could no longer remember a day when her stomach didn't feel tight from lack of food; a day in which she didn't feel faint from lack of nourishment or an hour in which her stomach wasn't complaining loudly of its emptiness. She didn't remember what her brothers and sisters looked like before they were reduced to skin and bones; couldn't remember Ma without deep circles under her eyes.

As families continued to disembark, she heard the familiar wail of babies and small children, their cries growing weaker even as they begged their mothers for food. And the familiar voices of their mothers as they told them tiredly that there was none.

Several men took the opportunity to hunt and Ike, Sam and Billy wearily joined them; though Mary knew they were as exhausted as she, it was their only hope for survival. Like Ike, Billy kept his wound bandaged but Mary had seen him more than once removing the bandage and cleaning fresh blood from the wound. It seemed the norm now, to see otherwise able-bodied men with bandaged arms and legs. But they were the lucky ones, she thought, as she remembered Mr. Payne and Simon and the Stuarts.

The few nets that had not been shredded beyond repair had not caught enough fish to sustain them. Complaining to Colonel Donelson did no good, as his own family was in the same dire straits as the rest of them.

Their numbers were fewer now. Captain Hutchings had left them three days ago with a group of men, women and children who no longer cared about reaching Fort Nashborough but were bound for the Illinois Territory, which they believed to be closer. Still others turned south to follow the strong current of the Ohio River to the Mississippi, where they hoped to reach Natchez. A few were bound all the way to New Orleans.

Mary lay for a long time, listening to the birds overhead and soaking in the first rays of the spring sun. Whenever she closed her eyes, her body felt as if it was still on the flatboat, still tumbling and rolling with the waves, and she was inclined to grasp the ground beside her to steady herself. She wanted sleep to come, but it did not; the sounds of the children and the voices of men and women around her seeped into her consciousness and roused her from any slumber she might find.

Finally, she opened her eyes and groggily sat up and peered around her. Perhaps, she thought, with the warmer weather she could find something to eat—nuts that had been hidden under snow for the winter, the first buds of wild greens, or even blades of grass.

Ma was seated nearby with Meg and Jane asleep with their arms around her neck; Jean was reading the same worn book she had read countless times on their long journey; and Beth was writing, presumably to her beloved, Jacob Spears. She didn't see Martha.

She came to her feet and to Ma's inquiring glance, she said, "I'm looking for food."

"Be careful," Ma said.

Mary nodded and wandered into the woods. At first, she saw many of the people from other boats—among them, Elizabeth Jennings, Mrs. Donelson, and Jed Cobb. But as she trekked further inland, the sounds died behind her and she was left with only the soft whistle of the trees swaying in the gentle breeze and the calls of songbirds.

She watched as several small birds foraged along the forest floor and she knelt to the ground and began picking through the dirt. She wondered if she dared eat grubs as she held one in her hand. She'd heard of others eating them and they were supposed to be rich in protein. But she didn't have the nerve to eat it raw and she didn't know how to cook them. Better that she should look for plants than return to their boat with an apron full of worms.

She kicked the ground, trying to find cattails or wild onions but she only found the humble beginnings of tiny mounds of grass.

She stumbled into a small clearing, her eyes focused on the ground, when a sudden noise caused her to jerk upward. Only a few yards away, one of the settlers had placed a skeletal dog on a tree stump and had sliced its neck open with an axe.

She gasped; her feet rooted to the forest floor, her eyes wide and mouth agape.

He turned and looked at her with a long, sad face. "The dog was dying," he said, "and I couldn't bear to watch it suffer no more."

Mary swallowed. She could think of nothing to say. He seemed to be waiting and as Mary stared into his face, she realized he wanted to know that she did not condemn him. Finally, she said, "These are trying times. May God have mercy."

"Mary," he said, "please don't mention this to my family. It was our pet; had been for years. But now we're starving…"

As his voice faded, the full realization of his words hit her. "So—so, you're going to skin it and eat it?"

He shook his head wearily. "We're starving," he repeated.

"The poor dog is out of his misery," she said, squaring her shoulders. "And if you don't eat it, the buzzards and worms most certainly will. Best that it be used to keep your family alive."

"Thank you," he said, his shoulders stooped and his back bent, "thank you, Mary."

Mary turned and walked back along the path she had just taken. When she was out of sight of the poor fellow, she dropped to her knees and dry-heaved until she collapsed in a heap on the ground.

C<sup></sup>

It was late afternoon when Ike, Billy, Sam and little Johnny returned from hunting. They had managed to shoot two rabbits and the Neely family came alive with energy and the kind of enthusiasm they might have shown if they had brought back a buck already skinned and quartered.

As Mary skinned one, she fought to remove the image of the man and his dog from her mind. But as she toiled, her eyes wandered along the shore until she caught sight of his wife cooking the meat over a fresh fire. He probably told them he'd killed a fox, she thought, as she watched the large eyes of the smallest children waiting for the meat to cook.

A buzz began at the northern end of the shore and traveled swiftly through their camp. As a cheer went up, Mary handed the rabbit to Jean and, wiping her hands on her dress skirt, made her way past the boats toward *The Adventure*.

Billy was rushing back from a gathering of men and almost bumped into her.

"It's the Cumberland!" he cried out. He grabbed her by both her arms and swung her around. "Jed Cobb says the Cumberland is just up ahead. And it's gentle, Mary, and it'll take us straight into Fort Nashborough!"

# 53

They reached the Cumberland River late that day. The Neelys' elation turned to disappointment as each boat left the vigorous waters of the Ohio River and journeyed northeastward.

"This can't be the Cumberland," Ma said.

Mary had to agree. It was too narrow and too shallow to be such an important waterway. They had certainly taken a stream and it would dead-end. She hoped it happened soon so they would not have wasted too much precious time.

But the current was gentle, as Jed Cobb had reported, and the winds were coming in from the west. Only the tiller was needed to steer them toward the center and away from the sandy shores. At last, they were no longer fighting a raging current, sandbars or rapids.

They journeyed only a short while before Jed Cobb made his way in his canoe along the fleet line, calling out to each boat that they would camp for the night at a spot just up ahead. And when they finally arrived and joined the others, Mary slept the deep sleep of the dead alongside the placid waters.

# 54

Mary sat on a wooden bench secured to the deck and watched the shoreline as the boats floated past. They'd been on this new river for almost six days now; it was wider now and Colonel Donelson, Jed Cobb and Captain Blackmore were convinced it was indeed the Cumberland.

The spring winds were gentle and continued blowing from the west, as if the angels were behind them offering puffs of air to speed them on their journey. Above her, two sheets had been erected for use as makeshift sails, and now the breezes were pushing them ever faster and closer to Fort Nashborough.

They could not arrive soon enough to suit Mary. Though she had to admit they had fared better since departing the Ohio River; the currents were gentle and they no longer had to struggle just to progress a short distance. They were making good time and the weather was getting warmer—so warm that they'd removed their heavier garments.

The trees were budding and on their stops along shore, they'd been able to find plenty of hydrophyllum, a beautiful plant that seemed to crop up out of nowhere, its white flowers waving to them from the edge of the woods. They were delicious and could be eaten raw, and they'd been plentiful enough to provide much needed sustenance. Some folks called it Shawnee Salad, and Mary hoped they would be the nearest thing to a Shawnee she'd ever have to face.

She realized as she watched the shoreline that they hadn't seen any sign of Indians in weeks, and for the first time in a very long time, she began to feel hopeful.

In addition to the flowers, they'd stopped several times in days past, killing various animals from swans to buffalo. At last, their pots were full of meat and their bellies were filled with something more nourishing than water.

"Mary," Ma said, breaking her train of thought, "you might want to check on Elizabeth."

Mary had almost forgotten that Elizabeth Peyton had joined them after their last stop. Ma thought she was in need of different surroundings, though Mary couldn't imagine that the view on their boat could be that much different than *The Adventure*. Jean, always the nurturer, had spent a lot of time talking to Elizabeth in hushed tones. It seemed the closer they got to Fort Nashborough, the more Elizabeth dreaded facing Ephraim and telling him of the fate of their firstborn son.

"Yes, ma'am," Mary said, rising and stretching. She turned toward the stern, but her line of sight was blocked by the sheets rippling in the wind. She meandered across the deck, ducking under the sheets even as Sam and Billy positioned them to take full advantage of the breeze.

When she reached the stern, she found Elizabeth lying face-up on the deck as if soaking up the warm sun's rays.

Mary sank to her knees beside her. "How are you?" she asked.

Elizabeth gazed upward at the blue sky filled with puffy white clouds. Then she rolled onto her side and propped her hand under her head. "Do you ever wonder if it was worth it?"

"The trip?"

"We had it so good, Mary. So good, and we didn't even know it."

"What's past is past. It doesn't help us any to compare the present against the past."

"Maybe. Maybe not…But I know, had we stayed back east, I'd be holding my little bundle of joy right now."

Mary gazed at her in silence for a long time. Her eyes were puffy and red; Mary imagined she'd cried more in the past few weeks than any woman ought to in a lifetime. "There will be more children for you, Elizabeth," she offered at last. "I know none will ever take the place of Baby Ephraim; I don't mean that—but you are so young and you have so much love to give."

"They say the Indians adopt children; I just hope and pray that Ephraim was found quickly and taken to a woman who will love him as if he were her own…"

Mary thought of the savages in their red and black paint, seeking war with the white man. She wasn't sure it would be merciful for a child to be brought up in an Indian village, especially a male child who would be taught their bloodthirsty ways. "He was in God's hands," she said at last, "and he still is—wherever he is."

Elizabeth turned toward her and smiled weakly. "I pray that is true." Her expression turned more somber. "I've thought of Jon so much, also."

The memory of Jonathan Jennings, Jr. untying the canoe and deserting his family in their greatest time of need came rushing back to Mary, and she felt the anguish once more of standing in the cabin doorway watching that horrific scene. Sam was right; they needed to burn this boat as soon as they reached Fort Nashborough. They needed to burn it and all the memories it represented—

"I've wondered so often what happened to him and Obediah," Elizabeth was saying. "Mamma saw Ezekiel fall into the river—she assumed he'd been shot but we were all so busy trying to get away that she couldn't—" Her voice caught in her throat and she stopped and took a deep breath before continuing. "She feels bad that we didn't go back and get him."

Mary's jaw dropped. "But if you had—The Indians would have gotten you for sure!"

"Maybe. Maybe not. Who's to know?"

When Mary didn't respond, she continued, "I forgave Jon. The thing is; everything happened so sudden-like. You think you know what you'd do in a situation like that, but you really don't. Something kicks in and you don't think; you just *do*."

Mary squeezed her hand.

"Jon and Obediah and Ezekiel—they must have all thought they'd be killed if they stayed on the boat. Or maybe they thought they could draw the Indians away from us and toward them. Who's to know what they were thinking—if they were thinking at all?"

"We don't know," Mary said quietly.

"I sometimes look behind us and I wonder if Jon is trying to catch up with us on the river; if we'll ever see him again."

"You won't know 'til you see him," Mary said. "None of us knows what the future holds. We just have to keep getting up, dusting ourselves off, and keep on a'goin'."

"And just where do you figure on getting the strength for that?"

"Sometimes you don't have much choice. You put one foot in front of the other. And you keep doing it until you've gone a yard and then a mile and then ten miles."

Elizabeth focused on the blue sky and feathery clouds. She opened her mouth to speak but her words were drowned out by Ike's shouting. "There's a canoe up ahead!" he shouted. "It's a white man!"

Mary sprang to her feet and rushed past the billowing sheets to the bow. The others joined them, their faces mirroring her sense of hopefulness. Shouts leapt from one boat to another as men took off their hats and waved them in the sunshine. Mothers hugged their children, tears of joy streaming down their faces.

"What is it?" Meg asked, pulling at Ma's skirt. "What's happening?"

Ma pulled her tight. "It's Richard Henderson," she said, choking back tears.

"Who's he?" Meg asked; her eyes wide and her voice filled with wonder.

Mary knelt beside her. "From Fort Nashborough!" she exclaimed. "We've got to be close to Pa!"

# 55

White Messenger stopped paddling and gazed admiringly at the beautiful springs that leapt from the otherwise placid river. It was said these waters could cure any ailment from flatworms in the belly to melancholia. Behind him, he heard the others as they also stopped paddling, and he knew that they, too, were enjoying the tranquil setting.

They were several weeks' travel from Tuskagee Island Town. They'd left the village the morning Noquali had gone mad; White Messenger's Shawnee mother, Medicine Woman, had been frightened of this curse that set itself upon the Cherokee villages and spread like a rolling fog. They'd joined the rest of their family at the caves that dotted the limestone bluffs along this river. After trading for canoes from another tribe, they'd made their way northwestward, following the current of this river the white man called Collins River.

He peered behind him at five canoes. His father, Eagle Feathers, sat erect and proud, his stocky chest breathing in the spring air. Directly in front of him in the small canoe was Medicine Woman.

His brother Msipessi silently paddled toward shore with their sisters Shooting Star and Silent Tree in the third canoe.

Black Heart, Strength of an Ox and Buffalo Woman came into view in the fourth vessel, followed by the last one in which three more braves leisurely navigated the gentle current.

White Messenger nodded at Doe-Deer, who sat behind him in the first canoe before following Msipessi to the shore. It was a good day for relaxing in the miracle waters.

They would remain here for a few days, perhaps a week or more, hunting game and enjoying the waters. Then they would head north on the Collins River until it gradually grew larger. Eventually, they would find their way to the river the Shawnee called the Warioto, but which the white man called the Cumberland.

He thought of the white men who traveled the treacherous Tennessee, or Tanase, River in their large, flat boats. He would never have navigated that wild river in those cumbersome vessels, he thought. And they could never have navigated this gentle one in them, either, as this river was neither wide enough nor deep enough for them.

He wondered if they had made it to the Cumberlands. Perhaps he would encounter them there, he thought as he reached the base of the limestone bluffs. It was prime hunting ground and his family would spend the hot days of summer hunting the plentiful bison, deer, boar, bear, and other game. Eventually, they would head north to Shawneetown. If Eagle Feathers remained resolute, he planned to lead the small family to places even further north.

But first, they would join their brothers in many raids planned over the long summer months: assaults that would take them into the heart of the white settlements, resulting in the slaying of as many white men as the Great Spirit allowed them; attacks that would reward them with many captive women and children.

He thought of the curse brought upon Noquali and his village and of those brothers and sisters who struggled even now to rid their bodies of the pestilence. What lesson was there to be learned from this? He wondered as he set ashore. His answer came swiftly and resolutely: to rid their lands of the white people and all the sickness they brought with them.

He inhaled the fresh air. Yes, he thought calmly. The battles between the two civilizations were only just beginning. And he had no doubt the Shawnee and their Cherokee brothers would be the victors.

# 56

It would be almost a month before the Donelson Party would sail past Fort Nashborough and come ashore along the banks beneath the bluffs. It was a month that felt like an entire year as the thought of arriving at their destination dangled tauntingly in front of them and yet just out of reach. It was a month of fatigue, of excruciatingly slow progress as they were forced to stop repeatedly and hunt for game, gather Shawnee Salad and wild onions, and spend hours upon hours cooking and caring for the ragtag fleet that limped onward. It was a month with nothing more than the promise of plentiful corn and bountiful crops awaiting them in the Cumberlands, of neighbors anticipating their arrival and of the hope for better days ahead.

When they first reached Eaton's Station, the first white settlement as they neared Fort Nashborough, it was almost anticlimactic. It was far from the images she'd harbored of houses basking in the sunshine and rolling fields cut short from grazing sheep and cattle; it was, instead, a small clearing encircled by a wilderness, the crude dwellings of a few families lay nestled beneath towering trees, of worn clothing drying on lines in the wind. Mary saw in their lined faces the hardship that hadn't dissipated after reaching these promised lands; and she heard in their voices, the fear that was ever present from repeated Indian attacks.

And as families began to drop out of the fleet in search of their own slice of paradise, Mary found herself with a mixture of anticipation and dread as they traveled still further. The river had become her safe haven; the cabin had become her familiar home. And when she stood in the doorway and looked back upon the worn and dusty mattress where she'd slept so many nights, she knew she would take a piece of this flatboat with her, carried gently in her heart. It was a journey she would never forget; a journey she might someday relate to her children and her children's children.

Pa met them just outside of Fort Nashborough. His skin was bronzed from hours in the sun; his black hair sported a few gray wisps; and his forehead was deeply lined. But when they fell into each other's arms, the months seemed to slip away until it was as though they were standing once again along the dusty Virginia road, the three hundred head of cattle fit and ready to move out, and her father's soft voice promising that she would spend Christmas with him at Fort Nashborough.

He introduced them to their new home amid the hills that rolled along beside the Cumberland River. He and the other settlers had built a log home in anticipation of their arrival: a two-room home with a dogtrot right down the middle. About fifty feet from the house behind some boulders was a chute; an Indian escape chute, Pa called it. The youngest children enjoyed sliding down the diagonal shaft until it landed them underneath the house in a room made completely of stone. If the Indians attacked, Pa instructed them, they were to ride that chute underground and remain there until all was clear. Even if the savages burned the house down, they would remain safe in the stone room.

Pa had located a salt lick and laid claim to it, naming it Neely's Salt Lick. He had a plan carefully laid out to boil down the sulfur water until they had enough salt to sell to the other settlers, salt that would be precious and costly for the only other competition was a week's travel over untamed land.

The first time Mary saw an Indian at the Lick, she froze in place like a stunned deer. But the Indian, resplendent in a buckskin loincloth and sporting a feathered band around one bicep, simply raised his hand in greeting before turning and making his way toward the river. They would arrive regularly after that; sometimes alone and sometimes in groups of two or three. Often they would trade food and furs for trinkets; trinkets that meant so much to their culture but which held little fascination for Mary.

Other times, she would learn of a fellow settler who had been killed or scalped, or of children plucked from their homes, never to be seen again. And at those times, she would remember her river journey; the days spent fighting for their lives, the gunshots ringing out, the rapids battering them, the Whirl attempting to swallow them.

She wrote letters to George and every few weeks would hand them over to a stranger passing through in the hopes they would make it back east to her beloved.

The flatboat was dismantled and the wood used to make furniture. The two mattresses upon which they'd lain so many months were burned in a ceremony that was both cathartic and melancholy. Their possessions were distributed now in their tiny home; possessions that represented the lives they'd left behind and the lives they hoped to have.

And as spring turned to summer, more settlers began to arrive. And each time she spotted another flatboat along the Cumberland River, it brought her back to the moment she stepped off the Neely boat for the last time; the day her river journey had come to an end.

# Epilogue

Fort Nashborough and Neely's Salt Lick did not offer the peace the settlers had anticipated. Instead, the spring gave way to a summer filled with Indian raids, of marauding and scalping, of murders and captures. The Revolutionary War stretched westward, reaching through the Cumberlands to the Mississippi River.

By early August, the settlers had been forced to leave their isolated log homes to seek refuge at the more fortified Fort Nashborough or a neighboring fort known as Mansker's Station.

On August 3, 1780, less than four months after Mary's arrival at Fort Nashborough, she left Mankser's Station with her father for Neely's Salt Lick. Hunters accompanied them; their plan was to bring back meat for their families while William and Mary boiled water down to make much-needed salt. The hunters left by mid-afternoon. Though they begged William to return with them, he wanted to finish their salt-making and return the following morning.

Shortly after the hunters left, William and Mary were attacked by Shawnee warriors. William was killed and scalped, his body left beside the Cumberland River. But Mary's ordeal was just beginning…

Captured by the Shawnee, she is taken hundreds of miles from home, deep into Indian Territory. She is renamed "Songbird" by her captors and enslaved by the chieftain's wife. She must depend on her own courage, faith and determination to escape from her captors and find her way back home over hundreds of miles of war-torn country.

It is a story that is told in *Songbirds are Free* by p.m.terrell. The first chapter follows...

# 1

## Neely's Bend, The Americas, 1780

Mary Neely was a mere slip of a girl; folks liked to say they could read the Books of Psalms clear through her. Her shoulder-length hair was as fine as cornsilk and changed colors with the seasons: in winter it was light brown with streaks of copper when the light hit just right; the copper would then turn to gold in the summer, as if the sun had kissed it. Now she pushed a strand of it off her forehead with the back of her hand, exposing beads of perspiration across her brow.

In the small clearing in front of her was a large iron cauldron suspended over a fire by four sturdy wood poles. It was filled almost to the brim with water that had just begun to simmer, which meant she would be standing over it the better part of the day, stirring it and stoking the fire until all that was left was salt residue.

She was a mix of Irish, Scottish, and English, which resulted in fair skin, sea green eyes and a rugged spirit despite her slight stature.

With one hand on the stirring stick, she used her other hand to grasp the end of her apron and wipe her face. It was an unusually hot August day, the air so thick even the flies didn't have the energy to move. It was even more scorching standing over the large black cauldron near the banks of the Cumberland River.

The bend in the river was known as Neely's Bend. Situated close by was Neely's Salt Lick, which consisted of a spring surrounded by rocks over which sulfur water would flow year round. The odor took some getting used to, as it smelled of rotten eggs, particularly when Mary was boiling the water as she was doing now.

Mary was the fourth of ten children. She'd be nineteen years old in less than three weeks; her oldest sister, Jean, was six years her senior and the youngest, Jane, was not yet four years old. But it was her brother Sam with whom she was closest.

Most of her sisters and brothers were at the homestead now, working to harvest a garden that had been woefully neglected because of the Indian threat. Elizabeth, who was three years older, had just become engaged to Jacob Spears and Mary knew she'd be talking up a storm about her anticipated change in status.

Part of the reason Mary wasn't with them was because she'd taken a liking to Jacob's brother, George. And George was right on the other side of those woods yonder, along with men from Mansker's Station, taking advantage of the animals' propensity for visiting the salt lick. They hoped to bring back enough meat to feed their families for several months.

The sound of footsteps on brittle twigs reached her ears and she turned to peer through the woods as Sam and George made their way into the clearing. George tipped his hat in greeting.

Mary glanced at him with a mischievous smile. His father was of German descent and George had inherited his thick, *sandy hair and gray-green eyes. He was taller than most and had wide, sturdy shoulders and beefy hands.* She knew she affected him. It was widely rumored they would marry someday and with two older siblings married already and a third betrothed, she would soon be expected to follow suit.

Sam dropped some dead rabbits near Mary's feet. "Hunting's good today," he said with a grin.

Mary tore her eyes away from George. "You need me to skin them?"

"Yep. We're leaving them for you and Pa. We're about to take them deer" —he nodded his head toward two bucks they'd shot this morning—"and head back to Mansker's Station."

"Leaving already?"

"We've got work to do, woman," Sam said with a sideways glance, a grin breaking out on his handsome face.

George led two pack horses to the deer, and Mary watched as they slung the carcasses over the horses' broad backs, the two muscular young men lifting the heavy deer as if they weighed no more than a sack of potatoes.

"Everybody's leaving except you and Pa," Sam said, growing somber. "The others from Mansker's are trying to talk him into letting you come back with us. I sure don't like the thought of you staying here."

"We'll be fine," she said. "I'll finish up this salt making and we'll be headed home first thing in the morning."

He didn't answer but his brow furrowed and he appeared to be chewing the inside of his lip.

"Where's Pa now?"

"Down by the river," he said as he mounted his horse.

Mary had a vision of her father toiling away, his shirt sleeves rolled up to his elbows, his black hair shining in the sunlight, his sharp green eyes scanning the horizon for meat befitting the Neely table. He was only forty-two years old, still a man in his prime.

George tossed the reins of one of the pack horses to Sam. They watched as the horses started along the old trail, their tails swishing in the still air.

George remained still, the reins to his own horse and the other pack horse still in his hands. They appeared to hold a great deal of interest to him.

"George," Mary said by way of parting.

He stood with a fixed smile on his face, his eyes glancing up beneath a stray lock of hair to find Mary's face, and then quickly dropping to peer at the reins again.

"What is it, George?"

"I was wondering," he began, his voice barely audible.

"Wondering what?"

"I was—I was wondering if you'd—if you'd go with me to Saturday's dance."

"Why of course," Mary said coquettishly. "I was figuring all along on going with you."

A broad smile graced his face from ear to ear before he visibly subdued it. Mary held back a smile of her own as she watched the color rise in his cheeks.

"I'll be leaving on Sunday to go back to Virginia."

She lowered her eyes and kept them focused on the boiling water, hoping he would not see the disappointment she felt welling up inside her. She swallowed. "You planning on coming back this way any time soon?"

Out of the corner of her eye, she watched him shrug. "My pa doesn't want to part with his tobacco farm in Virginia…" he started, his voice trailing off. "But I aim to come back, soon as I can."

She stirred the water in silence.

"Won't you go to Mansker's Station with us?" he asked as a group of men entered the clearing.

She glanced up as one of the men shook his head. "William won't leave," he said as they approached.

"Then I'm staying, too," she said, squaring her shoulders. "We'll be back tomorrow."

George hesitated until the men had passed through the clearing, leading horses burdened with game. "Bye, Mary."

"Bye, George."

"I'll be seeing you then on Saturday."

"I'm counting on it."

"Yes, ma'am. Me, too."

She thought he would trip over his own feet as he rushed to mount his horse and catch up with the others.

Mary turned back to the water. Humming, she reached to the pile of kindling beside the fire and tossed more under the pot. It wouldn't do to have the fire go out while she stood there chatting.

Her mind wandered to this Saturday's dance. There would be at least forty in attendance—maybe even more. She'd have to pull out her fine cotton dress, the one with the blue pattern on it. She'd borrow Elizabeth's hair pins and pull her hair into a top knot, and she'd probably even use some of Ma's flower water to make her smell especially nice. As she day-dreamed about the evening, the settlers in attendance, and the music provided by Daniel Norman and his fiddle, she broke into song. The hours crept by as the afternoon began to wane. Mary loved to sing and she listened to her own voice wafting through the summer air as she sang the hymns she'd memorized from the one church hymnal that everybody shared.

Musket fire pierced the air, sending a flock of birds above the trees, their panic-stricken wings beating the air in their hasty retreat.

Simultaneously, she heard the Indians, their distinctive cacuminal cry at once harmonious and terrifying, the sound growing in escalating intensity.

Mary felt the adrenaline course through her veins as she dropped the stirring stick and raced to the edge of the clearing, where she grabbed the musket they always kept loaded and primed.

She stopped abruptly at the edge of the woods. The Indian warriors seemed to be everywhere at once, their faces obscured behind grotesque red and black paint, their bodies clad only in breechcloths.

Her eyes fell on a lone Indian at the edge of the water, kneeling over Pa's still body. She leveled the musket and aimed.

The air was filled with the dust from hurried feet, momentarily blinding her. As the dust settled, she spotted Pa lying on the bank in a pool of blood that flowed to the river.

In the next second, she fired, the smoke blast momentarily blocking out her target. Then the air was filled with a deafening war cry. As she turned, she glimpsed another warrior as he rushed her, his arm raised high with his club held tight. She grabbed the musket by the barrel and swung it with all her might into his torso. As blood erupted from him, she was struck from behind by yet another Indian.

The world blurred around her as she tumbled backward. She was surrounded by warriors, their faces otherworldly in their red and black paint. She fought with all her strength, kicking and screaming, pummeling those who came near, while they continued to encircle her.

Her last memory was a lone war club sailing through the air, the perpetrator's face devoid of expression, catching the side of her head and slinging her downward. Her body hit the ground with such force that her breath was knocked from her. The last sound she heard was her own desperate gasp for air.

# Appendix A

## Passenger List

The passenger list for Colonel John Donelson's and Captain John Blackmore's riverboat journey consisted of the head of each family. Because William Neely accompanied James Robertson on his overland journey, Colonel Donelson used Isaac Neely's name; he was the eldest male in the Neely family on the riverboat journey. Names of females appeared only when they were unmarried, widowed or there was no adult male family member present.

Some reports have the number of boats as thirty while others list forty. The most common boat was the flatboat, though it also included a few canoes, scows, and pirogues. In all, one hundred and eighty men, women and children left with Colonel Donelson on the now-infamous riverboat voyage.

It is not known why a complete passenger list was not made, as some people mentioned in Colonel Donelson's daily journal are not listed in his passenger list. Passengers included (in alphabetical order):

Francis Armstrong and family;
Benjamin Belew and family;
John Boyd and family;
John Caffrey and family;
Robert Cartwright and family;
Daniel Chambers and family;

John Cockrill;

John Cotton and family;

William Crutchfield and family;

Colonel John Donelson, his wife and children (including Rachael, who later married General Andrew Jackson);

John Donelson, Jr. and family;

Daniel Dunham and family;

John Gibson and family;

Russell Gower and family;

David Gwinn and family;

Frank Haney and family;

Hugh and Thomas Henry and families;

Mrs. Mary Henry and family;

Captain (later Colonel) Thomas Hutchings and family;

Jonathan Jennings and family;

Mr. Johns and family (first name unknown);

Isaac Lanier and family;

Mr. Maxwell and family (first name unknown);

James McCain and family;

John Montgomery and family;

Isaac Neely and family;

Mr. Payne and family (first name unknown);

Benjamin Porter and family;

Mrs. Mary Purnell and family;

Isaac Renfroe and family;

James Robertson's wife and five children;

Hugh Rogan and family;

Mrs. Roundsever (first name unknown);

Thomas Stuart and family;

John and Solomon Turpin and families.

# Appendix B

# The Neely Family

The information below was obtained from a photocopy of Mary Neely's family Bible, supplied by one of Mary's direct descendents, Thomas Robertson. It should be noted that in the original Bible, Mary's last name was spelled Neeley. At some point over the years, the name was shortened to Neely.

William Neely, father, born 1730
Margaret Patterson Neely, mother, born May 25, 1737

Jean, born July 7, 1755
Elizabeth, born March 8, 1757
Isaac, born March 24, 1759
Mary, born August 20, 1761
Martha, born April 25, 1764
William, born December 12, 1766
Sam, born May 30, 1769
Margaret, born December 20, 1772
John, born May 16, 1774
Jane, born December 21, 1776

MARY NEELY AND GEORGE SPEARS MARRIED
February 24, 1785 in Lincoln County, Kentucky

# CHILDREN OF GEORGE SPEARS AND MARY NEELY

Hannah, born December 27, 1785
William, born October 17, 1787
Mary, born August 2, 1789
John, born August 1, 1792
Solomon, born May 17, 1795
David, born October 2, 1797
Elizabeth, born August 4, 1799
George, born March 9, 1805

Mary outlived all of her children except George, who died in 1892

# Appendix C

Adsila – female Cherokee name meaning "blossom"

Ambush – the first ambush on the Donelson Journey took place near present-day Moccasin Bend near Chattanooga, Tennessee

Apollina – French name meaning "Gift from Apollo"

Beersheba Springs, Tennessee – although this is not mentioned by name in this book, it is the location of White Messenger and his family in Chapter 55. Named after Beersheba Porter Cain around 1833, it is an iron spring in the Collins River Valley in central Tennessee in the Cumberland Plateau.

Blackmore, John – founder of Blackmore's Station, later to be known as Fort Blackmore, located along the Clinch River in Virginia. In 1793, Fort Blackmore changed hands when John Blackmore failed to pay the taxes on it, possibly because he had already relocated to Tennessee.

Bloody Fellow – changed his name to "Clear Sky" when the Chickamauga Indian Wars ended, and lived in peace among the Americans. His Cherokee name was "Iskagua."

Chickamauga – the phonetic spelling of the Indian word Tsikamagi. The Tsikamagi Indians were predominantly Cherokee who did not honor the treaty or the sale of Cherokee Territories west of the mountains. Their leader was Dragging Canoe. The town in which they originally lived was known to the settlers as Chickamauga or Chickamauga Town. Today the City of Chickamauga, Georgia has 2,245 residents and covers a 1.8 mile area. It is also near the scene of the Battle of Chickamauga (named for Chickamauga Creek) that occurred on September 18-20, 1863. Some Cherokee dictionaries have the definition of "Chickamauga" as "the river of death" while others have it as "stagnant water."

Clinch River – known as the Pellissippi River to the Cherokee

Cobb, Jedediah (Jed) – this is a composite character of the scouts who accompanied the Donelson Party. The name of the lead scout is not known.

Cotton, John – survived the trip to Fort Nashborough and received one of the original land grants from the State of North Carolina, then in control of Fort Nashborough and vicinity. Born in 1718 in Chowan County, North Carolina, he died on September 20, 1782 in Northampton County, North Carolina at the age of 64. His wife, the former Mary Wills, had three children from a former marriage that John adopted: Henry, William and James, who were aged 12, 10 and 8 respectively at the time of their journey. John and Mary had four more children together (shown here with their ages in 1780): Allen, 6; Willie, 4; Jonathan, 2; and John was born soon after reaching Fort Nashborough, which meant Mary Wills Cotton was pregnant during the journey. A fifth child may have been born in 1782. The name is also spelled "Cotten" in some records.

Danda'ganu' – a Cherokee word that means "looking at each other", it was used to describe the place in which two mountains looked across at one another over the Tennessee River. It was an ideal place for the Indians to monitor activity on the river and mount attacks against settlers. The original villages were torched by soldiers and militia in an attempt to eliminate the Indians' vantage point.

Dakwayi – known as Toqua to the settlers. This Indian village established by the Chickamaugas was located near the Chickamauga River close to the mouth of the Tennessee River.

Donelson, Colonel John – one of the founders of present-day Nashville, born 1718 and died mysteriously in 1786 along the trail between Kentucky and Nashville. He'd moved his family to Kentucky due to repeated Indian attacks in the Nashville area. He had eleven children; his tenth child, Rachel Donelson, later married Andrew Jackson, who became the seventh President of the United States. Rachel was only twelve years old during the riverboat trip in 1779-1780. Also see Captain Thomas Hutchings (below) for information on his daughter Catherine.

*Donelson's Journal* – written by John Donelson during the 1779-1780 riverboat journey, it chronicles the voyage and contains dates and facts that were relied upon in the writing of this book.

Dragging Canoe – an Indian warrior of mixed tribes; his father was of Cherokee and Shawnee blood and his mother was Natchez Indian. He did not abide by the Treaty of Sycamore Shoals (see *Henderson's Purchase*) and he declared war on all white men venturing west of the mountains. His followers became known as the Chickamauga Indians. The words he spoke in the Prologue are from transcripts made at the time of the Watauga Settlement meeting, made available through a variety of historical societies. His words have also been passed down through generations of Cherokee descendents and are available at various web sites (search for *Dragging Canoe snow balls in the sun.*)

*Early History of Middle Tennessee* – written by Edward Albright in 1908, one of the texts used in researching this book, particularly Chapters 14 through 16, which details the Donelson Journey and provides a list of passengers. Chapter 19 also chronicles the Indian attack that occurred in August 1780, in which William Neely was killed and Mary Neely was captured (covered in the book *Songbirds are Free* by p.m.terrell).

Gower, Nancy – survived the trip to Fort Nashborough and married Andrew Lucas (some textbooks have the name as Anderson Lucas.) She lived for fifty years after reaching Fort Nashborough. Nancy's husband was one of the signers of the Cumberland Compact.

Holston River – known as the Hogohegee River to the Cherokee.

Hutchings, Captain (later Colonel) Thomas – a land surveyor from Pittsylvania County, Virginia, he married Colonel Donelson's daughter Catherine in 1768. They left the Donelson Party near present-day Paducah, Kentucky and migrated to Kaskaskia, Illinois. They eventually joined another Donelson party headed for the Cumberlands in 1781. Tom Hutchings died in 1810 at the age of 70. Catherine moved to Madison County, Tennessee and died in 1835 at the age of 87. The son mentioned in this book was Christopher, who was about six years old during the winter of 1779-1780.

Jennings, Jonathan Jr. – was reunited with his family and lived for a time near Fort Nashborough. Last mentioned in his father's will as having been "scalped by Indians and rendered incapable of getting his living", the will directed that his mother become his ward.

Jennings, Jonathan Sr. – survived the trip to Fort Nashborough but died in July or August 1780 due to wounds he received in an Indian attack. His dream and premonitions of their ill-fated journey was chronicled in several journals that were passed down through his descendents.

Jo-leigh or Joleigh – a name meaning pretty or cheerful.

Henderson's Purchase – a term that referred to the Treaty of Sycamore Shoals, also known as the Treaty of Watauga. Richard Henderson, a land speculator and North Carolina judge, met with more than 1,200 Native Americans in March, 1775 in order to purchase approximately 20 million acres of land between

Virginia and the Mississippi River. Although representatives from the Shawnee, Delaware, and Wyandot tribes were present, the treaty was officially with the Cherokee nation. In reality, however, the Cherokee did not own the land they sold to Henderson and his allies; and Henderson's purchase was in violation of the Royal Proclamation of 1763, which prohibited the purchase of Indian land. Many younger members of various tribes did not recognize the purchase and the treaty and declared war on settlers moving west past the mountains. See *Chickamauga*.

Kaskaskia, Illinois – the village to which Captain Hutchings and his family originally migrated when they left the Donelson party. Once an Indian village, it was occupied by the British until 1763. George Rogers Clark overtook the British there in 1778. The Great Flood of 1844 almost completely destroyed the town, and the flood of 1881 destroyed all remaining remnants of it. The census of 2000 listed 9 people, 4 households and 3 families in the area. It is located along the Mississippi River south of St. Louis, Missouri.

Lookout Mountain and Signal Mountain – the locations of two Cherokee villages looking across the Tennessee River at each other; known as Danda'ganu' by the Cherokee

Msipessi – means "Spirit of a Lion" in the Shawnee language

Muscle Shoals – it is said the Indians originally named the portion of the Tennessee River that winds past present-day Florence, Muscle Shoals, and Tuscumbia, Alabama after the amount of muscle it took to navigate it. Mussels continue to be found in the area, and it is also possible the name was taken from "mussels" and the spelling changed. The Muscle Shoals Canal dropped more than 140 feet within 30 miles, creating formidable rapids that prevented travel eastward, upriver. The river was often shallow, rocky and filled with obstacles, sandbars and islands. The river here served to divide the lands between the Chickasaw and Creek to the south and the Cherokee to the north. The Tennessee Valley Authority (TVA) erected a number of dams in the area and this stretch of the river now bears little resemblance to the one that existed in 1780. Although James Robertson promised to leave provisions at Muscle Shoals for Donelson's Party, it is unknown whether his men ever waited for the Donelson Party there, or ever left anything that was taken by others before the Donelson Party arrived at Muscle Shoals.

Neely, Elizabeth (Beth) – married George Spears' brother, Jacob, on June 23, 1781 in Lincoln County, Kentucky, where they migrated after repeated Indian attacks in middle Tennessee. She died in 1791 at the age of 34.

Neely, Isaac (Ike) – married Ann Coppage (or Coppedge). By 1784, he was living on the north side of the Cumberland River in present-day Davidson County, where he was awarded a land grant for 640 acres. He eventually migrated to Kentucky and founded Neely's Gap, where he died in 1794 at the age of 35.

Neely, Jane – married Thomas Buchanan in 1796 and died in 1830 at the age of 54.

Neely, Jean – married a man named Caldwell, but as of this writing, her date of death is unknown.

Neely, John (Johnny) – was killed at the age of 8 in an Indian attack that also killed his mother, Margaret, near Neely's Bend (now in Madison, Tennessee).

Neely, Margaret (Meg) – was only eight years old at the time of the river journey. I could find no additional information about Meg once the family reached Fort Nashborough and do not have the date of her death.

Neely, Margaret Patterson (Maggie) – though she made it to Fort Nashborough, she was killed just two years later in an Indian attack near Neely's Bend at the age of 45. Her youngest son,

John, who was 6 years old at the time of the river voyage, was killed at the same time.

Neely, Martha – I could find no additional information about Martha after the family reached Fort Nashborough.

Neely, Mary – only four months after arriving at Neely's Bend near Fort Nashborough, she was captured by Shawnee warriors. Held in captivity for three years, she was taken hundreds of miles from home to northern Michigan, where she escaped and was captured by the British and held as a prisoner of war. Finally escaping the British, she journeyed overland through Canada and into New York, eventually making her way on foot to Fort Pitt, Pennsylvania, where she was rescued. She was eventually reunited with the remnants of her family; her father had been killed at the time of her capture and her mother and youngest brother, Johnny, were killed in a separate Indian attack while she was living in captivity. She married George Spears and had eight children: Hannah, William, Mary, John, Solomon, David, Elizabeth and George, eventually moving to Kentucky and into Illinois. She outlived all of her brothers and sisters and her own children except one, George Spears, III, and died in 1852 at the age of 91 at Clary's Grove, Illinois. The story of her capture, captivity, escape and journey home is told in *Songbirds are Free* by p.m.terrell.

Neely, Sam – married Mary "Polly" Watkins and had two children, Sam and Joshua. He lived the rest of his life in the home the Neely family built in the spring and summer of 1780. The home became known as the "Sam Neely Home" and was relocated to Clarksville, Tennessee in the 1960's, where it stands as of this writing at Hachland Hills. He became an Indian fighter and killed the Indian who killed his mother and little brother Johnny. Though his mother thought his hot temper would result in a short life, he outlived all his siblings except Mary. He died in 1845 at the age of 76. Mary and her great-grandson visited him only months before his death.

Neely, William (Sr.) – cleared the land around the original Fort Nashborough, founded Neely's Salt Lick at Neely's Bend (now Larkin's Sulfur Spring in Madison, Tennessee) and built the log home mentioned under *Sam Neely*, above. Only four months after his family joined him in the Cumberlands, he was attacked and killed at Neely's Salt Lick. He was only 49 years old.

Neely, William, Jr. (Billy) – married Jane Buchanan and after her death, married Esther Walker. He died in 1793 in Davidson County, Tennessee (near present-day Nashville) at the age of 27.

Nickajack – the Indian village where John Rogers, the trader who saved young Jonathan Jennings' life, made his home among the Chickamaugas.

Noquali – means "The Noble One" in the Cherokee language. The character in this book was a composite of various Chickamauga Indians who fought against the settlers as they migrated westward. It is unknown which Indian captured the two Stuart girls.

Pellissippi – the Cherokee name for the Clinch River.

Peyton, Elizabeth Jennings – was only 20 years old when she gave birth to her first child during Donelson's 1779-1780 Journey. One year after settling in present-day Tennessee, she gave birth to a son, John. Three years later, a second son was born, whom they named William. Elizabeth died in 1799 at the age of 40.

Peyton, Ephraim Jr. – the firstborn son of Elizabeth Jennings Peyton and Ephraim Peyton. He was lost in the Tennessee River in the vicinity of present-day Chattanooga, Tennessee during an Indian attack. There are no records indicating whether he survived and was picked up by the Indians or drowned in the river. He was less than one day old at the time of the attack.

Robertson, James – known as "The Father of Tennessee", he was one of the founders of present-day Nashville, born 1742 and died in 1814 while working with the Chickasaw Indians near present-day Memphis. He was a farmer, an explorer, a surveyor, and an Indian agent. He was instrumental in getting legislation that provided 640 acres to each of the original inhabitants or their heirs, including the William Neely family. His wife, the former Charlotte Reeves, is credited for teaching Robertson how to read and write.

Running Water – a Cherokee village in Tennessee near the present-day border of northwestern Georgia; the Shawnee and Cherokee joined there in 1777 to mount attacks against the white settlers along the Holston River area in northeastern Tennessee and Virginia. Other residents included the Shawnee warriors Tecumseh, Cheeseekau and Tenskwatawa (Tecumseh's brothers), their father, Shawnee Warrior, and many Indians from the Creek, Delaware, and Choctaws who did not agree with the treaty between the Cherokee and the white men.

Smallpox – this disease was unknown to the Native Americans before the Europeans brought it to their shores. It is said that 75% of the Cherokee Nation was wiped out by smallpox epidemics by the mid-1700's, as the Indians had no remedy or medicine with which to treat it. The capture of the Stuart girls on the Donelson Journey spread another wave of smallpox through the Chickamauga village where they were taken, decimating the tribe.

Tennessee – both the river and the state get their name from the Cherokee village, Tanase (also spelled Tanasi). Tanase and the Cherokee villages of Chota and Toqua are submerged by Tellico Lake as a result of the Tennessee Valley Authority's dams, except for a monument on the old Chota site.

Treaty of Sycamore Shoals – see *Henderson's Purchase*.

Treaty of Watauga – see *Henderson's Purchase*.

Tsikamagi – known to the settlers as Chickamauga (the phonetic spelling of the name) or Chickamauga Town. It was an Indian village near present-day Chattanooga, Tennessee in an area today known as Crawfish Springs. The village was comprised primarily of Cherokee under the leadership of Big Fool. But because Dragging Canoe was the leader of all the Chickamaugas, it was known more as his town than Big Fool's town. It was later the scene of the Battle of Chickamauga on September 18-20, 1863. See also *Chickamauga*.

Tuscumbia Landing – across from the mouth of Cypress Creek on the Tennessee River was once a village inhabited by Chickamauga Indians and Frenchmen, from which attacks were launched on the settlers as they came through Muscle Shoals. Seven years after Donelson's Journey, James Robertson, accompanied by men from Fort Nashborough, Mansker's Station and other forts in the Cumberlands, returned to this village and burned it to the ground. The Indians did not rebuild there, and the region was made a bit safer for settlers traveling westward.

Tuskegee Island Town – a Chickamauga Indian village that was established on present-day Williams Island near Chattanooga, Tennessee. The Cherokee name was Taskigi. The leader of this village was Bloody Fellow.

Virginia Territory – in Chapter 2, Mary Neely mentions that Fort Nashborough was included in the Virginia Territory. This was a misconception that many of the settlers believed. In reality, Fort Nashborough was included in the North Carolina Territory. This meant that George Rogers Clark and his militia were north of Fort Nashborough in what is now known as Kentucky; and the settlers south of the Kentucky-Tennessee line were unprotected from Indian attacks. As the attacks increased, many settlers including some of the members of the Neely family, migrated to Kentucky where it was considered to be safer.

The Whirl – also known as "The Suck" was a whirlpool and a particularly treacherous spot in the Tennessee River near Chattanooga. Until the 20th century, it proved to be a hazard to many settlers traveling the river, as small boats were easily caught in its rapidly swirling waters, capsizing and drowning the boat's inhabitants. In the 1930's, the Whirl was eliminated when the Tennessee Valley Authority built a dam nearby. (Recommended: Johnny Cash's video, lyrics and song, *The Whirl and the Suck;* see www.youtube.com)

Yunsayi – known as Buffalo Town to the settlers; this was another village established by the Chickamauga Indians. It was located at the headwaters of the Chickamauga River in present-day northwest Georgia.

# About the Author

p.m.terrell is the pen name for Patricia McClelland Terrell. She is the internationally acclaimed author of more than 20 books in five genres.

Ms. Terrell is the co-founder of The Book 'Em Foundation, a partnership between authors and law enforcement agencies dedicated to raising public awareness of the correlation that exists between high crime rates and high illiteracy rates, increasing literacy, and reducing crime. She is the founder of the Book 'Em North Carolina Writers Conference and Book Fair at www.bookemnc.org.

Ms. Terrell is also proud to serve on the Robeson County Friends of the Library Board of Directors (www.robesoncountylibrary.org) and on the Board of the Robeson County Arts Council (www.robesonarts.org). Both organizations are committed to supporting the arts, science, history and heritage of Robeson County, North Carolina.

Prior to writing full-time, Ms. Terrell was the founder of two computer companies in the Washington, DC area. Her clients included the U.S. Secret Service, CIA and Department of Defense, as well as various local law enforcement agencies.

She is also a staunch supporter of Crime Stoppers, Crime Solvers, and Crime Lines, which offer rewards and anonymity to individuals reporting information on criminal activity. She is proud to have served as the first female President of the Chesterfield County/ Colonial Heights (Virginia) Crime Solvers Board of Directors (2003-2004). Visit www.pmterrell.com for more information.

CPSIA information can be obtained at www.ICGtesting.com
Printed in the USA
BVOW06s0836151215

430328BV00034B/1802/P